HUMAN RIGHTS
and World Politics

It should be recognized that true respect for human rights is nothing less than a way of life.

Final Document, UNESCO Congress on Teaching Human Rights, September 1978.

HUMAN RIGHTS
and World Politics

Second Edition, Revised

by David P. Forsythe

University of Nebraska Press   Lincoln & London

Chapters 3 and 4 have previously been published, in different form, as "American Foreign Policy and Human Rights: Rhetoric and Reality," *Universal Human Rights* 2, no. 3 (July–September 1980): 35–54, and *Humanizing American Foreign Policy: Non-profit Lobbying and Human Rights*, Working Paper no. 12, Yale University, Program on Non-profit Organizations (1980).

Cartoons by David Luebke © copyright 1981 by the *Daily Nebraskan*.

Library of Congress Cataloging-in-Publication Data
Forsythe, David P., 1941–
    Human rights and world politics /
by David P. Forsythe. — 2nd ed. rev.
        p.   cm.
    Bibliography: p.
    Includes index.
    ISBN 0-8032-1978-4 (alk. paper)
    1. Human rights. 2. World politics.
3. United States—Foreign relations. I. Title.
JC571.F634   1989   88-39840
323.4–dc19   CIP

To Lindsey, again, and of course for Preppy, too.

Contents

Preface to the Second Edition ix

Preface xiii

Acknowledgments xv

Abbreviations xvii

1   Promoting Human Rights: Human Rights as Legal Ideal 1
    Introduction 1
    Historical Background 7
    Contemporary Developments 10

2   Promoting Human Rights: Some Fundamental Issues 24
    Introduction 24
    Further Reflections 29
    Conclusions 43

3   Protecting Human Rights: The Public Sector 45
    Introduction 45
    Formal International Control 47
    To Review 65
    Further Reflections 67
    Conclusions 82

4   Protecting Human Rights: The Private Sector 83

Introduction 83
Basic Functions 84
Steps 87
Further Reflections 93
Conclusions 98

5   United States Foreign Policy and Human Rights: Rhetoric and
    Reality 102

    Introduction 102
    Kissinger Rhetoric and Reality 105
    Carter Rhetoric and Reality 110
    Reagan Rhetoric and Reality 114
    Conclusions 121

6   Humanizing American Foreign Policy: Nonprofit Lobbying and
    Human Rights 127

    Introduction 127
    Lobbying and Foreign Policy 129
    Lobbying for Human Rights 130
    Beliefs about Influence 140
    Conclusions 154

7   The Political Philosophy of Human Rights 160

    Introduction 160
    Three Political Philosophies 163
    The Three Views in International Society 177
    The Practice of Rights and Value Sharing 181
    Conclusions 187

8   The Future of Human Rights in World Politics 189

    Introduction 189
    To Recapitulate 200
    Final Thoughts 214

    Notes 229

    Bibliography 259

    Appendix: The International Bill of Human Rights 265

    Index 307

Preface to the Second Edition

An author could become schizophrenic (then again, maybe not) read-ing reviews of his first edition. To some reviewers the first version was "well written," "fast paced," and characterized by a "writing style [that] is witty and occasionally jaunty." To another "the writing style is not lively." To one reviewer the first edition was "balanced and unbi-ased"; to another it was "less than impartial." There was common agreement among the reviewers, however, on essential points; and thus I believe I clearly accomplished several objectives which make an updated and expanded second edition worthwhile.

The second edition, like the first, remains oriented to undergradu-ate students and the (probably mythical) general reader as either an in-troduction to international human rights, or as a supplement on hu-man rights to the subjects of foreign policy and world politics. (To one reviewer, "Law Faculties and lawyers will benefit as well. . . ." And in-deed to my surprise the first edition was used in several human rights courses in law schools.) I try to demystify the subject of human rights by being "unpretentious," "matter of fact," "nontechnical."

There is no doubt that from the start of this project "the author's real concerns . . . [were] practical rather than theoretical." Another re-viewer was correct to note that I tried to minimize "abstract philo-sophical argument inappropriate to an introductory text." I seek to de-scribe and analyze action taken in behalf of internationally recognized human rights. That is why I have kept the original sequence of chap-ters, and thus kept the chapter on philosophies of rights as number seven rather than number one.

One of my main arguments in the first edition, which I have not revised, is that too much emphasis can be placed on theories of rights. That emphasis is bound to magnify abstract differences between liberals and conservatives, Marxists and non-Marxists, Westerners and non-Westerners, affluent and impoverished. One of my continuing objectives is to show that, despite various theoretical and philosophical differences which to be sure are very real in the world, a great deal of action can be—and has been—taken in support of human rights.

One of the more intriguing reviews of the first edition came from a law professor in Yugoslavia who picked out my statement that internationally recognized human rights constitutes "a standard overarching traditional ideologies . . ." In the words of that law professor, "[T]he present reviewer fully endorses" that view. "[The book] shares the cultural and political outlook of its most probable readers while not subscribing to their prejudices." Whatever that means, it certainly is nicely worded.

There was one reviewer above all who captured exactly what I was trying to get across in the first edition. "This book's effectiveness as an introduction to international human rights is achieved precisely because it is more than that. It also introduces the reader to many of the important issues of world politics and law, and to the development and operation of political institutions. Human rights are explained in terms of their relation to security and economic development and to the evolution of the international political system. As a result, one gets a tangible sense of what human rights and the institutions intended to promote them actually are, not what they might be in the mind's eye of a philosopher. Accordingly, one is asked to evaluate contemporary human rights law and practice, not against an ideal standard, but against real possibilities."

Concern for international human rights leads not simply to philosophical debate or cases in a court of law, but additionally to political action broadly defined affecting a person's relation to government and society. If international human rights are defined by international law, we should be aware of the broad impact which is possible from law not simply as a command but as an agent of political socialization. In the last analysis it is political process, international and national, which defines human rights and controls their implementation. It is on that process that the second edition, like the first, focuses.

In the second edition I have tried to update factual material to take account of events between 1983 and the first half of 1988. I have tried to correct errors and ambiguities noted by reviewers and correspondents, and I thank them for their careful reading of the first edition. My own thinking about rights has not changed fundamentally since I wrote the first version, but I think it has evolved. I certainly hope I have learned something from all the reading I have done on rights during the past five years, and I have tried to reflect that increased exposure in the second edition. Chapter 3, on U.S. foreign policy, has been completely rewritten to take into account reflection on the Carter period and a close following of Reagan's policies on rights. Also, I completed a sizable study of the U.S. Congress and human rights (*Human Rights and U.S. Foreign Policy: Congress Reconsidered*), and that too affected the revision of chapter 3. The final chapter has also been largely rewritten.

Preface

There are a number of books on human rights for the specialist in law, politics, and philosophy. This is not one of them. I believe in limits to growth and in the perils of inflation. On the other hand, there is a need for a new introduction to human rights for the university student—and for the interested general reader. It is for that audience that I write.

As a political scientist who teaches international law in political context and world politics in legal context, I am interested in the process of making and implementing rules about human rights. I am interested in human rights norms for what they tell about political values and about limits on the exercise of power.

The organization of the book is as follows. First I describe and critique the major values found in the most important human rights treaties. Then I describe and critique the international means—official and unofficial—of implementing the rules. The next chapters focus on the United States: the first analyzes governmental policy during the 1970s and early 1980s; the second analyzes the role of private groups in working for human rights during the period of renewed concern for human rights (1973–79). I then discuss the political philosophies underlying the global debate about human rights. Classroom testing in Denmark and the United States indicates that students prefer to have this philosophical discussion later rather than earlier in the book. Moreover, I will try to show that action on behalf of human rights is possible despite philosophical differences, which is another reason for taking up philosophy later rather than earlier. The final chapter gives a balance sheet on protecting human rights as of the early 1980s.

Through this organization I seek to provide a new synthesis of what we know about human rights. I stress the political process that controls the making and implementing of the rules, rather than an abstract discussion of what the rules should mean to a rational mind. I also try to integrate the human rights of armed conflict with human rights in general. And I attempt to place appropriate stress on unofficial or private means of implementing human rights, in addition to official or public means.

The subject of human rights and world politics is too large a subject for a single, simple thesis. The reader will find, however, several leitmotifs running throughout the following pages: the revolutionary nature of the global human rights effort; the importance of recognizing how far we have come, as well as how far we have to go; the pivotal position of the United States in the human rights movement; the significance of socioeconomic rights; the necessity of blending the liberal emphasis on individual civil and political rights with the communal emphasis on collective and socioeconomic rights.

The student just beginning studies of law and politics may first regard my chosen subject with skepticism, especially if brought up on the prevalent diet that international law is a myth and world politics a crude struggle for power. Such a student may initially see me as Vladimir Bukovsky, the well-known Soviet dissident, saw a colleague: "As for his theories on legality, his friends regarded them indulgently as a forgivable eccentricity, shaking their heads with a smile when he launched into one of his expositions." That student would certainly think that ethics and power made a strange mix, and in thinking about enemies in world politics, would agree with what Bukovsky said of his Soviet adversaries: "What sense was there in expounding our laws? It was like expounding humanitarianism to a cannibal."[1] My only response is that by the end of this book the student should be able to intelligently evaluate Bukovsky's assertion about his experience as a political prisoner: "I crushed them with laws, pinned them down with articles and stunned them with paragraphs."[2]

Acknowledgments

I am grateful to Yale University and its Program on Non-Profit Organizations under the Institution for Social and Policy Studies for an uninterrupted year of research which allowed me to complete this book. John Simon's support enabled me not only to collect new material but also to rework portions of the manuscript. I am also indebted to my colleagues in the program for their numerous comments, as well as the agreeable atmosphere, which was no less important to my work. Barbara Mulligan, Andrea Compton, and Ella Selmquist provided invaluable logistical support.

At an earlier stage of writing I benefited from a year at the Institute for Social Sciences of Odense University in Denmark. Helge O. Bergesen, now of the Nansen Foundation in Oslo, was especially helpful in giving me a Scandinavian view on human rights. Johannes T. Pedersen gave me insight on Danish policy, and Mogens N. Pedersen, then director of the institute, was most accommodating. Two Danish students provided stimulation and commentary: Helle V. Nielsen and Erik Henning.

At a still earlier stage the Department of Political Science of the University of Nebraska–Lincoln granted me the prospect of released time from teaching in order to prepare this project. William Avery encouraged me in my planning, and Susan Welch responded with good humor and cooperation to my many requests for leaves of absence. Final typing was done by Jacci Leger.

A number of persons commented on all or part of the book. At the risk not of violating their rights but of committing a sin of omission, I would like to thank especially Maurice East of the University of Kentucky for arranging a discussion of American policy on human rights when we both were in Norway; Richard Magat of the Ford Foundation; David Mayhew, chairman of the Department of Political Science at Yale; Jens Faerkel of the Law School at the University of Copenhagen; June Burton of the University of Akron; Phil Dyer of the University of Nebraska–Lincoln; and Jack Plano of Western Michigan University.

I am especially grateful to Richard P. Claude of the University of Maryland for his thoughtful comments on the entire manuscript, which led to many improvements. His knowledge of the literature and his insights into the protection of human rights greatly affected the final revision of my work.

Any errors which remain, as well as the interpretations consciously presented, naturally rest at my doorstep alone. In this latter regard I should mention that I have intentionally put forth a view on the various aspects of human rights rather than a descriptive balance sheet of pros and cons. Interpretations are more stimulating than a neutral description of the contents of this or that treaty, even if—as I hope—the reader makes up his or her mind concerning the validity of my interpretations.

A different version of Chapter 5 first appeared during 1980 in what is now titled the *Human Rights Quarterly.* A different version of Chapter 6 first appeared as part of the Working Paper Series, Program on Non-Profit Organizations, Yale University, also during 1980.

Abbreviations

ADA	Americans for Democratic Action
AI	Amnesty International
AID	Agency for International Development
ARA	Bureau of Inter-American Affairs, Department of State
CIA	Central Intelligence Agency
DOD	Department of Defense
ECOSOC	United Nations Economic and Social Council
EEC	European Economic Community; the Common Market
FAO	Food and Agricultural Organization
FCNL	Friends Committee on National Legislation
HA	Bureau of Human Rights and Humanitarian Affairs, Department of State
HCR	United Nations High Commissioner for Refugees
ICJ	The International Commission of Jurists
ICRC	International Committee of the Red Cross
IFI	International Financial Institutions
ILO	International Labor Organization
IMF	International Monetary Fund
NGO	Nongovernmental Organization
NSC	National Security Council
OAS	Organization of American States
OAU	Organization of African Unity
ODC	Overseas Development Council
PEN	Poets, Essayists, Novelists
UCC	United Church of Christ

UNESCO	United Nations Educational, Scientific, and Cultural Organization
WHO	World Health Organization
WOA	Washington Office on Africa
WOLA	Washington Office on Latin America

Chapter One

Promoting Human Rights

Human Rights as Legal Ideal

The concept [of human rights] *constitutes the very core
of the public debate on the preferred structure and
organization of society.*
Asborn Eide, *Human Rights in the World Society*
(Oslo: Universitetsforlaget, 1977), p. 7.

INTRODUCTION

By 1680, to select arbitrarily a nice round number, European political
elites had clearly started the process of dividing their world into
nation-states. Having tired somewhat of slaughtering each other in
the name of religion, they decided on the principle of territorial su-
premacy. Whoever ruled a given territory, that ruler was allowed to determine the religion therein—and eventually everything else therein.
Thus arose the principle of national sovereignty, which, as a result of
the religious wars and then the Peace of Westphalia (1648), was intended to produce international peace. As a by-product, the doctrine of
national sovereignty entailed the notion that how a state treated those
within its territory was a national, not international, matter. What is
now called human rights was not an established part of world politics
from more or less 1648 to 1948. National sovereignty, devised by Europeans as an idea supposedly useful to peace and order, and carried by
the dominant Europeans to the rest of the world where it was readily
accepted, implied that human rights was an internal affair of nation-
states.[1]

By 1980 and the administration of President Jimmy Carter, it
seemed that human rights was an idea whose time had finally come *as
a part of world politics*. After sporadic attention to human rights issues in international relations, which is to say that after various states

and other organizations had tried intermittently to make human rights part of world politics via treaties and diplomacy, one of the most important states in the world promised to make human rights the key to its foreign policy. For a time thereafter almost every international subject was encased in the rhetoric of rights. In 1978 the United Nations Educational, Scientific, and Cultural Organization (UNESCO) proclaimed a World Day of Animal Rights. In the same year the prime minister of Grenada addressed the United Nations and defended the rights not only of household pets but also of plants (he seemed highly concerned about stripping bark from trees). (Later, in 1983 when the United States invaded Grenada and overturned the ruling group, it made sure that this particular politician did not return to power.) In 1981 the United States government agreed to fund a study to see if the rights of livestock were being adequately protected in the slaughterhouse.[2] Given the saliency of human rights because of President Carter's speeches, there was much rhetoric about rights not only within nations but in world politics as well.

This euphoria about rights, however, especially as it applied to foreign policy and world politics, came under increasing criticism during the 1980s. The administration of President Ronald Reagan indicated that the key to its foreign policy would not be human rights but combating Soviet-led communism and especially communist-inspired terrorism. The first Reagan administration was part of a trend, warmly endorsed by many around the world, trying to downplay attention to specific human rights as defined by modern international law. While supportive in the abstract of the civil and political rights familiar to western political theory, these circles of opinion did not like the international version of human rights which included economic, social, and cultural rights. They also did not like the demand for an even-handed attention to rights around the world but preferred to focus on communist violations of civil and political rights. Whatever their view on rights at home, they were reluctant to make a broad, balanced attention to human rights an important part of foreign policy.

For this group, composed of many statesmen as well as mere academics, the competitive nature of world politics meant that any state should concentrate on winning the power struggle rather than protecting specific rights. For former president Richard Nixon the struggle against the Soviet Union was "the real war." For President Reagan's first nominee to be assistant secretary of state for Human Rights and Humanitarian Affairs, Ernest Lefever, this fight against communism was real ethics. And former secretary of state Henry Kissinger said: "In an age when nuclear cataclysm threatens mankind's very survival, peace is a fundamental moral imperative. Without it nothing else we do or seek can ultimately have meaning. Let there be no mistake about it: Averting the danger of nuclear war and limiting and ultimately reducing destructive nuclear arsenals is a moral, as well as political, act." Hence for this group, true to at least some of the writings of the late Hans Morgenthau, the nature of world politics requires an emphasis on power; ethics largely consists of projecting the power of the lesser evil over the greater evil; and the rights to be protected are primarily the rights to peace and life as implemented through traditional diplomacy aimed at avoiding war between the super-powers.[3] Ironically, as we shall see, this means that the arch-anticommunist Kissinger had much in common with Soviet spokesmen of his time, as each stressed international peace rather than specific concern for individual human rights.

Doonesbury   BY GARRY TRUDEAU

Yet by the 1980s much international law on human rights had been adopted and was legally in force for many nations. And several international agencies existed for the specific purpose of keeping an eye on such things as the British use of force in Northern Ireland or whether the government of Honduras was responsible for the "disappearance" of persons. Regardless of how much President Carter was ambivalent about his stated commitment to human rights, and regardless of comparable zigs and zags in the policies of the Reagan administration, this international law and these international organizations would not go away. Indeed, in 1980 a federal court in the United States used this body of international human rights law and U.N. resolutions to say, in the case of *Filartiga* v. *Peña*, that torture was prohibited by customary international law and that U.S. federal courts had jurisdiction over a human rights dispute arising out of events in Paraguay—even though the U.S. Senate had yet to consent to ratify the relevant human rights treaties.[4] (Subsequently another U.S. court followed up on the *Filartiga* case by ruling against the Argentine general Suarez-Mason, convicting him of torture and then in a separate action extraditing him to Argentina to stand further trial for his part in the "dirty war" that left at least 9,000 dead.[5])

It is a basic thesis of this book that the subject of internationally recognized human rights is here to stay on international and national policy agendas. There is too much international and derivative national law on human rights, and too many specialized agencies in existence, for the subject to disappear. Emphasis on human rights may vary depending upon the state of politics, but some human rights actor will remain concerned about torture in Paraguay, slavery in Mauritania, starvation and malnutrition in East Africa and Southeast Asia. Dissent in the Soviet Union and prison policies in the United States cannot be so easily swept under the rug of national sovereignty. Some state, some international organization, some private group like Amnesty International would keep the issue alive by making reference to the international law of human rights, no matter how much some national leader might find it more convenient to focus on other issues.

This book, then, explores the past, present, and future of human rights in world politics—albeit in an introductory way. Is it possible for states and other actors to take effective action to protect human rights globally? Or must they sacrifice human rights on the altar of national power struggles? What has been done, what is being attempted now, and what are the prospects of improved protection of human rights in the future? How has world politics changed because of emphasis on rights?

What is the exact origin, nature and extent of human rights? Such questions have bedeviled philosophers for years. We give a sense of that philosophical debate in a later chapter. For now it suffices to note some basic starting points. Human rights are entitlements that lead to fundamental claims against public authority. If one has an agreed-upon right, one is entitled to claim something positively or negatively from authorities—from mostly governments representing nation-states because they have most of the power to implement rights. If the right is said to be a human right, it is more fundamental, more basic than other rights.

The purpose of language about human rights is to make the governmental action more obligatory, more mandatory. If we say that a government would be wise not to torture its citizens, that is one approach to good government hinging on policy recommendation and appeals to the supposed reasonableness of governmental leaders. If, on the other hand, we say that persons have a human right not to be tortured, that is much stronger language implying a barrier that may never be crossed. Human rights are frequently pictured as "trumps."[6] They specify the most important policy values that presumably may not be contravened by other policy considerations (i.e., it is good to get information about an impending crime, even if one has to torture).

It is a debated point about whether human rights can ever realistically be absolute trumps in contemporary world politics, when that politics is characterized by the nation-state system in which the overriding practical priority for states must be their security—else they will cease to exist. We will return to this issue in chapter 7. At a minimum the language of international human rights implies that protecting human rights should not be contravened except in the most dire and unusual circumstances. The very meaning of the term "human rights," and the very reason for existence of such language, suggests that such rights are of the highest priority for public authorities. Indeed, a number of human rights treaties state that even in situations of "national emergency threatening the life of the nation," certain human rights may never be violated—such as the right to life, and to freedom from torture and mistreatment. (One can compare in U.S. constitutional history the argument that freedom of speech should be an almost absolute value, but still qualified in a few situations—i.e., no shouting fire in a crowded theatre.)

What is the ultimate purpose of language about human rights? Such rights are a means to the end of human dignity. In order to guarantee, or at a minimum increase the probability of, a life with dignity, it is said that rights must be recognized and respected. There are other means to human dignity. One can emphasize cultural traditions, *noblesse oblige,* the duties of rulers under religious precepts. But the human rights movement arose in the West, in part during the Enlightenment, out of the belief that these other means were insufficient and unreliable, and that the surest way to enhance the prospects for a life of dignity was to emphasize human rights.[7]

Human rights in a positive or empirical sense is a subject defined by international law. From this "positivistic" view, human rights is what the law says it is, however much philosophers may debate. Human rights legal instruments, in 1988 numbering some twenty treaties and about as many major resolutions and declarations, assert extensive rights for individuals and groups. It is traditional to group these rights into three categories, paralleling the French revolution and its slogan of liberty, equality, and fraternity. The so-called first generation rights pertain to civil and political liberty. The second generation rights cover economic, social, and cultural rights. The third generation rights, which are demanded by a majority at the United Nations but which have yet to be recognized in global treaty law, are the solidarity rights to peace, to development, to a healthy environment, to the common heritage of mankind, and to humanitarian assistance.[8]

How can this be? Even if we set aside the highly controversial third generation of solidarity rights, how can it be that states have agreed on a legal definition of universal human rights? We know that there are capitalists and communists, Westerners and non-Westerners, those who believe in the superiority of Islam and those who do not. Given the diverse world in which we live, how can agreement be reached, and just what does this agreement mean for action to implement the defined rights?

We will see in this book that extensive human rights law exists, that it is worded in a very general way to accommodate competing views, that the agencies created to monitor implementation are weak compared to many national institutions, and that the norms are so sweeping and demanding that they constitute more an ideal of world reform to be realized over considerable time than a program of governmental policies which can be implemented tomorrow by court order.

A central point about human rights law is that it establishes a set of rules for all states and all people. It reflects a moral demand for common, universal treatment of persons.[9] It thus seeks to increase world unity and to counteract national separateness (but not necessarily all national distinctions). In this sense the international law of human rights is revolutionary because it contradicts the notion of national sovereignty—that is, that a state can do as it pleases in its own jurisdiction. On the other hand, for the state that adheres to international standards on human rights, its legitimacy is enhanced and is position made more secure. Thus at one and the same time internationally recognized human rights constitute a challenge to national sovereignty and a source of national security.[10] This will not be the last time we find how complex is our subject.

The overriding concern in the rest of this chapter is the promotion of human rights through creation of legal standards. What human rights have been established through legal definition? What means are created to supervise the defined rights?

HISTORICAL BACKGROUND

The beginnings of international attention to human rights, at least from the standpoint of international law, can be traced either to slavery or to war. If the first multilateral treaty (or convention, which is not a meeting but a legal instrument) is the benchmark, then international concern for human rights dates back about one hundred and twenty five years. Ironically, the first multilateral treaty on human rights arose out of war, and the oldest branch of human rights law is that devoted to protecting human rights in armed conflict.

Human Rights in Armed Conflict

In 1864 the major states of that era—mostly Western—wrote the first Geneva Convention for victims of armed conflict. This treaty embodied the central principle that medical personnel should be regarded as neutral so they could treat sick and wounded soldiers. Such soldiers were no longer active combatants doing their national duty but were simply individuals in need. Another way of stating the central principle was that the individual soldier was entitled to at least a minimum respect for his essence as a person, to a minimum degree of humanitarianism—even in war, the greatest denial of humanitarianism. In human rights terms, although the treaty did not use this language, sick and wounded combatants had the right to medical attention, and medical personnel had the right not to be treated as military targets. Human dignity mandated such provisions.

It was a paradox—the effort to interject a minimum humanitarianism into a basically inhumane situation—that led to an entire branch of human rights law that was reaffirmed in 1977 and to the International Red Cross Movement. (The group of Swiss citizens led by Henri Dunant who worked for the first Geneva Convention of 1864 ultimately came to be known as the International Committee of the Red

Cross [ICRC]. The ICRC in turn was joined by National Red Cross Societies, which by 1988 numbered 144, and by their federation, the League of Red Cross Societies. This grouping is the International Red Cross Movement.) The 1864 treaty on medical personnel was revised in 1906, and a new treaty for prisoners of war was developed in 1929. In the modern period four treaties were produced in 1949 on the subjects of wounded and sick combatants, prisoners of war, civilians, and internal wars. The 1949 treaties were reaffirmed and supplemented in 1977.

For the historical background it suffices to note the following. In some respects the early law about human rights in war was *avant-garde*. It was general international law, some eighty years ahead of general human rights law for so-called peaceful situations. It articulated a limit to national objectives even when the nation-state saw its goals as important enough to merit violence: there were humanitarian limits beyond which the individual could not be legally ordered to kill and be killed for his state. In other respects the law for human rights in armed conflict was not so progressive. If we consider the early, pre-1949 law, we find no dramatic means of implementing the rights of sick and wounded combatants and prisoners of war. Belligerent states had primary responsibility for interpreting and implementing the law.

The law for human rights in armed conflict remains one of the major trends in human rights prior to the modern, United Nations period. There were two other major trends prior to 1945.

Human Rights under the League of Nations

The first of these major trends can be called League of Nations attempts to protect human rights between 1919 and 1939 and encompassed primarily minority rights, labor rights, and rights of individuals in mandated territories (there was also embryonic protection for refugees).

1. As for minority rights it was once again war that produced concern. After World War I there was a belief that unhappy minorities in central Europe had contributed to war's outbreak in 1914. Thus minority treaties were attached to the Versailles peace treaty of 1919. An extremely important principle lay behind these treaties: peace, order, and justice—in addition to human dignity—mandate that a national majority show tolerance toward minorities. Whatever the positive benefit from these treaties,[11] they collapsed within twenty years under

the pressure of persistent local animosities, not to mention Nazi expansionism and absorption of German peoples into the Third Reich.

2. International attempts to legally protect labor rights fared much better—at least in the sense that such attempts proved more durable. The International Labor Organization (ILO) was created by treaty at the time of the League, and it subsequently developed a series of treaties to protect the rights of labor. In so doing, the ILO attempted to oversee the labor policies of states. The effectiveness of the ILO and these treaties is considered in a later chapter. For now it suffices to note that the ILO commanded enough support after World War II for it to be incorporated into the United Nations system. Far from collapsing like the minority treaties, which were not duplicated post-1945, the ILO and its treaties expanded.

3. The rights of individuals in mandated territories were theoretically protected under the League Mandates Commission, which had the responsibility of seeing that Mandate Authorities (in reality, colonial powers) governed Mandated Territories (in reality, colonies) for the well-being of the inhabitants. The theory of international supervision over both national authority and individuals is more noteworthy than the actual practice in the inter-war years. The Mandates Commission consisted partially of the colonial powers, and individuals from Mandated Territories could not appear before the commission. Yet the general idea was accepted at this relatively early date that the League of Nations should guarantee the rights of peoples in these territories to national independence and well-being. This would not be the last time that a human rights provision was more important for long-term developments than short-term protection.

Human Rights and Slavery

In addition to Red Cross attempts to protect human rights in armed conflict and what may be loosely called League of Nations attempts to protect various rights, a third major historical trend was made up by the long effort to protect the rights of those held in slavery. This effort was not spearheaded by any one international organization but rather was led by an amalgam of nongovernmental organizations (NGOs), the Anti-Slavery League. These NGOs finally persuaded states to adopt the 1926 Convention outlawing slavery, a treaty that was supplemented in the 1950s.

Three points are worth noting briefly. First, as in the struggle to secure rights in armed conflict, the effort to ban slavery was led by non-governmental forces. Second, international law was ahead of, and a stimulus for changing, much national law: slavery was outlawed in a number of nation-states only in the 1950s. Third, as with the early Geneva Conventions for armed conflict, there were no treaty or customary provisions allowing individuals to take action to protect their rights; states were obligated to act for the rights of persons.

Humanitarian Diplomacy

Described thus far is the twofold effort to confirm by general inter-state agreement certain human rights, and on occasion to devise means of supervision (i.e., ILO and League monitoring). In addition to these legal measures and others, such as the Central American court on human rights (1907–17), to which individuals had access, diplomatic action occurred in support of presumed human rights prior to 1945. In particular, Western powers attempted to mitigate genocidal policies by the Turks against the Armenians and similarly harsh behavior in parts of Europe and Africa.[12] This combination of legal and diplomatic steps, spasmodic and uneven in development, constituted the background for the explosion of concern for human rights in the modern, United Nations era.

CONTEMPORARY DEVELOPMENTS

The United Nations Charter, dating from 1945, is a global constitution. But it is a constitution without a bill of rights and with only meager mention of human rights. Much diplomacy has been expended since 1945 to correct this deficiency, and the process is still in progress.

Conflict has produced endorsement of rights, and so it is in the United Nations era. We have just seen that the relatively small war for Austrian Succession led to creation of human rights in armed conflict in the 1860s. The larger World War I led to endorsement of minority rights. The greatest war to date, World War II, led to the greatest effort to promote human rights. The belief was evident after World War II that Nazi assaults against the human being and against the international political system itself must never be repeated. It is difficult to say exactly, but post-war leaders either displayed a moral reaction to fascist atrocities, or they believed that states engaging in gross violations of human rights were also likely to violate the law against aggressive war. These two views converged in some fashion so that the founding fathers of the United Nations paid more attention to human rights in general than had been the case in 1919 when the previous global constitution had been written.

The United Nations Core of Law

The reaction against Nazi aggression and genocide produced several references in the U.N. Charter to human rights, the most important of which is Article 55:

> With a view to the creation of conditions of stability and well-being which are necessary for peaceful and friendly relations among nations based on respect for the principle of equal rights and self determination of peoples, the United Nations shall promote: a. higher standards of living, full employment, and conditions of economic and social progress and development; b. solutions of international economic, social, health, and related problems; and international cultural and educational cooperation; and c. universal respect for, and observance of, human rights and fundamental freedoms for all without distinction as to race, sex, language, or religion.

1. It is this single if lengthy article on human rights that constitutes the cornerstone of subsequent U.N. efforts to protect human rights on a global basis. It is this legal norm in binding treaty form which almost all states of the world have accepted in principle. (Of important states, only Switzerland and the two Koreas remain outside the United Nations.) On the other hand, Article 55 is not self-explanatory. Indeed, it seems to suggest that human rights are limited to those subjects mentioned in paragraph c, and that the subjects in a and b are not rights at all but only policies that should be promoted.

2. Because of the general language of Article 55, states at the United Nations quickly turned to efforts to specify its meaning. The first result was the oft-celebrated Universal Declaration of Human Rights, adopted by the U.N. General Assembly in 1948 without negative vote. This declaration of thirty articles affirmed rights of immediate and mundane import ("periodic holidays with pay"), as well as rights of general and visionary scope ("Everyone is entitled to a social and inter-

national order in which the rights and freedoms set forth in this Declaration can be fully realized"). From the time of its adoption, the Universal Declaration was deficient in three aspects. It was not binding law but rather a U.N. recommendation to states. At places it was as general as Charter Article 55, as in Article 3, affirming that "everyone has the right to life, liberty and security of person." And the declaration offered no means of implementation other than state good will.

Yet the declaration was and is important for two reasons. First, it reflected a continuing effort to move beyond lip service to a real concern for human rights. Some articles of the U.N. Charter have, in practical terms, died a quiet if premature death (for example, Articles 43 and 47 requiring member states to coordinate their military policies for collective security). The declaration demonstrated that human rights was alive and kicking.

Second, while the declaration was not international law in 1948, it is legally important for two reasons. It is an authoritative statement of the meaning of Article 55, which is law: thus the U.N. member states did reach agreement on a meaning of Article 55 that was relatively more specific. And, the declaration has become either part of customary law or quasi-law. The Universal Declaration has been reaffirmed without opposition so many times, and so many states have incorporated it into their national constitutions (especially in the Third World) that the declaration is considered more than just a normal U.N. recommendation. We will know the legal status of the declaration most fully when an international court makes a binding judgment based on that document. Until then, it is clear that the declaration creates special expectations about compliance with it, above and beyond ordinary General Assembly resolutions.[13]

3. Still further efforts have been made to clarify the declaration and its foundation, Article 55. Almost twenty years of negotiation at the United Nations produced, as of 1966, two treaties on human rights. The first treaty, or covenant, pertains to civil and political rights; the second, to economic, social, and cultural (the two covenants, along with the declaration, are found in the Appendix). It took another decade for the treaties to enter into legal force for adhering states. By 1988 eighty-six states had adhered to the civil-political covenant, and ninety states to the economic-social-cultural covenant. From 1976, therefore, there was a legally binding, relatively detailed statement of the meaning of Article 55, which over one-half of the states in the world pledged to implement.

Thus, as noted, Article 55 has not withered away. On the other hand, it has taken some thirty years to define the meaning of the human rights language in the U.N. Charter, and just over one-half of U.N. member states so far have explicitly pledged their observance to that interpretation. The process of clarifying basic standards is still going on; only in 1987 was a serious effort begun to specify what was expected under the Socioeconomic Covenant (more on this later). It could not be said, therefore, that protection of human rights has been at the apex of state concern. After all, human rights treaties limit the exercise of state power.

Yet universal human rights are affirmed as never before by these two sweeping treaties. At a general level of analysis the two covenants are noteworthy in several respects. They further endorse the idea, also contained in the Universal Declaration, that human rights go beyond the civil and political rights familiar to the American Bill of Rights and include economic, social, and cultural rights (this point is discussed at some length below). They do not endorse the idea, which *was* in the 1948 declaration, that there is a right to private property. The covenants set up two systems of supervision (discussed in the following chapters). While weak, these control systems further the notion that more than good will is needed from states to ensure protection of human rights. The Political Covenant allows individuals to petition an international organization against their governments, under certain conditions. Further comments will be made about these 1966 treaties as our discussion proceeds.

Discussion of the Core

Contemporary developments about international human rights thus have a core or foundation consisting of Article 55, the 1948 declaration, and the two 1966 covenants. The charter and declaration were heavily influenced by a Western emphasis on "negative" or "blocking" rights. The individual was acknowledged to have civil and political rights to block certain governmental actions, hence affording the individual "freedom from" undesirable governmental action. But as U.N. membership changed in the late 1950s and 1960s, the increased number of non-Western states produced an emphasis on positive, communal, and socioeconomic rights. The rhetorical or general stress was on "positive rights" giving the "freedom to." Peoples and individuals were entitled to affirmative rights obligating governments to do certain things. Two basic and related tensions thus existed in the development of human rights norms: between civil-political and socio-economic rights, and between more and less government.

The tension between socioeconomic and civil-political rights is probably more important than that between positive and negative actions by public authorities. Concerning the latter subject one can say that the right to lawyers and a jury trial blocks a government from arbitrary action. But the government is obligated to take positive action to implement the rights. It must create a court system and even pay for lawyers to represent indigents. Positive action must be taken to implement negative barriers. Hence the difference between negative and positive is more in the semantics than in the actual protection of rights.[14] From an analytical point of view, it can be said that rights are rights; it is the duties of governments which might initially be viewed as negative or positive, but even some negative duties entail positive action.[15]

What was especially troubling to many Westerners was that some emphasis on socioeconomic rights seemed to exclude individual freedoms. According to a Soviet spokesman in 1975, "The question of guaranteeing individual rights is of secondary importance as compared with the social and economic consequences of scientific and technological progress for society in general."[16] Many national elites prevented individual freedom based on equal rights. The rationale frequently offered was that the socio-economic needs of society (and its ruling class) always overrode the rights of the individual. It was this formulation that the West especially opposed.

Different ideas about the hierarchy of rights, as well as a decision to use two different systems of supervision, led to the adoption of two human rights instruments in 1966—whereas one has been adopted in 1948.[17] The first Cold War and its associated ideological arguments had something to do with the evolution of human rights norms at the U.N., of course. It bears noting, however, that despite the reality of this conflict, the East-West division has been spotlighted to the neglect of other important facts (discussed below)—namely, the interest of parts of the West in economic rights.

Supplementary United Nation Developments

Beyond this core of human rights law, other law of global scope was developed through the United Nations. In some cases the already existing law received new attention, as in the case of ILO treaties concern-

ing unionization of agricultural workers and restrictions on forced labor. In the same year as the Universal Declaration, the ILO produced a
treaty on freedom of association and organization while the General
Assembly adopted a treaty against genocide. This treaty was quickly
followed by one on the rights of women—a treaty some twenty years
ahead of popular concern with "women's liberation" in many nations.
In the mid-1960s the Assembly adopted the treaty on racial discrimination. In the meantime, UNESCO had produced a treaty on discrimination in education. The ILO produced six more basic treaties to accom-
pany the two from the League of Nations period. These six covered
collective bargaining, forced labor, discrimination in employment, social policy, and workers' representatives.

Other human rights treaties were negotiated through the United
Nations on more limited subjects, and the General Assembly and Security Council passed recommendations on numerous subjects such
as apartheid in South Africa, the right to self-determination, the rights
of the Palestinian people, the situation of human rights in Chile, and
so forth. By the mid-1970s one source had found twenty-three U.N. human rights treaties and thirteen major U.N. declarations on human
rights.[18] A 1987 U.N. publication listed twenty-two basic human
rights treaties.[19] One of the more important of these specific treaties
was the one on refugees, which was linked to the U.N. High Commissioner for Refugees for help in implementation.

The legal norms in these treaties covered all types of rights. The
system for implementation varied with each treaty. Some called for
self-reporting by states. Some permitted review and commentary by
an international organization on these state reports. The Convention
on Racial Discrimination permitted adjudication by the World Court
(the International Court of Justice), but this article was reserved
against by a large number of non-Western states.[20] More will be said
later about the process of supervision, control, or monitoring.

Other United Nations Developments

In addition to the development of core human rights law and supplementary law, there was a third trend at the United Nations that merits
mention. Some of the specialized agencies, like the ILO and UNESCO,
had long been active in the human rights field. But others, like WHO
(World Health Organization) and FAO (Food and Agriculture Organization), had been considered program agencies not linked to human

rights. In the 1970s at least some of these specialized agencies increasingly overlay their activities with the rhetoric of human rights. In substantive terms, they increasingly tried to link their programs with the rights identified in U.N. human rights treaties. On the other hand, it should be noted that U.N. developmental and socioeconomic programs were not well coordinated, and were all too frequently carried on without attention to linkages with U.N. human rights resolutions and programs.[21]

Contemporary developments in the international law of human rights are found not just in the United Nations. There are two other lines of development of major importance: further law on human rights in armed conflict and regional human rights law.

Modern Human Rights in Armed Conflict

Human rights in armed conflict had received its most extensive development in 1949, as already noted. Significantly, the four treaties of that year were based on types of victims, reflecting their human rights orientation. Interestingly, these 1949 Geneva Conventions came to be almost universally accepted in principle. Virtually all states legally adhered to them (which is not the same as implementing them), regardless of political philosophy or geographical region. Indeed, signing these 1949 conventions seemed to constitute positive proof of statehood, along with joining the United Nations and being recognized by the great powers. For example, both the Algerian rebels in the 1950s and the Ian Smith regime in Rhodesia tried to deposit signatures with the Swiss government. Virtually no other treaty save the U.N. charter had the status of the 1949 conventions on human rights in armed conflict.

The 1949 law was inspired (if that is the right word) by the events of World War II. One example of this was the expanded legal attention given to civilians in the form of a separate treaty on the subject—the Fourth Geneva Convention of 1949. But this complex of four treaties looking backward to large-scale, conventional war proved partially deficient in regulating the less than fully conventional wars post-1949 in such places as Algeria, Vietnam, and southern Africa. Even in more conventional wars, such as occurred repeatedly in the Middle East, there were ample problems in applying the 1949 law. For these and other reasons (such as the Third World, nonhumanitarian interest in conferring political status on "freedom fighters"), the 1949 law was supplemented in the 1970s.

The two Geneva Protocols (or additional treaties) of 1977 are note-worthy in a number of respects. For the first time in world history, there is a relatively detailed treaty on human rights in internal war. In 1949 each of the four treaties contained but one article on internal war, an article plagued subsequently by disputes over meaning. As of 1977, it was clear as never before that a government was legally supposed to adhere to human rights standards in attempting to manage its own na-tionals who had revolted and carried their rebellion to the level of in-ternal armed conflict. Nirvana was not at hand, because each state re-tained considerable discretion about when an internal war existed and what the applicable law required. Yet there was a further inroad on state arbitrariness represented by this second protocol of 1977. If the inroad was partly symbolic rather than fully practical, this was offset by awareness of the fact that states had historically been reluctant to accept international regulation of events within their territory and es-pecially of events touching upon the security of the government.[22]

The two protocols extended legal protection of civilians to the point where starvation of civilians as an act of war was explicitly pro-hibited, for the first time in history. The first protocol extended legal protection to guerrilla fighters as well as regular army personnel, and the second protocol extended sweeping protection to any person de-tained in connection with an internal war.

These 1977 protocols are not likely to transform armed conflict into a Red Cross social event, despite the significant provisions noted above. The second protocol, on internal war, has yet to be widely ac-cepted in those states where a number of internal wars are likely to oc-cur. The U. S., when finally accepting the Second Protocol more than ten years after its adoption, rejected the first Protocol under the con-troversial argument that it endorsed terrorism.[23] This U.S. position undercut support globally for that protocol. States which do adhere to the protocols retain much freedom in interpreting the law, and there is not a reliable system of international supervision to promote a reason-able and equitable application of the law in either international or in-ternal war. The law has become terribly complex: the "good-old-boy average soldier" from Arkansas (or Madras or Shaba) will have trouble understanding what he cannot legally do.

Yet in the last analysis the 1977 protocols are a symbol of the strength of the idea of human rights. It may even be said to be amazing that they were adopted by a diplomatic conference and made available for state adherence. Especially when states employ violence, it is difficult to get them to mesh the ethics of human rights with state self-interest. And the usual philosophical and regional differences must be overcome.

These differences are, in the law of armed conflict, sometimes not so much overcome as papered-over, as in Protocol II, Article 11, where paragraph 4 states: "*Subject to national law* [emphasis added], no person engaged in medical activities may be penalized in any way for refusing or failing to give information concerning the wounded and sick who are, or have been, under his care." It is not self-evident how an inconsistent national law is to be blended with a clear norm of international human rights, in this instance the right of a doctor not to divulge information about a patient. The strength of the idea of human rights is thus reduced by vague language which permits conflicting interpretations. Only future state practice will provide a clear record of protection efforts.

Regional Human Rights Laws

Our final subject in contemporary developments of human rights is regional law. Four regions are worthy of discussion: democratic Western Europe, the Americas, Africa, and Europe as a whole.

1. Democratic Western Europe has produced the most highly developed system for the international protection of human rights that we know to date. The European Convention on Human Rights, which entered into legal force in 1953, affirms extensive civil and political rights. All twenty-one member states of the Council of Europe have adhered to this treaty.

Some of the rights specified in this treaty can be abridged during times of national emergency threatening the life of the nation, but others remain inviolable at all times. The latter category includes prohibitions against such acts as torture and murder. Equally or more important is the fact that states are not always entitled to interpret these provisions themselves. The convention creates regional machinery to aid in implementation, in the form of a conciliation commission and an international court. There now exists almost four decades of case law from the European Court of Human Rights and of decisions from the European Commission on Human Rights. Many of these cases and decisions originate from individual petitions. It is worth noting that even democracies violate human rights, and the past forty years show persistent use of European regional agencies to monitor democratic governmental performance on rights.

This regional international law for human rights in democratic Western Europe has worked slowly and cautiously but generally well. This is because the political culture (the total of political attitudes) in that region supports human rights. Indeed, so supportive is the political cal culture that under certain circumstances an international organization (the European court) is given the final say about human rights. Nation states have only intermediate jurisdiction.[24] No European democracy has ever refused to implement a binding judgment from the European Court of Human Rights. On human rights in Western Europe there is supra-national authority.

It has been said that this support of human rights in Western Europe stops at the edge of economic and social rights, since these are not found in the Convention on Human Rights. This point of view is largely in error. The Western European democracies have put their economic and social eggs in two separate baskets. Twelve of these states have joined the Common Market (European Economic Community, or EEC) to create a higher standard of living. And the larger Council of Europe, which spawned the Convention on Human Rights, has adopted the 1961 European Social Charter with its separate implementation machinery for economic and social rights. Thus it is clearly not true to say that Western democracies are uninterested in the economic and social dimensions of justice but rather only in procedural niceties.

The West European experience in constructing an international system for human rights has not been fully duplicated in any other region. It is only in the inter-American region that one finds another regional system which appears to resemble the European experience. The Inter-American Convention on Human Rights, dating from 1969, came into legal force in the summer of 1978. It is largely similar to the European convention in its overall legal structure: there are extensive political and civil rights, some of which can be abrogated in times of emergency, and there is a conciliation commission and a court. The Inter-American Convention contains brief but explicit references to economic and social rights in its Article 26.

It is difficult to say with assurance how successful this regional human rights law will turn out to be in the long run. It has been binding for only a short period. It is striking, however, that the Inter-American Commission for Human Rights had been functioning since 1960 without a human rights treaty for foundation (it had a legal basis in the Charter of the Organization of American States, or OAS). And the Commission has been able to achieve some protections of rights (covered in chapter two).

On the other hand, Inter-American provisions on human rights are obviously undercut by the denial of many human rights by the dictatorships and military oligarchies of the hemisphere. The inter-American region has long been characterized by a tension between a cultural tradition emphasizing the equal rights of the individual, and governmental policy emphasizing benefits to a chosen few—usually the military, aristocracy, and monied well-to-do. In parts of Latin America, the treatment of the indigenous Indian population may approach genocide.

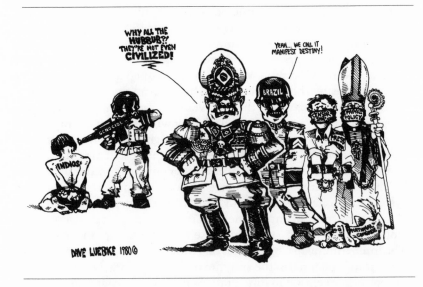

It remains to be seen how the human rights law of the region will function. At least the Inter-American Court had been accepted by enough parties to begin functioning, and it had begun to hand-down both advisory and binding legal judgments. Some of these cases were of major importance, such as whether Honduras was guilty of the forceful disappearance of its nationals. ("Disappeared persons" is a nice euphemism for state-sponsored unrecorded detention, frequently leading to torture and political murder.)

The Organization of African States (OAU) did approve a regional human rights treaty which entered into legal force in October, 1987. This African Charter on Individual and Peoples Rights, or the Banjul Charter, contains generally weak protections for human rights.[25] No doubt this is because most of the states which are members of the OAU manifest serious human rights problems in their territories. It is also said that the African Charter reflects a cultural emphasis on governmental and individual duties rather than rights, and on a group orientation (hence peoples rights) rather than individual rights. Be that as it may, there is no African court of human rights, and the African commission on human rights appears to be a weak agency without even the authority to use publicity directly to embarrass a government which has violated its obligations under the Banjul Charter. (The OAU had previously approved a regional treaty on refugees.)

2. The Islamic Middle East and the region of Asia have no regional treaties on human rights. The Arab League does have a Permanent Arab Commission on Human Rights, dating from 1968. The commission has fostered national delegations and a regional action plan, and it does comment on governmental reports. But it has given priority in its work to the important but limited question of protecting human rights in the territories occupied by Israel since 1967. Its work in Arab countries has been less assertive and characterized more by promotion than by protection of human rights. There is growing demand in many parts of Asia for more serious attention to internationally recognized human rights, but this demand has not, at the time of writing, led to the construction of regional machinery for the protection of human rights.

3. In Europe as a whole, however, there is the Helsinki Accord. In discussing this accord we must first note that the United States and Canada are considered honorary Europeans (much as Japan used to be considered an honorary European in the 1930s). Second, we should note that the 1975 Helsinki Accord is not, strictly speaking, law. It is not a treaty but rather a diplomatic agreement. Moreover, its specific terms rarely mention human rights but rather emphasize humanitarian principles. Its overriding significance is twofold: (1) this agreement creates the expectation that the thirty-five signatory nations will implement certain specific human values which transcend philosophical and other differences; and (2) the subject is important enough to merit periodic reviews by signatories to ascertain who is meeting the expectations and who is not. The accord thus performs the function of law while avoiding a legal label. More attention has probably been directed to these diplomatic standards than to most international

law. The accord addresses human rights in fact, even though the document speaks mostly of humanitarian subjects.

In part three of the accord, which deals de facto with human rights (the first two parts concern security and economics), the thirty-five states agree to do such things as reunite families divided by the East-West conflict, promote the movement of journalists and the freer flow of ideas across that conflict, and take other steps recognized de facto as the rights of individuals. The Marxist states, not philosophically supportive of individual rights in general, accepted these norms for at least two reasons. First, the Eastern states received in return Western support for the geopolitical status quo in Europe (the meaning of the security part of the Helsinki Accord is that the thirty-five states accept the legitimacy of a divided Germany, present Polish borders, etc.). And second, no international organization was created to implement the accord. True, a diplomatic conference was held in Belgrade in 1977, and in Madrid in 1980–82, and in Ottawa and also Stockholm in the mid-1980s in order to oversee implementation, but conference resolutions were not binding and moreover had to be adopted by consensus. Thus state jurisdiction was not seriously eroded.

Nevertheless, by design or miscalculation, the thirty-five states involved started a process in the 1970s through which their national policies were evaluated by others according to international standards. The values specified in basket three of the accord (all sorts of things were "thrown into the basket"), insofar as they were not already included in other human rights agreements, ceased to be matters of purely domestic concern and became matters which could be legitimately debated by the other states. This debate covered a wide range of subjects, from Soviet use of psychiatry on political dissidents to American restrictions on the use of passports.

Summary of Contemporary Developments

In summary, there is a clear if incomplete answer to the question "What are human rights, anyway?" Universal human rights are defined by international agreements, the most important of which are treaties. There are the core U.N. agreements, the supplementary U.N. agreements, the law of human rights in armed conflict, and regional agreements. All of these constitute the human rights affirmed by states. Some of the most important human rights agreements along with the extent of their acceptance can be noted in table 1.

TABLE I

Acceptance of Major Human Rights Agreements, 1987

Agreement	Open	State #	Adherence #	Ratio
UN Economic Covenant	1966	159	90	.56
UN Political Covenant	1966	159	86	.54
Optional Protocol	1966	159	38	.23
UN Racial Discrimination	1965	159	124	.78
UN Apartheid	1973	159	86	.54
UN Women Discrimination	1979	159	93	.58
UN Genocide	1948	159	97	.61
UN Slavery	1956	159	102	.64
UN Prostitution	1949	159	59	.37
UN Torture	1984	159	40	.25
UN Refugees	1951	159	99	.62
Protocol	1967	159	100	.63
ILO Association #87	1948	160	98	.61
ILO Bargaining #98	1949	160	114	.71
ILO Forced Labor #105	1957	160	108	.68
ILO Discrimination #111	1958	160	108	.68
Geneva Conventions	1949	171	165	.96
Protocol 1	1977	171	67	.39
Protocol 2	1977	171	61	.36
European Convention	1950	21	21	1.00
Art. 25 Decl. (Ind. pet.)[1]	1955	21	17	.81
Art. 62 Decl. (Ct. juris)[2]	1958	21	19	.90
American Convention	1969	32	19	.59
Art. 45 Decl. (St. pet.)[3]	1969	32	8	.25
Art. 62 Decl. (Ct. juris)[2]	1969	32	9	.28
Helsinki Accord	1975	35	35	1.00

1. Individual petition

2. Court jurisdiction

3. State petition

Chapter Two

Promoting Human Rights

Some Fundamental Issues

*If we can make sense of human rights, and bring our
conceptions of them down to earth a little, the
intelligibility and usefulness of appeals to human
rights in social and political discourse will be
strengthened.*
James W. Nickel, *Making Sense of Human Rights*
(Berkeley: University of California Press, 1987), p. 39.

INTRODUCTION

It should be clear by now that much international law and diplomacy
is concerned with human rights. From the international view, human
rights is a subject firmly established on the policy-making agenda. The
crux of the concern of this book focus on the question, so what? But before proceeding to that most important question of whether all these
international agreements have any impact on political behavior, it
may prove useful to engage in a short further discussion of this process
of establishing norms—usually called promotion. We should not gloss
over the establishment of human rights standards, for promotion may
be fairly considered a type of indirect protection.

Rights and Politics

The very notion of human rights may obscure the fact that the human
rights endorsed in international agreements result from a political process. To describe the ideas that went into human rights agreements, to
describe how human rights treaties were negotiated, and to describe
the principles in those agreements is to describe the international legislative process for human rights. And the legislative process is always

a political process. States, the only full subjects of law (the only actors with full legal personality from the international view), are the primary actors who make law. States are political animals which act in political ways. It is ironic that while rights have been mostly studied by philosophers and lawyers, rights standards clearly result from a political process. Making human rights rules (and even more so implementing them, as we shall see) is part of a political process. The abstract debate over human rights may be a matter for philosophers, but establishing (and implementing) rights is a proper subject of politics—although I would allow a role for my lawyerly friends.

The relationship between politics and law has been well captured by Ivo Duchacek:

> The dynamic force behind all constitution making [with bills of rights or human rights provisions] is primarily political: however legalistic a national constitution as a supreme law of the land [or a global or regional constitution—e.g., the U.N. Charter] may sound, it basically deals with the hard core of all politics, namely who leads whom, with what intent, for what purpose, by what means, and with what restraints.[1]

It is precisely because of the reasoning of this quotation that states pay so much attention to the details of international human rights agreements. The norms specify the purpose of national rule, the restrictions on state policy, the relative authority of states and international organizations and individuals. In a word (more or less), human rights norms are supposed to affect the exercise of power, and states are always concerned about power—especially in a basically nation-state system where their security depends upon their power. Above all, human rights norms establish a source of legitimacy for states. States which implement human rights standards have an unimpeachable claim to being legitimate from the international point of view. Legitimacy contributes to stability and the successful exercise of power. Human rights is thus very much part of world politics.

Centrality of Socioeconomic Concerns

The making of international human rights has paralleled national lawmaking in this sense: both international and national law have been increasingly concerned with social and economic subjects. At the national level almost all states aspire to some version of the welfare state. Virtually all states reject the idea that the state should only control violence and do nothing about social and economic justice. The same evolution is now occurring at the international level. Some authors have already observed increased international regulation of economic matters, so that the old division of international law between public (order) and private (economic) no longer holds completely.[2] We are now witnessing a spectacular growth of legal regulation not just because of a concern with order per se or with economic transactions, but because of a concern with justice—read human dignity—for persons (whether as individuals, groups, or peoples).

This concern for justice, a.k.a. human dignity, certainly has a political and civil dimension, above all to the Western mind. But the fact bears emphasizing that the evolution of international human rights reflects a growing emphasis on economic and social matters. I have already noted that some states tend to downplay or exclude the civil and political dimension to human rights. What I would like to emphasize here is that some Western states and nonstate actors do *not* downgrade the idea of socioeconomic rights. The Catholic church has been at least sporadically interested in economic rights for almost a century. The constitutions in Mexico and Ireland in the 1930s contained a charter or bill of social and economic rights. President Franklin Roosevelt spoke of the importance of freedom from want. President Lyndon Johnson spoke of the "right to earn a living."[3] Economic rights have been debated periodically in the U.S. Congress.[4] A number of past and current Western constitutions, especially those in Scandinavia, contain social and economic rights. Thus there is now an embryonic attempt to create an international welfare state, and most Western states support this principle. Individual social and economic rights figure prominently in this effort.

The demanded third generation rights of solidarity can be seen as part of this evolution of moving from individual civil and political rights to other subjects. This evolution remains controversial. Some believe that human rights can only be individual and must be restricted to civil and political rights. Some are willing to accept individual economic and social rights but resist collective rights. Some argue that the solidarity rights are too amorphous as demanded, entailing no specific duties on specific actors; who is obligated under the "rights" to peace and development, for example, and what exactly is required? On the other hand, supporters argue that the first two generations of rights are meaningless and do not lead to human dignity unless one avoids such situations as major wars, abject poverty, a polluted environment. After all, they say, what good is the right to vote if there is no ozone layer to protect us from the sun?

Uneven Development

The development of international human rights has been uneven. Indeed, as noted, human rights in armed conflict preceded more general human rights, in some cases by more than a hundred years. The concern about slavery long preceded the concern for women's rights. And so on.

To some, this unevenness is cause for relegating human rights to the "back burner" (as they say in the State Department). Consider the view of the distinguished diplomat and historian George Kennan:

> One notes that even among those Americans who profess the most passionate attachment to [guaranteeing liberties], the actual enthusiasm is highly selective. . . . They show no comparable concern for the nameless and numberless Chinese who may have fallen victim to the rigid intellectual and physical discipline of the Chinese Communist regime; for the several tens of thousands of Africans slaughtered . . . by other black Africans . . .; for the Indians abruptly and brutally expelled from Kenya and Uganda; for the thousands of Angolan blacks forced to flee . . .; nor indeed, in the case of the Soviet Union, for the hundreds of thousands of non-Jewish people . . . who are still suffering from the measures taken against them in the Stalin period. These and other such peoples simply do not fit into the highly selective limits to which the enthusiasm of various Americans for other people's liberties is normally confined."[5]

In this view, if one cannot give a "very fair and principled devotion to the cause," one should not pursue it very much, if at all.

But an uneven development of human rights, and indeed an uneven concern about human rights, is a normal condition. In no society does development of human rights occur all of one piece, at one time. In Western societies the right to vote was progressively achieved—e.g., from property-owning males in England to, say, women in Switzerland in contemporary times. (And some Swiss women in the German, agrarian cantons still do not have the right to vote in local elections.) In the United States, concern about the rights of black Americans antedated in most cases concern for the rights of Spanish-speaking Americans. Thus it is reasonable to expect promotion and protection of human rights to remain uneven and to be dependent upon shifting perceptions and political coalitions.

It is not reasonable—in an international society of varying cultures, philosophies, and levels of economic development—to expect the rights of migrant workers in the West, political dissidents in the East, or Western journalists in the Third World to be developed fully and simultaneously (to pick three examples at random). In the light of this reasoning, the argument that one must have practical action for all individuals everywhere before one should do anything about anyone anywhere is simply at odds with the reality of human rights in historical perspective.

One may want to keep a totally even-handed or balanced attention to all human rights everywhere as a moral ideal.[6] But one should keep the practical point in mind that no actor, national or international, possesses the wisdom and resources to tackle all human rights problems at once. To expect the moral standard to be the practical guide is to condemn human rights action to paralysis. We will return to the subject of biased or double-standards in the chapter on U.S. human rights policy.

Legitimacy of Human Rights

Over half of the member states of the United Nations have clearly accepted the obligation to fashion their policies in accordance with internationally agreed standards of human rights. (At a first stage of analysis, it would seem that states are far ahead of their student critics. Students are still asking, "What are human rights?" States have been acknowledging international human rights for over a century in a process which started with the *bête noire* of student radicals—the military. [At least when the author was a student several millennia ago, there were such things as student radicals.] However, appearances can be deceiving, and we will subsequently observe a number of truths on the side of the critics of governments.)

Human rights is clearly an established issue-area of world politics. What was once a matter of domestic jurisdiction has been internationalized. As the Permanent Court of International Justice once said, what is international and what is national depends on the state of international relations; things change, and what is international is what international law says is international.[7]

Debate about human rights in the Soviet Union, the United States, or anywhere else is not an impermissible interference in domestic affairs. And other types of international action may be permitted, depending upon the human rights at issue and what the relevant norms permit. Two serious questions exist, however, about state obligation to uphold international standards: (1) What is the precise content of the rule? and (2) To what extent is a state prevented from being judge and jury in a case involving itself? An obligation is fully serious only if it can be understood clearly in a concrete situation and if an impartial party is allowed to resolve differences in interpretation.[8] This point will be expanded subsequently.

Extensive Scope

International human rights standards are indeed extensive. As Ernst B. Haas has dryly observed, "The world thus seems to have a code which leaves out very little."[9] Like Haas, we use this statement not as a final analysis but rather as a transition to further questions. Unlike Haas, we do not do so quite so cynically.

FURTHER REFLECTIONS

There are detailed compendia of human rights norms for law professors and those bothered by insomnia. It is not possible to describe all rules here or to give a textual analysis of all important, substantive rules in order to logically deduce their surface meaning.[10] One can, however, identify certain basic points (at least they seem so, on less than scientific grounds) important to a discussion of human rights.

Why Do We Have the Norms?

According to the United Nations Charter and other sources, human rights exist because they contribute to international peace. The charter's Article 55, quoted above, speaks of "the creation of conditions of stability and well-being which are necessary for peaceful and friendly relations among nations based on respect for the principles of equal rights and self-determination of peoples." In this view, human rights are necessary as a means to a peaceful world society.

This view has also been expressed in this form: authoritarian governments that deny human rights cause war, whereas democracies are peace loving.[11] Hence Woodrow Wilson spoke of making the world safe for democracy (and not, as some wag put it after observing especially American policy, of making democracy safe for the world). This view seems part of American political culture. Franklin Roosevelt expressed it: "We in this nation still believe that [self-determination] should be predicated on certain freedoms which we think are essential everywhere. We know that we ourselves will never be wholly safe at home unless other governments recognize such freedoms."[12] Secretary of State George Marshall said it: "Governments which systematically disregard the rights of their own people are not likely to respect the rights of other nations and other people and are likely to seek their objectives by coercion and force in the international field."[13] Jimmy Carter said something similar: "Because we are free, we can never be indifferent to the fate of freedom elsewhere.[14]

And Stanley Hoffmann, an eminent political scientist at Harvard who does not have to make high-sounding speeches, has said much the same thing: "If one believes in the values of liberalism, it is not enough merely to have them practiced at home; and if one wants to establish a livable world order, human rights must be taken into account, since governments have a disturbing way of connecting their behavior at home and their behavior abroad."[15]

Discussion of the complex relationship between human rights and peace can be organized according to three arguments. (1) There is probably a connection between how a state treats human rights at home and the nature of its foreign policy. This relationship, however, is complex. And it is not so clear that a state which violates human rights at home will necessarily be aggressive in its foreign policy. (2) Denial of human rights at home may lead to intervention by a foreign power to correct the injustice, but pure humanitarian intervention happens rarely since other expediential factors are usually present encouraging the intervention. (3) The denial of human rights may lead to an international armed conflict, but such a situation is likely to transpire and be officially recognized as such when the right denied is that to national self-determination against racist colonialism.

1. In its bold form the linkage between denial of human rights and aggression is probably more complex than the thinking, affected by

Nazism, that went into the U.N. Charter. There is considerable evidence to support the proposition that democracies (viz., those governments respecting civil and political rights) do not make war on each other, but they do make war on others.[16] One searches in vain for a clear-cut case of international war between two democracies in modern times. On the other hand, democracies do make war on others (the three democratic states of Britain, France, and Israel invaded Egypt in 1956; democratic America forced war on the Spanish Empire at the turn of the century). Moreover, not all authoritarian states (viz., those that violate civil and political rights to varying degrees) act aggressively in international affairs. Fascist Spain, for example, was neutral during the Second World War.

In its more subtle form the linkage between human rights and a peaceful world is worth exploring. The peace research school, associated primarily with academics in Scandinavia, equates the denial of human rights ipso facto with the denial of peace. Peace is defined to mean the absence of psychic dissatisfaction. Denial of rights leads to perceived deprivation and hence to psychic anguish. One problem with this approach is that peace comes to mean justice. Another problem is that awareness of deprivation may not bring psychic peace but a feeling of tension and frustration in the struggle to correct the problem.

Perhaps more convincing is the argument that a Soviet Union which denies human rights at home via forced labor is not likely to be genuinely interested in consistently trying to eradicate forced labor abroad—although it may support such an effort when directed against an American ally like South Africa. Likewise, a United States uninterested in economic injustice at home is not likely to be genuinely interested in trying to implement economic rights abroad—although it may use the language of economic rights to defend an ally like the Shah of Iran, who had engaged in some land reform. Hence governments probably do connect their behavior at home with their behavior abroad. The nature of a regime—meaning the thrust of its major policies—does have a bearing on its foreign policy.[17] This will become clearer in chapter 7, where we examine American foreign policy in detail.

In general, if states do not accept a common standard of rights, the probability of long-term international conflict increases. But it is much too simple to say with validity that authoritarian states are inherently aggressive. Some authoritarian states, moreover, may have a good record at implementing socioeconomic rights. And it is equally simplistic to say that democratic states are inherently peace loving. The U.S. in particular displays a sizable history of violent actions especially in Central America.

2. Denial of human rights can provoke violence in the form of foreign armed intervention, but usually other considerations are present. Foreign intervention is humanitarian intervention when undertaken to correct a violation of human rights and when there is no intention to change the political or legal structure of the offending regime.[18] But cases of pure humanitarian intervention are rare. The United States used "Operation Stanleyville" to rescue some whites from internal violence in the old Belgian Congo in the 1950s. More recently, Israel launched the raid on Entebbe airport in Uganda in the 1970s to free hostages from a hijacking situation. (There is some debate about whether the concept of humanitarian intervention covers action by a state to rescue its own, as opposed to foreign, nationals; such debate need not detain us here.)

After the U.S. used force in Grenada in 1983 not only to remove U.S. nationals from that tiny Caribbean island, but also to overthrow the Marxist ruling authorities and enforce elections which led to a new government, there was a spate of writing about whether armed intervention in a state was permissible when intended to correct human rights abuses and install a government sympathetic to internationally recognized human rights.[19] Some argued that such coercive intervention was permissible when for the purposes recognized in the U.N. Charter. Others argued that parts of the U.N. Charter recognizing domestic jurisdiction of states, along with other parts requiring peaceful settlement of disputes, precluded the legality of such armed intervention. Complicating the picture was the argument that the U.S. only used force, along with supporting legal claims, when it could attack a leftist government which was supposedly violating human rights— i.e., Grenada, Nicaragua 1979–88, Cuba in 1961; the U.S. never used force to correct human rights violations in rightist regimes.

The case of Grenada is one more example of the biggest problem with the claim to humanitarian intervention: states are prone to use the claim as a mask for ideological or strategic objectives. (Actually in the Grenada case the U.S. used a variety of shifting and largely ex post facto claims, in an effort to rationalize its use of force.) Vietnam occupied Democratic Kampuchea (Cambodia) ostensibly to oust the genuinely genocidal regime of Pol Pot, but in so doing it installed a puppet regime of its choice and thereby engaged in denial of self-determination, along with other denials of individual human rights. India intervened in what is now Bangladesh in the early 1970s to stop the slaughter of young Bengali males by the Punjabi of West Pakistan, but India also took the opportunity to dismember its arch rival Pakistan.

Moreover, even a major violation of human rights does not always—or even usually—lead to violence. The Idi Amin regime in Uganda compiled a horrendous human rights record but was not invaded by Tanzania until Ugandan troops crossed into Tanzanian territory. There are many examples of an obvious, consistent pattern of gross violations of internationally recognized human rights but not followed by armed intervention to stop the abuses.[20]

3. As for the denial of human rights leading to escalation to international armed conflict (which can overlap with the idea of foreign intervention), this undeniably happens. (A good example of escalation to *internal* armed conflict is that of El Salvador from 1979 to the time of writing. Repression and oppression led to the overthrow of the ancient regime and to a continuing civil war recognized as such by subsequent governments.) The relation between human rights and international war is most clear in cases involving denial of the right to self-determination.

Self-determination of peoples is an internationally recognized right of long standing but unclear meaning. It was a favorite subject of Woodrow Wilson and became a favorite subject at the United Nations, whose Charter mentioned it in several places.[21] The two 1966 covenants contain a common first article whose first paragraph reads: "All peoples have the right of self-determination. By virtue of the right they freely determine their political status and freely pursue their economic, social and cultural development."

This hoary principle is important. Recognition of self-determination is the key to participation in the making of international rules and in influencing the distribution of international benefits. An actor cannot participate fully in world politics unless widely recognized as a state. To be recognized as a state, the actor must represent a people that has achieved self-determination.

But recognition of states, which is based on recognized self-determination, is a subject considerably muddied by the troubled waters of world politics. In fact, recognition and self-determination have no transcendent meaning. Do the Eritreans have the right to self-determination from Ethiopia, the Kurds from Iraq, the Armenians from Turkey, the Basques from Spain, the Scots from Britain, the Native American Indians from the United States, and so on ad nauseam?

The waters become less muddied when the issue is self-determination from colonialism. It is in the denial of this type of self-determination, especially when racism is involved, that the denial of human rights is most likely to escalate to an international armed conflict. Indeed, the U.N. Security Council—in the Rhodesian case—has given an authoritative, binding ruling that a threat to international peace can result from denial of human rights.

How can we distinguish self-determination vis-a-vis colonialism from unjustified claims to self-determination? According to a U.N. document negotiated by states from all regions and approved by the General Assembly, the key is whether the territory in question is "possessed of a government representing the whole people belonging to the territory without distinction as to race, creed or colour."[22]

Thus from 1965 to 1979 the black majority of Zimbabwe was said to be entitled to self-determination because the two governments claiming authority over the territory, the Rhodesian and the British, did not represent the whole people and did discriminate on the basis of race. And the Security Council made not just a recommendation but an international law to this effect. (The Security Council is entitled to adopt a binding resolution when dealing with a threat to the peace, breach of the peace, or act of aggression. Thus in the situation of Rhodesia/Zimbabwe, the council decided in 1966–68 that the denial of human rights—especially by the Ian Smith government, which was itself illegal—constituted a threat to the peace.)[23]

Legal perspectives aside, as they are all too frequently, factually there was an international war over Rhodesia (with participation in various ways by various foreign parties) because of denial of the right to self-determination (and other rights). In the view of the majority of states at the U.N., the armed struggle for self-determination from colonialism is by definition an international armed conflict, regardless of the level of violence or the degree of participation by outside states.[24]

Thus the idea of self-determination, and the relationship between this human right and international peace, is clear in places like Zimbabwe and Namibia.[25] Yet there remain many fuzzy aspects to the idea and the relationship. These aspects may be clarified by the following questions: when does ethnicity within a state lead to justified demand for a new state? Does the U.S. government represent American Indians? Does the Soviet Union discriminate against Latvians? Does Ethiopia place a negative distinction on the creed of Eritrean-ness? Do the peoples of the Chittagong Hill Tracts in Bangladesh have a right of secession because they are discriminated against by the Bengali majority?[26]

Whatever the objective answers to these sorts of questions about the relation of ethnicity to statehood, two essentially political questions must then be answered: what is the prospect of violence from the situation in question, and will the Security Council or other authoritative body (e.g., World Court) clearly characterize the situation as one of legitimate self-determination and/or armed conflict? The objective and political answers to these questions are likely to remain less than fully clear in places beyond Namibia—the last vestige of formal colonialism. Other dimensions to the concept of self-determination, which cannot be examined here for reasons of space, such as the meaning of free determination of economic development, will also remain debatable and debated.

Hence (in case you have forgotten how we started this discussion), the simple notion that human rights is necessary for peace turns out to be complicated. Denial of rights does not lead to aggression in many cases, may or may not lead to foreign intervention (and the nature of the intervention is itself not so clear), may or may not escalate to armed conflict (but probably will be so viewed when the claim of self-determination is made against racist colonialism). A state's view of human rights in general is probably connected to its behavior abroad, and denial of internationally recognized human rights is certainly a source of potential conflict.

The push for human rights, however, may produce more conflict than peace. The reverse of the idea in the U.N. Charter may be true in the short run. As Hoffmann has written, human rights breeds confrontation.[27] How can the United States speak about human rights in Russia without challenging the Kremlin's jealously guarded control over Soviet nationals, without challenging the very legitimacy of that authoritarian, totalitarian government, without reintroducing the cold war and the dangers of superpower confrontation and conflict? There are answers to these questions (although the answers are not always universally accepted). They will be discussed subsequently. For now, we repeat that we have human rights norms officially because of the view that they contribute to peace. And that, in itself, is a debatable notion.

It should be noted additionally that the Charter theory about the relationship of human rights to peace may be a formality, anyway. As mentioned previously, it is possible that human rights are addressed in the Charter, and in international law more generally, because of morality or moral demand.[28] Charter language about a functional interest in human rights—viz., that rights contribute to peace—may be a convenient theory that makes rights language more acceptable, but is perhaps a cover for the moral view which sees violations of human rights as wrong in and of themselves, whatever the connection between rights and peace.

Can We Know What the Norms Mean?

Human rights norms are sometimes very clear, as in Article 9 of the 1966 Covenant on Economic, Social, and Cultural Rights: "The States Parties to the present Covenant recognize the right of everyone to social security including social insurance." A second perspective is that international human rights law is sometimes no more vague than national law. Note the American Constitution, which declares in the Fourteenth Amendment that every American has the right to "equal protection of the laws." More than a hundred years after those words were written, Americans are still in the process of deciding what the words mean. Likewise, one can expect some time to elapse before we have a clear meaning for some human rights norms, such as this wording from Article 2 of the 1965 Convention on Racial Discrimination: states shall take "concrete measures to ensure the adequate development and protection of certain racial groups."

We will see in the next chapter that compared to most national processes, the process for interpreting international human rights norms is underdeveloped. That international process, regardless of particulars, will confront three fundamental problems because of the nature of the norms.

First, some rules *are* vague, and sometimes there is no clear meaning from the record of negotiation (this is called the legislative history of the rule). We have noted this already with regard to rights in armed conflict, where the interjection of national law coexists with a clear rule of international law (see above, first chapter, p. 18). Or note Article 12 of the 1966 Covenant on Civil and Political Rights, which first affirms liberty of movement and of emigration, and then states: "The above-mentioned rights shall not be subject to any restrictions except those which are provided by law, are necessary to protect national security, public order . . ., public health or morals or the rights and freedoms of others." Whatever agency may exist to interpret this article, there is massive ambiguity compounded by lack of guidance from the diplomatic record.[29]

Second, some rules permit both a broad and a narrow interpretation. Those who interpret must confront the problem of what scope they will give to the rule. For example, paragraph one of Article 6 of the 1966 Political Covenant states: "Every human being has the inherent right to life. This right shall be protected by law. No one shall be arbitrarily deprived of his life." The narrow interpretation includes such ideas as prohibiting summary execution—that is, death without proper examination and reflection by appropriate officials.

The broader interpretation has been well explained by Professor Asborn Eide of the Norwegian Peace Research Institute. This approach is that the right to life also prohibits structural violence. In this view, "social structures which are such that possibilities for survival and the life expectancy of the individual fall below what is avoidable according to contemporary capacity" represent systemic violations of human rights.[30] Eide points out that the structure of the global distribution of food causes the death each year of perhaps 14 million people. From a global perspective, the food exists but simply does not get to those who need it. This is structural denial of the right to life, since in objective terms the ruling elites of the world do have the material means of feeding the starving. Eide also observes that some people in Third World countries consistently get less nutrition than forced laborers in a "special punishment regime" in the Soviet Union. Lack of adequate nutrition shortens life, among other debilitating effects, and thus is a denial of the full right to life. There is, thus, a broad and socioeconomic dimension to the right to life which goes beyond making sure the police do not commit murder. As Eide has written, "Whether a child dies in infancy due to poverty and consequent malnutrition and lack of hygiene, or if it grows up and at a later stage is executed as a political opponent, the society in which this happens must be considered hostile to human rights."[31]

This second problem confronting those who would interpret human rights—the problem of a narrow versus a broad approach—relates to a third problem. Some language in human rights treaties calls on states to assure human rights; other language says to take steps to end human rights violations.[32] The difference is legally important. On

the one hand, you can have an international rule which can be legally implemented by passing a national law which is then enforced by national means. Consider Article 7 of the Political Covenant: "No one shall be subjected to torture or to cruel, inhuman or degrading treatment or punishment. In particular, no one shall be subjected without his free consent to medical or scientific experimentation." Thus signatory states are under an obligation to assure that torture is not committed. That legal assurance can be rather quickly enacted (even if controlling torture in practice takes considerable time and effort).

On the other hand, you have paragraph 1 of Article 2 of the 1966 Economic Covenant: "Each State Party to the present Covenant undertakes to take steps . . . to the maximum of its available resources, with a view to achieving progressively the full realization of the rights recognized in the present Covenant by all appropriate means." This general rule is loaded with troublesome words such as "progressively," "maximum of its available resources," and "appropriate means." Since Article 13 of the Economic Covenant requires states to take steps to progressively introduce free higher education, does the U.S. government have to stop Princeton, Harvard, and Yale from charging tuition, and if so, how soon?

The distinction between assuring a right and taking steps to progressively realize a right does not always neatly coincide with the distinction between political and socioeconomic rights. For example, Article 10 of the Political Covenant forbids prison for the sake of punishment and insists that prison be for the purpose of "reformation and social rehabilitation." The executive branch of the United States has suggested to the Senate that when and if it ratifies the covenant, it should state that Article 10 is to be realized progressively.[33] Hence some civil-political rights may require progressive implementation. But it is the broad approach especially to socioeconomic rights that frequently requires a long time for implementation. And in this process it will be very difficult to say precisely who has violated the norm, and when. How much nutrition is enough for tin miners in Bolivia, relative to Bolivia's other problems and to where Bolivia stands in the charts today compared to five years ago?

These, then, are three basic problems in understanding human rights norms in general. Some rules are indeed ambiguous. Some rules allow both a broad and narrow interpretation. And some rules require progressive implementation, which raises the question of how much is enough. Theoretically, the problems are not insurmountable. In the next chapter we will see to what extent the problems have been overcome.

Is There a Hierarchy among Conflicting Norms?

This is one of the most troublesome questions about international human rights. Where should one start in working for human rights? What should one emphasize? Is there a historical or logical or moral sequence which should be followed? If rights conflict, what is the priority?

Some theorists say that all the rights internationally recognized are of equal moral value.[34] This is not helpful in terms of practical action, given the wide range of recognized rights and the limited resources of all human rights actors. Some say that one should concentrate on implementation of minimum standards of basic rights: subsistence, security, freedom.[35] Others have other schemes,[36] including one that stresses material provisions and political participation.[37]

Unfortunately neither theorists nor statesmen have agreed on either a moral or practical hierarchy of human rights standards. One could argue as follows: (1) The most important right is the right to life broadly *and* narrowly understood. One must have sufficient nutritional and hygienic conditions in order to survive and mature with sound mind and body. But one must also be free from murder, torture, and mistreatment in order to develop with human dignity—viz., personal integrity.

(2) The second most important right is the right to participation. It is political participation which allows one to exercise most rights and allows one to control all manner of decisions affecting one's rights. Participation takes many forms, and there is no one form of participation—e.g., a multi-party, Western-style democracy—which must be followed by all. But all legitimate forms of participation entail the rights of freedom of thought, expression, and association. It is the right of participation which guarantees the right to life in both meanings. As Professor Eide notes: "It is the wider political participation which has made possible more equality in some rich countries, such as England and Norway, and it will only be when general political participation becomes a reality in the Third World that the income disparities will be rectified."[38] Hence these first two rights form a dynamic circle, one reinforcing the other.

(3) Third in importance comes the right to education, which makes participation most meaningful. (4) Other rights follow. Of course, this argument is just that—an argument. National courts, the World Court, the U.N. Security Council have not provided an authoritative statement on the subject. And the debate will surely continue.[39]

At least two further points can be made with regard to a hierarchy of rights. First, one should be wary about an easy distinction between socioeconomic and civil-political rights. The distinction sometimes exists: the right to a lawyer is not the same as the right to work. Yet the two categories are sometimes meshed, so that it is not so easy to say which category takes precedence. The classic example is the right to free trade unions (economic or civil?), but other examples exist as well (education: civil or social?). The right to food stamps in the United States (civil or economic right) has been linked by Congress to not living in a commune (civil right of association), with congressional action being overruled by the courts.[40] On an international scale, racial discrimination (involving civil and political rights) has been shown to affect negatively life span and health (involving socioeconomic rights). Thus one legal principle—e.g., right to life, or right to equality, or right to freedom of association—may involve both categories of specific rights. It may prove useful to think of rights as rights, and not to debate which categories they fall in. If this be true, it makes little sense to debate which category of rights comes first. They could lead to an integrated, composite whole.

It can be further noted in the light of the above that another easy and sometimes false statement is that civil-political rights are enforceable, whereas socioeconomic rights are not (we have already observed that both categories may be enforced progressively). We should note that some national constitutions explicitly state that socioeconomic rights are not judicially enforceable.[41] But we should equally note that socioeconomic rights are sometimes adjudicated, either as socioeconomic rights or as civil rights (and this is apart from the implementation/enforcement of these rights in non-judicial ways). In the United States, courts have adjudicated the right to social security, as well as the right to shelter (a New Jersey court said there was none), as well as the right to child support. Some U.S. courts have issued injunctions having to do with material prison conditions (is that social or civil?). In Sweden one can bring suit to establish paternity (social, civil, economic?). Also in Sweden, delinquency is dealt with not by courts but by a social agency. So we find a meshing or overlapping of socioeconomic with civil rights. Such rights, viewed as fitting in whatever category, do get adjudicated. And there are means of implementation beyond the court room. Rights may be viewed as rights, and the implementation process can be very broad. When categories of rights become so blurred, it does not prove very helpful to think in terms of hierarchies of categories of rights, at least not according to a division between political-civil and socio-economic-cultural.

Our second and last point is that some rights clearly do conflict, and for practical action on rights this conflict must be resolved. For example, in the West national constitutions have sometimes been defined so that freedom of speech includes freedom of advertising by corporations. On the other hand, there is in some national law and now in international law a right to adequate health. Factually, we have had in the 1970s and early 1980s a situation in which the Nestle Corporation of Switzerland has advertised, sometimes by questionable means such as salespersons dressed as doctors or nurses, its nursing substitute for babies. When advertising of this baby formula is combined, as it factually is in parts of the Third World, with ignorance about nutrition and hygiene on the part of parents, the result is profit for Nestle and damaged health for the infant. The marketed formula as used by badly informed parents is inferior to the mother's milk and can—and has—damaged lives. The only humane answer—viz., one based on a concern for human dignity—is that the right to life and health must take precedence over freedom of advertising. As Stanley Hoffmann has written, "Private groups cannot be above internationally recognized rights, business is not above humanity. . . ."[42] If we accept this view, it is reprehensible that the Reagan Administration was the only state to vote against WHO guidelines on the marketing of infant formula in 1981, on the grounds that they infringed on free-market principles of economics.

Likewise freedom of religion can conflict with women's right to equality, especially in the Islamic world. Here again a choice must be made between affirming a people's right to practice the religion of its choice and affirming the right of a group to attain equal status. Many students of this problem opt for the superiority of women's rights, but the view of Muslims is not always the same.

One of the more salient disputes over conflicting rights occurred in the late 1970s over freedom of the press. On the one hand was the right

to free speech and movement, on the other the right to a specified public order. The conflict was sometimes presented as that between a free press and a responsible press. In UNESCO meetings the Marxist delegations introduced the idea of broad governmental restrictions on the press in the interests of responsible order. This position had strong support from parts of the Third World where governmental authority, control, and legitimacy were not strong and where there was a concomitant desire to have the press report events (or not report them) in a way favorable to national development and integration (or, more simply, in a way comfortable to ruling elites). The Western delegations opposed this position.

The debate in UNESCO was precisely about conflicting rights, it was fairly clear-cut between the West and non-West, and when the conflict was resolved it left freedom of the press undiminished as a principle, although the Third World did gain some attention to its concerns and some promises of Western assistance in building up media located in the Third World.

Therefore, in review, it can be said that the matter of a hierarchy of rights presents many questions; answers are frequently absent, which is a situation partially provoked not only by the complexity of the subject but also by the fact of meshing of the two basic categories of rights. Some rights obviously conflict. When they do, those who interpret the norms frequently make a judgment based on what seems "reasonable" in context.[43] What is reasonable in context cannot, of course, be discussed in the abstract. One must look at particular decisions in particular situations. This we do in the next three chapters.

CONCLUSIONS

The norms from international agreements on human rights are indeed "visionary." Those norms do provide a view of the "preferred . . . society." The norms do seek to counterbalance the unbridled claims of national sovereignty.[44]

That human rights agreements should create vague and conflicting norms is not surprising. One reason is the need to negotiate across different philosophical positions. A second reason is found in man's vague and conflicting aspirations. Professor Duchacek has put the matter well:

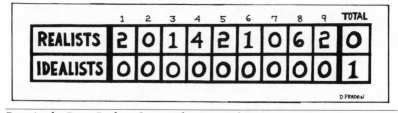

	1	2	3	4	5	6	7	8	9	TOTAL
REALISTS	2	0	1	4	2	1	0	6	2	0
IDEALISTS	0	0	0	0	0	0	0	0	0	1

D.FRADON

Drawing by Dana Fradon; © *1976 The New Yorker Magazine, Inc.*

Men are bound to reach conflicting conclusions as to what is best for them individually and for society collectively—and to be self-righteous about their opinions. In addition men are in conflict not only with other men but also with themselves. They simultaneously desire mutually exclusive goals. Sometimes a balance between partly contradictory goals is possible, often it is not. Men dread both unemployment and employment that is so rigidly planned that it resembles conscripted labor. They want to be free, yet to have a sense of direction; to go it alone and to go it with others. Such inner conflicts in men's hearts as well as conflicts between individual and general welfare, have been described but not solved in millions of pages written by philosophers, political scientists, psychologists, sociologists, anthropologists, religious leaders—and constitutional lawyers. It is too much to expect that a few [legal] articles will do more than add another brave attempt to the general search for an acceptable balance between the conflicting aims and hopes of men.[45]

Since contradictions are therefore inherent in all societies, the task for those who interpret human rights is to manage the contradictions.[46]

The management of vague and competing norms in human rights agreements raises again the question of implementation. Which norms have been implemented? In what political situations and socioeconomic conditions? It is to such questions of protecting human rights that we now turn.

Chapter Three

Protecting Human Rights

The Public Sector

Even when a right exists, it can hardly be taken for
granted that a remedy is close behind.
Stuart A. Scheingold, *The Politics of Rights* (New
Haven: Yale University Press, 1974), p. 5.

INTRODUCTION

Human rights have been promoted through the development of international agreements. These international documents frequently contain general, competing, or idealistic statements. Have some human
rights been realistically interjected into world politics from these documents? To what extent has the "law on the books" become the "law
in action"? What is the nature of the process that seeks to translate the
norms from paper to behavior? In sum, now that human rights have
been promoted through legal standards, to what degree have human
rights been protected in fact?[1] This chapter seeks answers to such
questions in the public sector of governmental and intergovernmental
agencies.

But we must first clarify our expectations about law. What should
we expect from international human rights norms? The question may
seem frivolous. A college sophomore at 8:30 on Monday morning
might say, "Why, of course we expect the law to tell individuals what
they can't do." Law, however, is more complex. As part of its general
function of providing order law manifests three roles: it constitutes an
ideology; it seeks to directly control behavior through commands; it
seeks to indirectly control behavior via political socialization—viz.,
informal education.

From the previous chapter it should be clear that much law is an
ideology. The goals of society are frequently stated through law, as is

the desired nature of governing authorities. National constitutions as well as the U.N. Charter and the human rights treaties can be considered ideologies outlining views of the just society and good government.

The traditional understanding of law is that it seeks to directly control behavior. This the law supposedly does by creating not only rules for what is permissible and impermissible behavior but also a system of implementation. At the national level this formal control system is traditionally thought of in terms of a court system which issues commands and a police system which enforces them.

Another understanding of law is that it seeks to control behavior indirectly or informally. Law is an agent of political socialization (viz., informal political learning). Seen thusly, law may affect politics less by court order and more by stimulating a new distribution of influence in the political system. Hence an important question is whether reference to law "can be useful for redistributing power and influence in the political arena."[2] If one is dissatisfied with the values dominant in existing public policy and the pattern of power which undergirds those controlling values, one may appeal to law in various ways to change that situation. The ultimate expectation may be not so much to advance one's cause through strictly judicial processes, but rather to mobilize political support for a political solution. Appeals to law, petitions based on law, attempts to go to court are all frequently used to redistribute power and change policy short of a complete judicial process. One can implement law in a variety of ways, in addition to enforcing it via courts.[3]

We will find in this chapter that the international law of human rights, while an ideological ideal, also attempts to control behavior both formally and informally. The official international means of control are weak, compared to much national law, which is the price paid for having the ideology officially adopted in treaties.[4] Most states, in negotiating human rights agreements, do not want authoritative international means of protection. The weak international control agencies, for the most part, exist to nudge states into national steps for protecting rights. Thus the international monitoring agencies act for indirect protection over time, with a few exceptions, trying to urge states to directly protect human rights.

As we shall see in the chapter following, the unofficial means of control, in the form of private groups, seek to push international and national actors into more vigorous protection. These groups may yet mobilize significant political support, so that the official means of control are eventually strengthened.

In other sources one can find a treaty-by-treaty description of the formal means for implementing each instrument.[5] Attempted here is an analytical overview of the sum total of the global process of officially protecting human rights. Stressed is the magnitude, diversity, and complexity of that process. Emphasized especially is the distinction between bodies made up of state representatives and those composed of uninstructed individuals. Finally underlined is the importance of the difference between a recommendation and a binding judgment or decision. If we take a representative sample of the major human rights agreements mentioned in chapter 1, table 1 (all are treaties except the 1948 Universal Declaration and the 1975 Helsinki Accord), we find that there is an array of measures available for the formal protection of human rights. The formal protection of human rights, entailing implementation and enforcement, is a broad and complex process.

In terms of increasing obligation on the part of states and increasing authority on the part of international organizations, the measures range from states' having to file a report with an international organization to states' having to accept a binding judgment from an international organization. Intermediary measures (1) permit an international organization to make a recommendation or suggestion to a state, either through an intergovernmental body or through a special organ composed of uninstructed or independent individuals; and (2) permit an international organization to create a conciliation body to work for resolution of a problem. There is also the matter of states' allowing their nationals to petition directly to an international organization, a process which may lead to either a recommendation or a binding decision, depending upon the law in question.

Reports

Eight of the seventeen agreements call upon states to make periodic reports concerning their implementation of human rights. Some reporting is by tradition rather than treaty obligation, as is true of reports to the International Red Cross concerning human rights in armed con-

TABLE 2
Official Measures, International Implementation of Human Rights

Agreements	IO Receives State Reports	IO Suggests: (Instructed)	IO Suggests: (Uninstructed)	IO Conciliates: (Uninstructed) Special Body	IO Receives Individ. Pet.	UNSC (Instructed)	Court (Uninstructed)
Core							
U.N. Charter		x	x	x[2]	x	x	
'48 Declaration[1]		x	x	x[2]	x		
Pol. Covenant	x	x	x		x[3]		
Econ. Covenant	x	x	x				
General							
Racial Discrim.	x	x	x	x	x[3]		x
Genocide		x					x
Women's Rights, '52		x					x
ILO Association	x	x	x	x[4]	x[5]		
Refugee	x	x		x	x		x
UNESCO Education	x	x		x	x		x
Slavery	x	x		x			x
Armed Conflict							
1949 Conventions	x[6]	x[7]		x	x[8]		
1977 Protocol 1	x[6]	x[7]		x	x[8]		
1977 Protocol 2	x[6]	x[7]		x			
Regional							
European		x	x	x	x[3]		x[3]
Inter-American	x	x	x	x	x[3]		x[3]
Helsinki[1]		x[9]					

NOTE: The chart does not suggest that any sequence of measures is required. Certain measures, such as state reporting, may be obligatory under law, but the reports do not permit binding judgments to be rendered. There is a fine—e.g., delicate—distinction between instructed suggestions and uninstructed conciliation.

[1] Not treaty law.
[2] Secretary-general diplomacy.
[3] Optional.
[4] Instructed and uninstructed.
[5] Union petition.
[6] By tradition, RC conference.
[7] Instructed and uninstructed.
[8] Detainees only.
[9] By unanimous vote.

flict. Reporting in and of itself may cause states to rectify some types of human rights violations. The reporting may produce new perceptions of perhaps technical or inadvertent deficiencies. For example, New Zealand was led to change some of its national law affecting individuals because of reporting and follow-up questions in the U.N. Human Rights Committee which operates under the U.N. Covenant on Civil-Political Rights.[6]

We know very little about how national bureaucracies act when required to do this kind of reporting. Under national law there is some evidence that required reporting on human rights does lead to increased attention to rights.[7] As for reporting to international agencies, we do know that many of these state reports are not filed on time and not taken seriously. If we look at reports under five major human rights treaties (U.N. Economic Covenant, U.N. Political Covenant, U.N. treaty on Racial Discrimination, U.N. treaty prohibiting Discrimination against Women, and U.N. treaty prohibiting Torture) by 1986 more than 460 state reports were behind schedule.[8] Some of those that were submitted were thin in substance. Reporting requirements lead to a particularly heavy burden on the less developed countries, since they frequently lack numerous and well-trained experts in this policy area (as in others). But above all the reporting record shows that rhetoric about rights, and willingness to promote rights through legal codification, has not been matched by serious efforts at implementation.

There is little if any evidence that reporting *per se* can correct major problems or deficiencies resulting from decisions made by top national leaders. Reporting is obviously not a panacea. The Soviet Union adhered to the 1966 U.N. treaty on civil and political rights (which entered into legal force in 1976) and was therefore, like New Zealand, obligated to submit a report to the U. N. Human Rights Committee created under that treaty. The thrust of the first Soviet report, submitted in 1978, was that there were no major civil-political problems in the Soviet Union. The Soviet constitution protected those rights, and thus any problems were eliminated.

Obviously, certain civil-political problems inhere in any authoritarian and totalitarian society (and the Soviet leadership occasionally, in ideologically correct terms, refers to itself as a dictatorship of the proletariat), and it is equally obvious that reporting alone will not correct them. By the mid-1980s Soviet representatives were still arguing in the U.N. Human Rights Committee that there was no discrepancy between obligations under the Covenant and the Soviet practice of civil-political rights.[9] By the late 1980s the Gorbachev regime was admitting that political prisoners existed, along with other human rights problems; one would want to watch carefully to see if Soviet reporting eventually changed.

Reporting may be a partial step in eventually securing some improvement in a situation. It may turn out to be historically significant that 1979 was the first time ever that the Soviet Union was legally obligated to respond to questions about its policies on civil-political rights. There is the view that the Soviet leadership is sensitive over time to criticism of its rights policies. This view sees the Soviet Union as wanting to be accepted above all in Europe, but in the wider world as well, as a legitimate, civilized state. It is at least possible, at the time of writing, that the Gorbachev era will lead to some fundamental changes in the practice of especially civil but also possibly political rights. From 1985 to 1988 some limited changes did occur with regard to press and cultural freedoms and also on the question of political psychiatry. If further changes in rights policy occur, various pressures from abroad (U.N. agencies, the ILO, the World Psychiatric Association, Amnesty International, Helsinki follow-up meetings) may have contributed to those changes. While changes have not yet occurred in Soviet reporting to the U.N. Human Rights Committee, the story is not over yet. If it is unlikely that the U.N. Human Rights Committee alone would prove to be a major influence on Soviet policy, its actions combined with others might be a contributing factor. (Given the fact that the Soviet Union remains a largely closed society despite the changes of the Gorbachev era, we are not likely to know exactly what led to the changes in rights policy that do occur.)

Recommendations

Implicit in the discussion above is the notion that state reports shade into comments by members of monitoring bodies. While the reporting itself may on occasion lead to changes, a major purpose of state reporting is to give international organizations an official source of information in order to make comments which become recommendations about implementing human rights. All human rights agreements permit such suggestions in one form or another, whether or not state reports are obligatory under an agreement. Even the Universal Declaration of Human Rights, which was not immediately binding and which said nothing about measures for supervision of its implementation, can lead to a recommendation by the U.N. General Assembly and/or the U.N. Human Rights Commission. (The Human Rights Commission operates under the Charter and reports to the Economic and Social Council—ECOSOC. It should not be confused with the Human Rights Committee, which operates under specific treaty provisions and is independent of the major U.N. bodies.) If one thing is clear about international human rights, it is that discussion of the subject, leading to recommendations, is now a legitimate part of world politics and is not an impermissible interference in domestic affairs.

Despite this last statement, and even though recommendations constitute a relatively weak form of attempted implementation, some states oppose the process as much as possible. States with something to hide in their rights record frequently try to limit the exercise of the authority to recommend. Under the African Charter of Human and Peoples Rights, African states require the African Human Rights Commission not to address states directly and publicly, but only the OAU itself. The Eastern European states have tried to limit recommendations by the U.N. Human Rights Committee. Particularly the Eastern European states have argued that it is up to each individual state to determine what the human rights agreement requires, and to block the development of a right to recommend by international agencies.[10] This stance by the East European states pertains to socio-economic rights as well, supposedly their strong suit.[11] Of course these same states are not reluctant to have the General Assembly make strong recommendations to states like Israel or Chile, since the Soviet Union and its allies are in the majority on those issues; sheer opportunism prevails.

While the U.N. General Assembly and the U.N. Human Rights Commission are composed of states and make numerous recommendations on human rights, a trend in the U.N.—and globally—is for suggestions to be made by bodies of individual experts. The reason for this can be seen in the history of monitoring the U.N. Economic Covenant. For a time the U.N. Economic Covenant was monitored, at least theoretically, by a working group of governmental experts acting under the intergovernmental ECOSOC. This process worked so poorly that by 1987 a group of uninstructed (personal or individual) experts was created to take over that process. The previous working group of governmental experts had done virtually nothing by way of serious supervision, and the parent ECOSOC had been content to drift with the status quo. Forces for change finally succeeded in breathing some life into the monitoring process, and to make the supervision of socio-economic rights similar to civil-political rights. Both the 1966 U.N. Covenant on Political and Civil Rights and the Convention on Racial Discrimination create special bodies of uninstructed individuals to process and make recommendations about the state reports.

It is clear that instructed (that is, intergovernmental) bodies contain a built-in brake on effective protection of human rights. The foxes (states) are charged with protecting the chickens (human rights). Those bodies place a state, which is generally interested in protection of power and national sovereignty, in a position to elevate those interests over human rights. The history of the U.N. Human Rights Commission demonstrates just that tendency, although that history also shows an interesting evolution. The commission, made up of states, first denied to itself the right to make specific recommendations about specific countries. When it did agree to undertake that activity, for years it acted only against such international pariahs as South Africa and Israel—and later Chile *post*-Allende. Only some thirty years after its creation did it begin to look more systematically at countries violating human rights.[12]

This broader concern by the U.N. Human Rights Commission, however, remained limited. Major powers did not become targets. So Chile tried to defend itself by asking why the Soviet Union had never been the target of concerted U.N. action, thus challenging the fairness of the U.N. process. (Moreover, Chile used critical U.N. suggestions to buttress its repressive regime. In 1978 the junta called a plebiscite which rejected U.N. criticism by a three-to-one margin. This constituted a de facto vote of confidence in the regime, at least from the junta's point of view. Thus the regime manipulated Chilean nationalism into a vote against U.N. action on human rights. This was accomplished by a government which certainly allowed, and in some cases directly caused, gross violations of many human rights.)[13]

Recommendations from the U.N. Human Rights Commission or from ECOSOC and the General Assembly on human rights have not had notable impact on target states—most certainly in the short run. It is evident that suggestions by instructed representatives are inadequate as a formal means of implementing human rights. Such recommendations, especially of a critical or negative nature, smack of foreign pressure, which can be used to mobilize emotional and defensive nationalism—particularly when the process of recommending is characterized by majority politics rather than impartial inquiry, as is all too frequently the case with intergovernmental action. That is to say, particularly U.N. intergovernmental bodies have not established a record of balanced concern for human rights *per se*, as compared to using human rights criticism as a means to a strategic or ideological goal.[14] It can be said, however, there by the late 1980s there was some increased balance in U.N. instructed bodies, compared to the first twenty or twenty-five years of U.N. deliberations.[15]

Unfortunately, recommendations from uninstructed bodies frequently meet an impotent fate also. In theory these suggestions should be more effective, being more free from the expediential (viz., self-interested or self-serving) considerations of states. Impartiality should lead to acceptability. But the price of impartiality has been weakness. For example, the implementing committee of individuals under the Racial Discrimination Convention has been suggesting to the United Kingdom that it disclose its dealings with South Africa. The committee wishes to know, ostensibly, whether the United Kingdom is contributing to racial discrimination in the Republic of South Africa. But the United Kingdom rejects this recommendation, saying that such a subject does not fall under the convention. And Britain has the power to make its rejection effective.

One of the more encouraging trends on human rights at the U.N. is the use of expert rapporteurs or working groups in order to by-pass, as much as possible, majority politics based on state self-interest. The U.N. Human Rights Commission, and its Sub-Commission, have employed such rapporteurs or working groups on general and specific problems: torture, summary executions, disappeared persons, religious discrimination; human rights in Afghanistan, Guatemala, El Salvador, Chile. Such independent actors can make recommendations without tint of ideological or partisan or strategic bias. This process gives an intellectual or moral authority to their recommendations. Unfortunately, the process does not appear to lead to improved protection in the short run, whatever its contribution to long-term implementation of rights, because of the power of recalcitrant states to resist.

The fate of international recommendations can also be studied through the interesting history of the ILO and its Convention on Freedom of Association. The ILO is an almost global organization, and this convention had led to state reports over about three decades. In other ways this ILO convention presents a picture of what Ernst B. Haas calls "conditions optimal for value sharing."[16] Almost all states of whatever ideological stripe profess an interest in the working class and endorse labor rights. To what extent is that sharing of values reflected in state compliance with ILO recommendations? First we should note that the ILO's process of making suggestions in relation to freedom of association is complex. The process is partly by instructed bodies, but key parts are played by independent agencies (the details need not detain us here).

Through the 1960s the process was widely regarded as equitable. That is, it was largely free of simple majority voting based on power considerations and on concerns distant from trade union freedom. The process was therefore unlike those in the U.N. General Assembly and the U.N. Human Rights Commission.

When looking at the ILO through the 1960s, one could be an optimist. There was some state compliance with ILO suggestions, especially when an established state policy to the contrary had existed for some time but was not strongly held at the time of suggested change by the ILO. There was other evidence, noted by Professor Haas, of state cooperation with ILO recommendations:

> Human rights are increasingly made the objects of complaints; voluntary organizations at the national level manifest a growing concern: the legitimacy of supervisory machinery is developing nicely, as are its methods of inquiry; the scope of rights to be protected is gradually expanding; . . . authoritarian regimes are more and more often defendants; and the distorting influence of international, politically charged issues is being more and more pushed to the side.[17]

A worker's paradise, however, was not yet at hand. In the period surveyed, 60 percent of ILO recommendations critical of given policies or practices remained unexecuted. Many types of states were found in this group which failed to implement ILO suggestions. Professor Haas ultimately concluded: "The authority of the international machinery is not improving; the overall record of national compliance is very poor and shows no signs of improvement; compliance is concentrated among countries least in need of international prodding, whereas those most in need remain uniformly unresponsive. . . ."[18]

One can say either that a rate of 40 percent compliance with ILO recommendations for change is good, or that 60 percent non-compliance is bad. The more pessimistic view seems justified by events in the 1970s. Majority power politics increased, and impartial voting on labor freedoms declined. The Marxist and Third World states within the ILO became more and more concerned with criticizing Israel on less than fully persuasive grounds—a development occurring simultaneously within UNESCO. The United States withdrew from the ILO from 1977 to 1980, for this and other reasons.[19] One lesson to be drawn from the ILO of the 1970s is that the governmental sector refused to allow the independent sector to function in an impartial and effective way. (The ILO is unique in that its membership is made up of state delegates, private business or management delegates, and private labor delegates. Much of the vigor for ILO action on rights comes from the labor delegations, although those from Eastern Europe are really under the control of the state.)

In the 1980s, when the ILO was the beneficiary of renewed emphasis on labor rights and a related decline in political battles over non-labor issues, other problems arose. The ILO took a clear, tough stand on the suppression of the independent labor movement, Solidarity, in Poland. Strong recommendations deploring martial law and the legal banning of Solidarity by the ILO led to the withdrawal of Poland. Its East European allies fought a minority battle against recommendations by the ILO concerning labor rights throughout Eastern Europe. It was clear that recommendations, even from respected international organizations, were frequently insufficient to curtail major violations of recognized rights, whether those recommendations stemmed from instructed or uninstructed bodies.

Conciliation

Because formal and public recommendations, whether by interstate or nonstate bodies, are obviously not fully effective, considerable effort has been made to implement human rights by conciliation. Most of the conciliatory efforts have been carried out by nonstate actors. Their goal has been to secure compliance by quiet persuasion rather than public meetings, public suggestions, or judicial judgment. As a final step, however, these conciliation bodies may issue a public statement of their conclusions.

The U.N. secretary-general, an independent actor in an intergovernmental network, sometimes uses his "good offices" in behalf of human rights. Dag Hammarskjold did so when he obtained the release of American military personnel from China in the 1950s. U Thant did likewise during and immediately after the struggle to create Bangladesh when he helped repatriate prisoners and provide relief to refugees. Other examples abound of this quiet diplomacy.[20]

Some agencies are especially created by resolution or treaty for negotiated solutions of human rights problems—what is being called here, in summary, conciliation. One of the most highly respected is the U.N. High Commissioner for Refugees, whose office was created by U.N. resolution but now functions under specific treaty. His independent office exists in part to persuade states to give protection and assistance to refugees. This is essentially a job of conciliation between individuals and states, or between states. The U.N. HCR cannot tell states what to do. This point was very clear, for example, when the United States refused to label fugitives from "Baby Doc" Duvalier's Haiti as legal refugees or when the U.S. government intercepted fugitives from Haiti in international waters to keep them from reaching American territorial waters, where they could have exercised claims to refugee status under treaty and municipal (national) law. While many refugee problems remain unresolved, the HCR is widely regarded as performing well its job of making it as easy as possible for states to help refugees—and of course for the refugees to escape situations of a well founded fear of persecution.[21]

Another highly respected nonstate actor which serves essentially as a conciliator is the International Committee of the Red Cross. The ICRC was not created by states and is not completely an official means of protecting rights. Nevertheless, it is linked to state agreements because of its official recognition in the 1949 Geneva Conventions and related 1977 Protocols. Among other tasks, this private group of Swiss individuals tries to persuade states to implement as fully as possible the human rights of armed conflict. It seeks to resolve problems between states, and between individuals and states. Its effectiveness in armed conflict is difficult to measure precisely, but is believed to be high by many elites around the world. The ICRC not only was awarded the first Nobel Peace Prize but also was one of five 1978 winners of the U.N. Prize for Human Rights.[22]

Another conciliator is the European Commission on Human Rights, charged under the European Convention with trying to obtain an "out of court" settlement of human rights problems—but a settlement within the terms of the convention. It has successfully carried out this mandate on a number of occasions, both between govern-

ments and between individuals and governments. When it is unable to secure such a negotiated solution, and when the states involved have agreed, the commission is authorized to send the dispute to the European Court of Human Rights along with its recommendations. The Commission seems highly regarded by the European states, and its position in continuing disputes has been subsequently endorsed by the Court on a number of occasions. Its position has also been subsequently endorsed by the European Committee of Ministers, which constitutes further proof of the Commission's high respect.

We have already discussed the U.N. Human Rights Committee, and other examples could be drawn from specialized organs made up of individual experts, such as the committee under the UNESCO Convention on Discrimination in Education and under the Treaty on Racial Discrimination. A particularly interesting example is the Inter-American Commission on Human Rights, which functioned from 1959 without a specific human rights treaty for foundation, which accepted individual petitions on the basis of its own practice, and which did important work for human rights in tense situations like the Dominican Republic in 1965 and Somoza's Nicaragua in the late 1970s.[23]

These diplomatic efforts by specialized international agencies in pursuit of negotiated solutions to human rights issues may be summarized thusly: Beyond state reports and international recommendations, human rights may be implemented by quiet diplomacy carried out by independent actors. The goal is to secure a mutually satisfactory interpretation and implementation of human rights, rather than a judicial judgment. This process is somewhat analogous to activity by ombudsmen, or, to a lesser extent, by lawyers negotiating for their clients. It is a prevalent feature of international implementation of human rights. The relatively recent treaty on torture contains a similar monitoring mechanism. The process has demonstrated considerable effectiveness—although like other means, conciliation is not a complete answer to the problem of implementation. In the case of Greece under military rule (1967–74), the highly respected European Commission was unable to persuade the Greek junta to change policies which violated the European Convention. The European Council of Ministers also failed.

Individual Petitions

Under a number of human rights agreements individuals can petition directly to an international organization for redress of alleged violations of human rights. The standard rule is that petitioner must first exhaust local (that is, national) remedies. (Under the European Convention, however, the Court of Human Rights has significantly held that when the petition is against the highest levels of national government, the regional organs may proceed without waiting for exhaustion of national avenues.)

The United Nations Human Rights Commission and especially its uninstructed Subcommission on Protection of Minorities have, after a considerable number of years, agreed to accept private petitions which meet specified regulations.[24] Some fifty thousand petitions are received each year. These are treated in a confidential process, thus removing much of the pressure on an offending state derived from negative publicity. Only the names of states are released which have been the subject of confidential proceedings. Given this record, obviously private petitions to the U.N. are insufficient as a means of protecting human rights. Moreover, the petitions which are processed by the U.N. Human Rights Commission and Sub-commission are not supposed to deal with individual cases, but with a consistent pattern of gross violations of internationally recognized human rights. Thus they do not lead, normally, to direct protection efforts but rather to attempted indirect protection over time.

Nevertheless, state willingness to allow nationals direct access to international organizations is one mark of the seriousness of state interest in protecting human rights. Under the European Convention, 17 of twenty-one eligible states have made the optional declaration activating the right of individual petition. This right can lead to binding judicial decisions, with the European Human Rights Commission representing the individual in court and with the individual having the right to submit written comments in that court.

Under the 1966 U.N. Political Covenant, by 1987 only thirty-eight out of 159 eligible states had accepted the optional protocol permitting individual petitions to the U.N. Human Rights Committee. Individual petitions have never been accepted by any European Marxist regime, nor by most of the authoritarian regimes of the Third World. When the Carter Administration signed the Political Covenant and submitted it to the Senate for consent to ratification, there was no action on the Optional Protocol pertaining to petitions. The U.N. Human Rights Committee has been more vigorous in acting on individual petitions than acting on state reports, and it has brought considerable embarrassment to Uruguay in particular.[25]

In the last analysis, individual petitions help to provide some check on governmental violations of human rights by giving international organizations another source of information. It is not by accident that the most effective international system of protection, in Western Europe, relies extensively on individual petitions, even if over 95 percent of such petitions are rejected by the regional machinery as ill-founded. The European Convention shows clearly that states do not like to bring claims against other states. Only a handful of state-to-state cases have been brought to the European Commission or Court, and most of these had some ethnic flavor (that is, only one or two complaints by states were free of ethnic concern). Most of the European protection of rights is triggered by individual complaints, not state complaints. Individual petitions have also been important, with less decisive results, concerning the Inter-American Commission.

Binding Measures

More important than individual petitions is the authority of the bodies acting on the petitions. If an international organization is entitled to give a binding judgment, which is to say that if it is entitled to have the last say about what should be done, then we have moved completely away from the principle of national sovereignty, which is the idea that states should have the last say. Binding judgments do not, in and of themselves, assure protection. Judgments must still be applied, and this does not happen automatically. In the most stable and effective of legal systems, courts are constantly concerned about securing cooperation from lower courts, the police, executive agencies, and the population—all of whom may be involved in enforcement. But it obviously does make an important difference if protection of human rights is through binding judgment rather than recommendation or conciliation. This is the essential difference between enforcement and implementation.

We have already noted that the U.N. Security Council may reach a "decision" (constituting a binding judgment) that a violation of human rights constitutes a threat to the peace, breach of the peace, or act of aggression—and that the council has in fact done this with regard to Rhodesia (1966 and 1968) and South Africa (1977). This is not the place to examine the large question of the effectiveness of the resulting economic sanctions on Rhodesia for over ten years, or of the mandatory arms embargo against South Africa. Neither action completely denied the sanctioned items to the target regime (sanctions were "busted" in several ways). And neither action quickly changed the major violations of human rights in southern Africa. In the case of Rhodesia, however, it is clear that U.N. sanctions, combined with military pressures, brought successive concessions from the ruling white minority and that in the end the right to self-determination was achieved for the black majority, along with much greater attention to other rights, including education.[26]

The fact that the U.N. resolutions on Rhodesia and South Africa were legally binding does not solve all problems, obviously. But legally binding decisions make national enforcement more compelling. The Springfield Rifle Company in the U.S. was successfully prosecuted for selling arms to South Africa after the U.N. and U.S. laws banning such transfers went into legal force. And if a governmental agency violates binding U.N. regulations, as did the U.S. Congress in the Rhodesian

Drawing by Booth; © 1977 *The New Yorker Magazine, Inc.*

case, the binding nature of the international decision gives other political actors a persuasive argument in the quest for compliance.[27]

The U.N. Security Council, while both a political and legal organ, is more political than legal. Its actions are based primarily on power considerations, tempered by concern for rules of law. This being so, the council cannot be relied upon to protect human rights through binding resolutions in a systematic way. It is not because of absent-mindedness that the council has reached only two binding decisions on human rights in thirty-five years. It is because the five states possessing the veto could only agree twice to use their power in behalf of human rights in a definitive way. Beyond certain actions against white regimes in southern Africa, it is not certain how—or if—the council will act to try to protect human rights.

Courts, too, are both legal and political. But they are more legal and less political than the U.N. Security Council. They give more attention to rules of law. They give relatively less attention to considerations of strategic interest, profit, and ideology. The World Court (International Court of Justice at the Hague, Netherlands) is available to settle any legal dispute arising among states under international law. And the court has handled what we would now call human rights cases concerning such subjects as political asylum and guardianship of infants.[28]

But states can easily avoid going to the World Court. They must give their consent before they are obligated to appear.[29] Thus in the early 1970s, when Pakistan brought a claim to the court against India concerning human rights in armed conflict, the court decided it could not handle the case because India had not given its consent to be sued on this subject. This maneuver, however, remains a good example of states using legal steps to try to mobilize pressure on another state. The United States also did this in the Iranian crisis of 1979–80, using the World Court at least in part to diplomatically isolate Iran and make U.S. diplomacy appear stronger—even if the United States thought strictly juridical steps would be unsuccessful. (While the Iranian Hostage Case was popularly perceived as a human rights case, it was technically a case arising out of law on diplomatic and consular immunity.)

A number of human rights treaties explicitly state that if a dispute under the treaty cannot be resolved by other means, the dispute shall go automatically to the World Court. At least six major human rights treaties contain such an article. The World Court, however, has yet to produce a series of cases under these treaties. Some states reserve against this type of article in the treaties—that is, they accept the treaty but not the article. This has been the policy of the Eastern European Marxist regimes and also of some Third World regimes. Other states may choose not to reserve against the article, but they do not sue other states in the court, perhaps fearing a turning of the tables in the future whereby they themselves would become defendants. Thus the court remains on the sidelines in major human rights cases. The last time the World Court handled a binding human rights issue was in 1966 in a case concerning self-determination for Southwest Africa/ Namibia. In that case the court was badly divided, and after prolonged internal debate the court avoided ruling on the central substance of the dispute.

The World Court did, in the case of *Nicaragua* v. *the U.S.*, manage to make some binding pronouncements on human rights in armed conflict during the 1980s. In this complicated case, which dealt primarily with aggression, self-defense, armed attack, and intervention, and from which the U.S. withdrew just as the Islamic Republic of Iran had done in the Hostage Case, the Court ruled that some actions by the Nicaraguan rebels violated international humanitarian law—which is the law otherwise known as human rights in armed conflict.[30]

The one international court which has produced a series of binding judgments on human rights is the European Court of Human Rights. All of its judgments, whether resulting from state-to-state proceedings or commission-to-state proceedings, have been implemented by the states concerned. (This can be compared with the record of the World Court, in which Albania, Iran, and the U.S. have refused to implement substantive judgments which went against them.) The European cases range from the highly technical (whether Austria has permitted sufficient rights to cross-examination so as to meet the due process required by the European Convention) to the highly sensitive and emotional (whether the United Kingdom has used torture in Northern Ireland). Nineteen states of twenty-one had agreed by 1988 to accept the court's authority as final.

The Inter-American Court of Human Rights, which has been in legal existence only since 1979, has handed down several advisory opinions and was, by 1988, just beginning to handle its first binding cases. One advisory ruling led to considerable attention. The court ruled that a Costa Rican law requiring journalists to graduate from certain schools of journalism (a legal policy for the professionalism of journalism) violated the rule in the American Convention of Human Rights pertaining to freedom of expression (Article 13). Thus the controversial effort to license journalists was, in effect, held a violation of internationally recognized human rights. While the judgment was not fully binding, it was expected to have considerable influence on the policies of many Latin American countries—and by extension on many countries outside the Western Hemisphere. There were similar human rights provisions in the U.N. Covenant on Civil and Political Rights, and the European Convention on Human Rights. At the time of writing, the Inter-American Court had just held—in a binding decision—that Honduras was responsible for death squads in that country and that compensation was owed to private families. The government said it would comply with the ruling.[31]

While this chapter focuses primarily on international protection efforts, we should note that international and national action can be merged. In particular, it is important to observe that national courts may make binding judgments on the basis of international law. Indeed, much international law is enforced in this way. With regard to international human rights law, however, national courts in the United States and elsewhere have been reluctant to become activist courts in protecting human rights. The historical pattern in the United States has been that both federal and state courts have been restrained in accepting arguments based on international human rights laws and resolutions. The courts have tended to avoid ruling on the merits and to make narrow and technical judgments.[32]

Nevertheless, perhaps because of the numerous cases in which one or more parties referred to international legal instruments, there has probably been an educational effect on American judges. Their consciousness has probably been raised about the importance of international human rights instruments. In the 1980s there were several cases in which U.S. courts became activists in defense of international human rights. They made creative rulings discovering customary international human rights law or in reading new interpretations into existing statutes and precedents. The 1980 *Filartiga* case (referred to in chapter 1) was perhaps the most striking, but there were other cases dealing with the rights of aliens and refugees.[33]

By the late 1980s it was too soon to say definitively that national courts were becoming an effective means of enforcing international norms on human rights. As mentioned in chapter one, the Filartiga case was used a precedent in the Suarez-Mason case. But courts in other nations might continue their conservatism. Courts in countries lacking an independent judiciary could not be expected to protect human rights against the wishes of the other branches of government.

Yet because of developments in some U.S. courts, there has been increased hope that national courts might play a larger role in protecting internationally recognized human rights. Much could depend on the nature of the American executive. The Carter administration had encouraged the court in the Filartiga case to break new ground in its ruling.

TO REVIEW

A summary is very difficult to fashion about these formal or official measures for protecting human rights. The state reports, international recommendations, conciliation attempts, petitions, and binding decisions and judgments certainly demonstrate that much action is expended in behalf of implementing and enforcing human rights rules. Indeed, while implementation efforts may compare unfavorably with some national procedures, international measures for supervision of rules are probably stronger in the human rights field than in some other areas of international law. But beyond that generalization, it is difficult to separate the official international measures from unofficial steps and from unilateral state efforts (to be analyzed subsequently). It is also difficult to make summary evaluations in the face of so many other intertwining variables: types of regimes, types of regions, types of human rights involved.

For the moment we attempt some tentative summary statements based only on the nature of the international official means of protection. (At a later point we will try further generalizations based on four interacting variables: official protection, unofficial protection, nature of rights involved, and nature of the target state involved.)

1. The protection of human rights cannot always be entrusted to states and to international bodies of state-instructed delegates. No matter how much states must be committed to protecting human rights in order for that protection to transpire, paradoxically, states alone cannot be trusted to protect. First of all it is clear that states simply do not like to press human rights issues. Such efforts interfere with other interests and set a precedent which can be used against them in the future.

Even under the European Convention, cited frequently as the best model of international official protection, states have sued other states really only five times. Only one of these cases, the Scandinavian states versus Greece, was free of ethnic factors. In the other four cases the petitioner had some ethnic relation with the individuals for whom protection was sought—e.g., the Republic of Ireland sued the United Kingdom for mistreating and torturing suspected members of the Irish Republican Army. Thus there has been only one European case in which states have initiated suit for purely human rights reasons. (One pure human rights case against Turkey, launched by states, was dropped as part of a diplomatic bargain.) Other cases stemmed from individual petitions which the commission or a defendant state took to the court.[34]

Especially the U.N. diplomatic record indicates clearly that states prefer protecting their sovereignty to protecting human rights, and that when they have competing interests they will largely forgo the latter for strategic or economic gain. It is for this general reason that U.N. agencies not insulated by treaty from state instructions have failed to protect human rights adequately. And it is for the same reason that one should not expect very much from regular U.N. bodies in the future. The few uninstructed regular organs like the U.N. Human Rights Sub-Commission report to instructed bodies. Thus the independent agencies are effectively restricted in what they can achieve. It can be argued that attention to human rights at the U.N. has become more serious and more balanced over time, but this does not suggest that direct protection efforts have been successful; most U.N. efforts comprise either promotion or indirect protection in the field of human rights.

2. It follows from the first point that a necessary, but not sufficient, condition for the effective protection of human rights through international official means is the use of uninstructed or independent agencies. It is not by accident that the most highly respected official actors in the human rights field are of this type—e.g., the U.N. HCR, the European Commission and Court. The protection of human rights will never be consistently effective until that process is shielded from the strategic and economic short-run interests of states. Impartiality, defined here to mean the exclusion of reasons of state, is a prerequisite for adequate protection.

3. One way to reduce reasons of state is to provide for individual petitions after use of national procedures. Such provision is a good litmus test of a state's commitment to protecting human rights. As long as a state like the Soviet Union legally adheres to a treaty on human rights like the 1966 Civil-Political Covenant, then refuses to permit individual petitions and submits a state report that can only be

termed propagandistic and a cover-up, one can legitimately doubt such a state's interest in the rights of the treaty.

4. Impartiality without authority, however, remains an inadequate halfway house in the protection of human rights. The U.N. Human Rights Committee under the Civil-Political Treaty and the committee under the Racial Discrimination Treaty seem impartial and are definitely independent, but they have no authority to command obedience from violators of human rights. Hence states find it relatively easy to disregard their recommendations. Therefore another necessary but insufficient condition for the protection of human rights is that review bodies be given the right to have the last say about what should be done.[35]

5. Authority without cooperation, however, leads to legalisms rather than legality and to the demise of authority rather than its use in protecting human rights. Effective authority depends on voluntary cooperation for the most part. If authorities had to implement all of their decisions with force, the legal system would collapse. It is voluntary cooperation that allows, for example, American courts to implement their judgments. Extensive opposition produces at least delays— note, e.g., the subject of school desegregation—and sometimes collapse of the law enforcement effort—note, e.g., the failure of the law on prohibition of alcoholic beverages.

The Security Council commanded economic sanctions on Rhodesia from 1968 to 1979. The World Court and Security Council commanded Iran to release American hostages in 1979. The World Court said in 1986 that the Nicaraguan rebels, as an agency of the U.S. government, were engaging in illegal attacks which also, at times, violated the international law on human rights in armed conflict. But lack of state cooperation made these exercises of authority ineffective in the short run. Binding judgments rather than recommendations increase the pressure on states to comply with the judgments, because the obligation to comply is greater, but the key factor remains the attitude of cooperation.

FURTHER REFLECTIONS

We have tried already to get a preliminary understanding about the impact of formal steps to protect human rights. In so doing we have considered the steps rather generally, with a few examples drawn from practice. We can say a bit more by speaking about different types of political systems and different types of rights. A state's disposition toward a right is one of the most important factors in how a state responds to international rules and organizations. In chapter five we will deal with this subject from the view of political philosophy. In this chapter we try to deal with it empirically. In such a discussion the following table is useful.

The table indicates several generalizations. Of states in the democratic First World, only three states have not signed either of the two covenants. Only the U.S. has ratified neither. Half of First World states have accepted the optional protocol permitting individual petitions concerning civil-political rights. Only Greece and Israel accepted the socioeconomic covenant but refused the civil-political one.

In the Second World of Marxist, industrialized states, only Albania deviates from the pattern of adhering to both covenants while rejecting the optional protocol.

In the authoritarian Third World, just over 41 percent of the 71 states accept the two covenants. Again, the two are usually treated as one package. Only 12 percent of these 71 states have adhered to the optional protocol. Most states have not given legal effect to either covenant.

In the democratic Third World, slightly over half (23) of these 41 states have adhered to both covenants. About half have accepted fully the optional protocol. However, outside of Latin America, there are few states which have accepted the covenants. Most of those accepting the protocol are Latin American tates.

It cannot be stressed enough that we are speaking of formal adherence to international standards. This may say very little about actual enforcement and implementation of those standards. Just as a number of Latin political regimes hold elections but are not really democracies because those who win the elections do not really exercise effective power, so a number of regimes may formally endorse international rights agreements without implementing their substance. A few further points can be made about types of states, types of rights, and types of protection at work.

First World Democratic

The industrialized democracies, with their historical tendency to define human rights in civil-political terms, have adhered to many treaties on those rights. The Western Europeans, and particularly the

TABLE 3
Acceptance of the Two 1966 United Nations Covenants

State	Civil/Political Covenant	Optional Protocol	Socioeconomic Covenant
First World			
Australia	x		x
Austria	x	s	x
Belgium	x		x
Canada	x	x	x
Cyprus	x	s	x
Denmark	x	x	x
Finland	x	x	x
France	x	x	x
West Germany	x	x	x
Greece			x
Iceland	x	x	x
Israel	s		s
Italy	x	x	x
Japan	x		x
Liechtenstein			
Luxembourg	x	x	x
Netherlands	x	x	x
New Zealand	x		x
Norway	x	x	x
Portugal	x	x	x
Spain	x	x	x
Sweden	x	x	x
Switzerland			
Turkey			
United Kingdom	x		x
United States	s		s
Second World			
Albania			
Bulgaria	x		x
Byelorussia	x		x
Czechoslovakia	x		x
East Germany	x		x
Hungary	x		x
Mongolia	x		x

State	Civil/Political Covenant	Optional Protocol	Socioeconomic Covenant
Second World (continued)			
Poland	x		x
Romania	x		x
Ukrainian SSR	x		x
Soviet Union	x		x
Third World — Authoritarian			
Afghanistan	x	x	x
Algeria	s		s
Angola			
Bahrain			
Bangladesh			
Benin			
Bhutan			
Burkina Faso			
Burma			
Burundi			
Cameroons	x	x	x
Cape Verde			
Central African Republic	x	x	x
Chad			
Chile	x		x
China			
Comoros			
Congo	x	x	x
Cuba			
Kampuchea	s		s
North Korea	x		x
Vietnam	x		x
Democratic Yemen	x		x
Egypt	x		x
Equatorial Guinea			
Ethiopia			
Fiji			
Gabon	x		x
Guinea-Bissau			
Guyana	x		x
Haiti			

State	Civil/Political Covenant	Optional Protocol	Socioeconomic Covenant
Third World — Authoritarian (continued)			
Indonesia			
Iran	x		x
Iraq	x		x
Jordan	x		x
Kenya	x		x
Kuwait			
Laos			
Lebanon	x		x
Liberia	s		s
Libya	x		x
Madagascar	x	x	x
Malaysia			
Malawi			
Maldives			
Mali	x		x
Mauritania			
Monaco			
Morocco	x		x
Mozambique			
Niger	x	x	x
Nigeria			
Oman			
Pakistan			
Panama	x	x	x
Paraguay			
Qatar			
Rwanda	x		x
Saudi Arabia			
Sierra Leone			
Somalia			
Sudan	x		x
Swaziland			
Syria	x		x
Togo	x		x
United Arab Emirates			x
Tanzania	x		x
Upper Volta			

State	Civil/Political Covenant	Optional Protocol	Socioeconomic Covenant
Third World — Authoritarian (continued)			
Yemen			
Zambia	x	x	x
Zaire	x	x	x
Third World — Democratic			
Argentina	x	x	s
Bahamas			
Barbados	x	x	x
Bolivia	x	x	x
Botswana			
Brazil			
Colombia	x	x	x
Costa Rica	x	x	x
Djibouti			
Dominican Republic	x	x	x
Ecuador	x	x	x
El Salvador	x	s	x
Gambia	x		x
Ghana			
Grenada			
Guatemala			
Guinea	x	s	x
Honduras	s	s	x
India	x		x
Jamaica	x	x	x
Lesotho			
Malta			s
Mauritius	x	x	x
Mexico	x		x
Nepal			
Nicaragua	x	x	x
Papua New Guinea			
Peru	x	x	x
Philippines	x	s	x
Samoa			
San Marino	x	x	x
Sao Tome y Principe			

State	Civil/Political Covenant	Optional Protocol	Socioeconomic Covenant
Third World — Democratic (continued)			
Senegal	x	x	x
Singapore			
South Korea			
Sri Lanka	x		x
Surinam	x	x	x
Thailand			
Trinidad and Tobago	x	x	x
Uruguay	x	x	x
Venezuela	x	x	x

SOURCE: *Human Rights International Instruments* (New York: United Nations), 1 January 1979.

NOTES: x = adheres to; s = signed.

The difference between "democratic" and "authoritarian" is based on the following: the presence of meaningful elections in which there is choice and after which power changes or is unchanged according to the electoral outcome. According to this standard there are always some borderline situations. Mexico, for example, which scores 50 on the Freedom House's scale of 100 for measurement of freedom, is a judgment call. Nevertheless, the approach remains broadly indicative of the difference between democratic and authoritarian regimes.

The total number of adherences and/or signatures depends on the resolution of several questions. For example, the government of the Republic of South Vietnam and that of the Republic of China took certain decisions with regard to human rights treaties. Both of these governments have been superseded by other governments. While the general principles of international law provide certain rules for changes of governments, governments do not always agree on the effect to be given to previous acts whose legitimacy may be challenged.

Scandinavians, have led the way. Others, such as the United States, have been much more reluctant to accept formal international obligations. No doubt one of the major reasons for general Western acceptance of official protection measures is the belief that national policies on civil-political rights will not be challenged under international procedures.

Speaking relatively and in global context, one can say that Western national records in protecting civil-political rights are indeed exemplary. Problems exist, nevertheless, and it is important to recall that the machinery for protection under the European Convention has not atrophied from lack of use. The United Kingdom finally acknowledged, by ordering a change of policy, under pressure from the European protection machinery, that detainees had been abused in Northern Ireland.[36] The fact is that genuine democracies violate human rights on occasion. In West Germany there was the policy of denying jobs (berufsverbote) to those with a Nazi background. This violated the internationally recognized right to work. On the American side of the Atlantic, unregulated by any of the specific treaties on civil-political rights, there was a long history of rights violations by, for example, the Federal Bureau of Investigation,[37] and President Carter's first ambassador to the United Nations, Andrew Young, created a stir when he alleged that there were many political prisoners in the United States.

The case of the Wilmington Ten merits recall. A group of ten human rights activists in Wilmington, North Carolina, finally were freed by a federal appellate court after the Carter administration legally intervened on their behalf. But before that time serious injustices transpired. As described briefly by an irate American journal, these were that:

> Ten people have been wrongly imprisoned for periods of up to four years, for which they will receive absolutely no recompense; a local prosecutor violated his constitutional and professional obligations and escaped without even a reprimand; a state trial judge issued grossly biased rulings which denied the defendants a fair trial, and then he hit them with heavy sentences; an entire state court system approved all this not once but twice; a state governor saw nothing unfair about the case and a Federal District Court denied any relief.[38]

While the case of the Wilmington Ten shows that occasionally an elaborate national system to protect civil rights can fail, it is in the field of socioeconomic rights that a number of observers, particularly non-Westerners, are keenly critical of the policies of the industrialized democracies. Again, many Western European states have accepted the Covenant on Economic, Social, and Cultural Rights, along with other socioeconomic standards noted in chapter 1. The critics tend to focus on the United States, partly because it has not fully adhered to that covenant and partly because its national economic history has been founded upon economic freedom rather than either equity or equality. Even for those states that have accepted international formal procedures for protecting socioeconomic rights, it is not easy in the short run to evaluate their impact. Acceptance by the United Kingdom of the Convention on Racial Discrimination (involving civil, political, social, and economic rights) has not ended the debate about British discrimination in immigration, housing, education, and employment.

Second World Authoritarian

The Soviet Union as well as the other Eastern European regimes have adhered to both of the 1966 covenants as well as to many other human rights official measures. It cannot be blithely assumed, as Henry Kissinger did in his memoirs, that the Soviets—or communists in general—have an inferior record compared to the West in meeting socioeconomic human rights standards or meeting basic human needs.[39] They probably have not fashioned their socioeconomic policies to any great extent *because* of the formal international measures, but on many socioeconomic issues their policies may be substantially in compliance with international standards.

It fits not only with ideological precepts but also with considerable national traditions in Eastern Europe that great attention should be given to equal distribution of *adequate* nutrition, housing, and social services. It seems a historical fact that in, say, the Soviet Union the average citizen is better off and more equal in material terms than at any time in Russian history. While figures on infant mortality in the Soviet Union seemed to be rising during the 1980s, it cannot be denied that many public policies seek to deal constructively with socioeconomic basic needs. (Moreover, *U.S.* figures on infant mortality ranked toward the bottom of the Western group of states.)

This is not to say that certain party members do not receive *preferential* benefits, thus qualifying party and state pronouncements about equality. And this is not to say that socioeconomic benefits are not made dependent on political conformity. It is well known that being allowed to work at a job for which one is qualified is sometimes made conditional in the Soviet Union (and other Marxist states) on not dissenting from party-state orthodoxy. Thus while there is minimum attention to the right to work, access to qualified work is treated more as a benefit than as a right. The same is true for access to excellent higher education. Yet the Soviet record seems far better than the democratic

First World's in providing free medical services, free day-care institutions for working parents, free higher education, and other socioeconomic goods and services. Such provisions may not be provided in response to human rights without distinction. Still, minimal goods and services to meet basic human needs are provided.

It is, of course, in the field of civil-political rights that the authoritarian Second World shows the greatest discrepancy between state practice and the generally understood meaning of official rules regarding these rights. The Soviet Union and other eastern states like Czechoslovakia have clearly violated a number of rules in the Helsinki Accord, certainly so with regard to encouraging a freer flow of ideas through publications between east and west. Only the requirement for unanimous decision-making in the follow-up conferences prevented formal registration of eastern (and some western) violations. And private groups which sought to monitor state compliance with the Accord have been harassed and detained by most Marxist states. Groups like Charter 77 in Czechoslovakia, a popular response to the Helsinki Accord, were driven underground.[40]

This type of crackdown, and continuing use of forced labor, political detention, political psychiatry, non-competitive elections, censorship, and the other usual practices of totalitarianism also clearly violated the spirit and letter of the Civil-Political Covenant in a number of respects. Indeed, the extent of violations of international standards on civil and political rights defies documentation and interpretation in the type of overview presented here.[41]

Why the Soviets ever adhered to the 1966 Civil-Political Covenant is not so clear, unless they saw it as a good move—when combined with rejection of the optional protocol on individual petitions—to deflate foreign criticisms. It appears to have been a major miscalculation for the Soviets and the other European Marxist regimes to have signed the Helsinki Accord, hoping that their citizens would not notice the humanitarian principles contained in Basket Three, despite the fact that the Accord called for its publication and dissemination. Particularly the latter agreement has led to widespread demands throughout the Soviet Union and Eastern Europe for serious attention to the human rights provisions accepted as humanitarian principles.

At the time of writing, the Gorbachev reforms are beginning to be implemented in an important test of the ability of the European communist systems to restructure and open up (peristroika and glasnost). Many Western observers believe the motivation for both lay in economic decline and the concomitant need to stimulate economic creativity. One of the contradictions of communism is how to get and maintain economic creativity and productivity while enforcing political and social censorship and orthodoxy. Whatever the precise origin, Gorbachev's reforms did lead to liberalization, meaning relaxation of some controls, in culture, journalism, and in general in Soviet civil society. Human rights offices were created in the Foreign Ministry and the Soviet Academy of Sciences. Human rights exchanges were pursued with Western scholars and activists. There was even public discussion of competitive elections at the lower levels of party-state activity, and dissidents were tolerated to a greater extent than previously—including the end of internal exile for Andrei Sakharov, the persecuted father of the Soviet atomic bomb. Given that policies are in a state of flux in particularly the Soviet Union as this is being written, one cannot say whether glasnost is essentially a propaganda move or represents a fundamental effort to implement Marxism with a human face in the Soviet Union—as the Czech communist elite attempted in the mid-1960s under Alexander Dubcek. When the Soviet Foreign Minister, Edward Shevardnadze, was asked the difference between Gorbachev's glasnost of 1987 and the "Prague spring" of 1968 which was crushed by Soviet troops, he is reported to have quipped: "Nineteen years."

Between 1985 and 1988 there were indeed some important changes in civil rights in the Soviet Union. For example, with regard to political psychiatry, mental hospitals were removed from the jurisdiction of the Ministry of the Interior (and therefore from the police, including political police), and Western doctors were invited to visit those hospitals.[42] If such changes continue, there would be much greater prospect for a closer fit between Soviet practice on civil and perhaps even political rights, and international standards on these subjects. Note that the argument here is not that the international standards have *caused* the changes in Soviet policy (although I would not rule out some impact from United Nations, Helsinki, and private circles). The argument is only that *perhaps* changes are underway which will allow the Soviets to claim with increased validity that they are in compliance with international standards, whatever the ultimate origin of or motivation for these changes.

While in some ways other European Marxist states were far ahead of the Soviet Union in both restructuring and liberalization, as shown by past events in Czechoslovakia, Hungary, and Yugoslavia in particular, changes in the Soviet Union in the 1980s rippled across its allies. Stalinist regimes in East Germany and Czechoslovakia began to experiment with some human rights changes of their own, such as increased contacts with Western scholars and increased tolerance for unofficial peace, ecological, and human rights groups—although the process was neither clear nor consistent.

Authoritarian Third World

The overwhelming number of Third World states are authoritarian. Their ruling elites, in so far as they use the language of international human rights, put rhetorical emphasis on the collective right of national self-determination and the claimed collective right of national economic development. If the 1979 Havana Conference of (nominally) Non-Aligned States is any indication of true perceptions, these states see human rights as primarily an effort against imperialism.[43] Many human rights resolutions at the United Nations, where Third World states exercise a majority, focus on South Africa and Namibia, Israeli occupied territory, development, and the necessity of combining human rights with a New International Economic Order beneficial to the less developed states.

On a subject like socioeconomic rights, a number of these elites would argue that they have less a problem of principle than a problem of capability. The will is there, they argue, but the resources are lacking. In some cases this is no doubt true. South Korea, for example, when it was authoritarian (prior to 1988) implemented relatively equitable socioeconomic policies leading to land reform and a relatively dispersed sharing of the wealth of the country. So did Taiwan, and a few other authoritarian states.[44] These states, while authoritarian, scored relatively well in rising on the Physical Quality of Life scale developed by the Overseas Development Council (see the following chapter), reflecting commitment to health, nutrition, and educational goals largely in keeping with international rights standards. (Such progressive policies may not have been instituted *because* of commitments to human rights; they could have been followed because of economic interests of the elite—i.e., in a healthy and educated labor force; but the result seems largely compatible with rights requirements.)

But in a number of other cases there is compelling evidence that ruling elites are no more willing to respond to basic socioeconomic needs of their people than to implement civil and political rights. One thinks readily of recently deposed strong men like Somoza in Nicaragua, Duvalier in Haiti, Marcos in the Philippines. In all too many Third World authoritarian countries the ruling elites exclude much of their population from socioeconomic benefits as well as civil and political liberties. Throughout Latin America, historically and despite a more recent trend toward formal democracy, much of the population is left outside the system of socioeconomic benefits from the economic system. The subject of a human right to basic socioeconomic needs does not even arise in dominant political discourse. In Latin America especially, but also in parts of Africa, the Middle East, and Asia, the health, education, and welfare of peasants, indigenous peoples, the proletariat, and other poor and uninfluential parts of the population hardly register in the minds of leaders like Mobutu in Zaire, Pinochet in Chile, Mengistu in Ethiopia, the military junta in Brazil, and so forth.

Virtually all of these authoritarian less developed countries (LDCs) are likely to be in significant violation of international civil-political standards and to resist for some time official protection procedures. Some states like Mexico may be able to combine some civil and even political rights within a political system that is dominated by one-party. Most one-party states, like Kenya, or no-party states where dictators or the military rule without political parties, will by definition violate international standards. Elites become very comfortable without significant opposition, and they therefore do not look with favor on critical statements from the likes of Amnesty International, U.N. officials, or pressures from other states.

Yet all of these authoritarian Third World states are likely to be continuing targets of international action demanding attention to internationally recognized human rights. Given the public and private agencies which exist and which function in relation to numerous human rights treaties, the international pressure is not likely to disappear. This is particularly true in Latin America where the Inter-American Commission on human rights has now been joined by a functioning human rights court.

The Commission played an important role in helping to delegitimize the Somoza dynasty in Nicaragua, issuing critical reports which facilitated internal and international opposition. That international withdrawal of legitimacy was an important factor to the United States, Venezuela, Costa Rica, and others who aided opposition forces. It was particularly Somoza's violation of human rights in internal war (covered by parts of the 1949 Geneva conventions and now by Protocol

II of 1977), including the killing of an ABC journalist filmed by American television and the killing of young males en masse as documented by the International Red Cross and the OAS commission, that finally accelerated the dictator's departure in 1979. Thus there was an important role for transnational human rights actors, even if major events could not be laid at the doorstep of those bodies.

Many Third World authoritarian regimes have cooperated with the ICRC concerning human rights in armed conflict and the human rights of "persons detained by reason of political events" (to give the reader a taste of the diplomatic jargon used to circumvent political sensitivities). This is no small matter, given the fact that most armed conflict now occurs in the Third World and that political detention is also prevalent. Especially when there is an armed conflict, but also where there is extensive political detention, it is rare for the ICRC to be totally excluded from Third World situations—despite the fact that the ICRC is staffed by white Westerners. Many authoritarian Third World authorities have had no unusual difficulty in accepting that opponents have minimum human rights which should be checked by the ICRC. Only communist Vietnam proved totally intractable on the question of ICRC access to American prisoners of war, thereby failing clearly to implement sections of the Third Geneva Convention of 1949.

Other controversies of course exist, as demonstrated by Syria's delay in admitting the ICRC to Israeli prisoners of war during and after the 1973 armed conflict in the Middle East. And it cannot be said that either Iran or Iraq was sensitive to humanitarian and human rights issues arising out of the Persian Gulf War. A long list of violations of rights could be written with regard to authoritarian Third World regimes. The point here is that international pressures to ameliorate those violations are in process and will continue, with some occasional successes.

Democratic Third World

The democratic Third World shares many affinities with our preceding group. The number of regimes, however, is not one of them. The clear cases of democracy in the Third World are exemplified by Venezuela, Costa Rica, Argentina after 1983, Colombia (which seems to be sliding toward demise of rights and even governmental control at the time of writing), Zimbabwe (for the moment), Senegal, India (except for the time of emergency decrees under Indira Gandhi's first tenure), Botswana, the Dominican Republic, Jamaica and a few others. Other nations which had democratic polities have fallen on hard times, such as Lebanon, Sri Lanka, Nigeria, and Malaysia. Some states display formal democracy via periodic elections, but the real holders of power are the military senior officers as in Panama and Honduras, or Thailand. Without getting bogged down in a discussion of requisites for true democracy, the point can be made that the lesser developed non-western world has fully implemented civil and political rights only with considerable difficulty.

By the end of the 1980s, at least in Latin America there was something of a trend away from military politics and toward a return to civil and political rights—at least formally. Elections in Guatemala, Nicaragua, El Salvador, Bolivia, Uruguay, and Argentina (and earlier in Peru) ushered in civilian presidents. A big question remained, however, as to whether civilian political leaders could exert control over a military leadership with a long tradition of authoritarian politics. An immediately pressing problem for these new civilian governments was whether they should move against military leaders which had engaged in gross violations of human rights. The Alfonsin government in Argentina started down this road, since the previous military government had engaged in a "dirty war" leading to the "disappearance" of some 9,500 Argentine citizens and the torture of many more, but stopped short in the face of several military coup attempts. Other civilian leaders thought the wisest course was to give amnesty to military violators of human rights in an effort to get them to stay out of politics.

The same tension between civil-political rights and military politics was manifest in other parts of the (sometimes) democratic Third World, as in Turkey. There, as in Nigeria, Bangladesh, Liberia, etc., the military moved to curtail civil and political rights, only to eventually withdraw to their barracks after finding that they had few answers to the economic and other problems plaguing the nation. Only in a few countries like Chile did military leaders persist for long periods in denying most civil and political rights to polities which had sizable histories of democracy. Numerous academic studies existed about democracy, a.k.a. civil and political rights, in the Third World, but it was not clear what factors led to the creation and maintenance, or return to, such political systems.

These democratic regimes, almost without exception, are favorably oriented also to socioeconomic rights. Most of them have accepted the 1966 covenant on the subject and devote significant portions of governmental spending to the health, education, and welfare sector. There seems to be considerable truth behind the argument that once civil and political rights are implemented, those rights are exercised to implement socioeconomic rights as well. Indeed, some Third World democracies, like Uruguay (before military rule) have extensive experience with a very broad welfare state, so much so that Uruguay was once called the Switzerland of Latin America. Sri Lanka, too, prior to civil war and the arrival of the Indian army, did very well not only in maintaining democratic politics but also in implementing equitable socioeconomic policies within the bounds of its lesser developed condition. (We return to how such situations can so deteriorate in rights terms in the final chapter.)

CONCLUSIONS

Public efforts to protect human rights, whether international or national, do not exist in a political vacuum. Rather, it is usually the case that rights are recognized and then protected, through enforcement or implementation, at least partially because of pressure from private sources. Without denigrating the importance of leadership in rights matters from above—that is, from governmental and intergovernmental agencies, one should also pay attention to action from below—that is, from the private sector. It is to that subject that we now turn.

Chapter Four

Protecting Human Rights

The Private Sector

*The increased influence of interest groups oriented
toward humanitarian values is a reality.*
Lars Schoultz, *Human Rights and United States
Policy toward Latin America* (Princeton:
Princeton University Press, 1981), p. 373.

INTRODUCTION

Just as there is an array of public means for formal implementation of
human rights, so is there a wide range of private or informal or unofficial steps that can be taken.[1] These efforts are carried out by non-
governmental or independent institutions. One can draw an academic
distinction between a human rights group and another group not oriented toward rights but toward humane reform of governmental policies, justice, or improved well-being of persons. In the real world, however, rights groups and these other groups frequently merge into one
coalition striving for improved human dignity.

It is because of this that one can say that any group can be called a
human rights group when it becomes interested in an issue related to
internationally recognized human rights. Thus when a labor union becomes active against repression abroad, on the basis of political reality
we can say that such a group has become a lobby for international human rights, even though the group does not describe itself as a rights
group. The AFL-CIO is not just a labor union concerned with hours of
the work week and members' fringe benefits; it is also a lobby for international human rights—pertaining to labor rights and other fundamental rights. It was partially because of AFL-CIO lobbying that the
U.S. Senate approved two further treaties protecting international labor rights in 1987.[2]

Many of these groups are basically national, especially as defined by membership or main focus of activity. But insofar as they become active on issues linked to international documents on human rights, then they can be said to be part of the means for implementing human rights on an international basis. Hence a group like Americans for Democratic Action (ADA) is usually thought of as an American lobby. But when it is active in protesting, say, Chilean repression, then it is accurately viewed as part of the unofficial and international process of implementing human rights.

It can be easily recognized, therefore, that the informal process of implementing human rights is as broad as international society, or, if the reader prefers, as broad as the 170 national societies of the world. Families, schools, and churches are in fact part of this process. One might keep in mind the UNESCO statement reprinted at the front of this book: "It should be recognized that true respect for human rights is nothing less than a way of life." Needless to say, the entire process cannot be examined here. What is attempted is: an identification of basic functions (indirect protection through education; direct protection through shielding from harm or positive actions); a description of some of the leading unofficial actors; and a discussion of the basic steps that can be taken.

BASIC FUNCTIONS

In one sense to promote human rights is to protect them. To educate people about human rights is to acquaint them with the subject. Such education is usually thought of in terms of promoting rights, but that step is also a form of indirect protection or a first step in protection efforts. In addition to universities such as Columbia or Cincinnati which have formal programs in international human rights, there are private groups which exist to encourage education in human rights. A well-known example is the International Institute of Human Rights in Strasbourg, France, which conducts seminars and other training programs on human rights and publishes a journal on the subject.

Beyond education, whether considered as promotion or indirect protection, independent institutions engage in direct protection. This means that they contact either the ruling elites that control human rights situations or those whose rights are denied. Such direct protection can be defensive, in the sense that Red Cross prison visits try to protect the victims of war and political battles from further harm, or they can be positive, in the sense that the International Rescue Committee tries to find new homes for refugees. Some groups undertake both kinds of actions. The International Commission of Jurists protests certain political violations and also consults with governments on how to create improved judicial procedures and better trained legal officials.

By way of concrete illustration, the better-known private groups most active in basically defensive protection of human rights can be listed. A very few of them are transnational or international: Amnesty International (concerned to protect prisoners of conscience and all prisoners from torture and execution); PEN (concerned to protect the right of writers, such as philosophers, essayists, and novelists); the International League for Human Rights (concerned to protect a wide range of rights); the International Commission of Jurists (concerned with implementing a humane rule of law); the ICRC (concerned, beyond protecting rights in armed conflict, to protect political prisoners); and the Watch Groups coalition (concerned to protect rights under the Helsinki Accord and other regional standards on rights). Less well-known (to Americans) transnational NGOs include the Anti-Slavery Society, the Minority Rights Group, Survival International, and the International Defense and Aid Fund.

Membership in these transnational groups is of three basic types: individuals, national groups, individuals and groups. The Anti-Slavery Society is made up directly of individuals; AI and PEN of national groups (which may have subdivisions); the ICJ and International League for Human Rights of individuals and groups. The ICRC is a special case.

Most of the unofficial groups that seek to help protect or implement human rights are national rather than transnational. In addition to the national components of a transnational organization (AI–U.S.A., PEN–American Center), there are three types of groups and one type of movement active within certain nations.

There is the national coalition group, which is a human rights organization actually made up of many other interest groups. A leading example here is the Human Rights Working Group in Washington, D.C., which is made up of some forty-five other groups as members and another thirty-five groups as affiliates. A similar coalition group in the United Kingdom is the Network.

Then there is the separate human rights group, which acts not through a coalition but on its own. Examples here are Freedom House, and the Working Group on the Internment of Dissenters in Mental Hospitals (a British group).

Finally, there is the group that is not originally or primarily a strictly human rights group but rather is concerned basically with a different interest. That is, the group does not take its raison d'etre from international agreements on human rights. Rather, it may be basically interested in a particular country or in a general concern (e.g., labor benefits, progressive government). The group, however, moves into the issue area of human rights from time to time. In fact, this is the most numerous type of human rights interest group—the nonhuman rights group which becomes temporarily or partly a human rights group. Any interest group may make this shift or expansion in focus, and many have—for example, Americans for Democratic Action, the American Federation of Labor–Congress of Industrial Organizations, and so on. Moreover, a church or even a political party can function as an international interest group—that is, be nongovernmental and seek particular policies without running candidates. It is quite clear that parts of the Catholic church in various parts of Latin America have increasingly acted as a human rights "lobby" and have apparently troubled a number of repressive regimes.

In addition to these three types of national organizations, we should note that certain less organized groups, or movements, exist to support certain human rights on an ad hoc basis. In 1979 in the United States, for example, a citizens' movement made up of scientists tried to protect the rights of two Soviet scientists, Yuri Orlov and Anatoli Scharansky, by sending signed petitions to the Kremlin. At the same time, a group of publishers banded together and sought to protect the rights of the Soviet writer Mykola Rudenko by threatening nonparticipation in a Moscow book fair. A decade earlier American citizens had come together briefly to demand that food be sent to Biafrans suffering from acute protein deficiency during the Nigerian civil war. Thus there are ad hoc human rights movements, in addition to the more structured and relatively more permanent groups.

Hence there is a melange of nongovernmental actors seeking to help implement human rights. Boundary lines are decidedly not neatly drawn within this swirling activity. Many of the temporary human rights groups join or affiliate with the national coalition actor. Also, AI–U.S.A. affiliates with the Working Group on Human Rights: thus a national component of a transnational organization is linked to a strictly national group. Moreover, an official of the American Civil Liberties Union may also be a member of the American section of the League for Human Rights. Boundary questions aside, the really important issue is, What do these human rights unofficial actors do, and how effective are they?

STEPS

It is much easier to say what these groups do than to measure with any accuracy their effectiveness. The foundation of all unofficial activity is research, in the sense of obtaining information about human rights situations. Other steps are organizing citizen pressure, directly persuading governmental elites, engaging in trial observation, visiting prisons and other places of detention to improve conditions, and taking direct action to provide a service such as legal counsel or a good such as food or medicine.

1. *Research*

Without research on human rights nothing could be done by these unofficial groups. The first step in the work of Amnesty International, for example, is the collection of reliable information about prisoners of conscience (those who have been imprisoned for their beliefs and who have, in general, neither advocated nor used violence) and about prisoners facing torture or execution. Such is the importance of this fundamental role of data collection that high U.S. governmental officials in the 1970s called for the creation of a nongovernmental institute to collect information on a broad range of rights. The proposal was almost approved by Congress. Others have noted the need for reliable indices of human rights progress and human rights violations, both in the civil-political and socioeconomic fields.[3]

Some private agencies have already pioneered in this area of data collection and indexing. The Overseas Development Council, a private agency based in Washington, has constructed a quality of life index on the basis of data concerning literacy, life expectancy, and infant mortality. The ODC also measures governmental performance against this index. Performance ratings give some indirect indication of a government's record in implementing certain rights, such as "the inherent right to life" (U.N. Civil–Political Covenant, Article 6), "the right of everyone to an adequate standard of living for himself and his family, including adequate food, clothing and housing" (U.N. Economic, Social, and Cultural Covenant, Article 11), and "the right of everyone to the enjoyment of the highest attainable standard of physical and mental health" (ibid., Article 12). The ODC in the late 1970s cited Japan, Spain, and Taiwan as the three countries making the most progress on the quality of life index over the past twenty-three-year period. Other indices exist, and there is continuing debate over problems of conception, definition, and measurement.[4]

It remains a widely accepted fact that data collection and interpretation is the first and fundamental step in protecting human rights. It is a step that will continue to be taken primarily in the private or unofficial sector, since only private interpretations will be free of the charge of serving particular governmental interests. While at some point governmental or intergovernmental bodies may approve a particular data collection or means of interpretation, it is clear that pioneering work will be done by unofficial agencies. The government of Norway, for example, has contracted with an academic institute, the Michelsen Institute in Bergen, to provide a report on the human rights situation in nations receiving Norwegian official developmental assistance.[5] By comparison, the U.S. Department of State publishes its own annual report of human rights conditions in all members of the United

Nations; this report is then reviewed not only by the Congress, which commissioned it, but also by private human rights groups.[6]

2. *Grass roots lobbying*

To organize citizen pressure in support of human rights is to engage in a type of grass-roots lobbying. One form of this activity is associated with Amnesty International. On the basis of its research, AI's international headquarters in London identifies certain prisoners who become focal points for a letter-writing campaign by individual members in Amnesty's various sections. No section is supposed to write about prisoners in its own country, but rather is expected to write to or about one prisoner in a communist country, one in a Third World country, and one in a developed democracy. The letters may go to national officials, international organizations, or to the prisoner himself. The objective may be to free the prisoner or to improve his situation.

The result of this process is difficult to analyze in general. AI itself does not like to call attention to its successes, for such claims may affront governments and hence make Amnesty's work more difficult. Governments themselves do not give AI credit for released prisoners, general amnesties, and the like, for this makes the government appear weak or erroneous in its policies. And AI's influence is normally merged with a myriad of other factors, which makes the separation of Amnesty's influence objectively difficult and sometimes impossible. There are instances, however, in which AI's impact on particular persons seems undeniable, and some of these particulars have been recorded elsewhere.[7]

Amnesty is perhaps the best-known unofficial organization which engages in the mobilization of citizen pressure. A number of other organizations engage in similar behavior. The American Psychiatric Association has organized letter-writing campaigns vis-a-vis the U.S. Congress concerning the politically inspired abuse of psychiatry in Eastern Europe and elsewhere.

3. *Direct Lobbying*

Direct lobbying of public officials by unofficial agencies can be related to the preceding role or can exist independently. AI officials from the international office frequently undertake lobbying or diplomatic missions (the two are the same) in order to try to persuade public officials, against the background of AI's letter writing efforts. The ICJ does the same, but without the effort at citizen pressure which characterizes

AI's activity. Chapter four below goes into some depth to analyze the impact of direct lobbying or persuasion on U.S. officials in the 1970s and 1980s.

The results of direct lobbying or negotiation are no easier to ascertain than is true for other unofficial efforts to protect human rights. In some cases one is able to say something about the correlation between direct lobbying and resulting legislation, as chapter four will demonstrate. But it is very difficult to be precise about direct lobbying and executive decisions, as well as direct lobbying by unofficial groups active at various intergovernmental organizations such as the United Nations.[8] Many private agencies criticize public documents and present information in an effort to persuade policy-makers at both national and international levels of decision. But whether these inputs have effect or are simply lost in the flow of words engulfing most policy-making processes is very difficult to determine. There is a widely held view that private groups have been influential at the U.N. on human rights matters over time in working with sympathetic states to improve international monitoring of state policy.[9] But if true, such non-governmental influence is meshed with other factors such as secretariat influence and public opinion. Using reverse evidence, one can say that if some of the private groups were not viewed as influential by governments, there would not be such a battle—as does transpire—to limit their rights to speak and circulate documents at the United Nations. Some governments fear NGOs, which can be taken as evidence of their presumed influence.

4. Trial Observation

Trial observation is practiced by a small number of groups. Especially in so-called political trials, where the trial is alleged to be more persecution than prosecution (and the two are not so easily separated in demonstrable fact), AI or the ICJ or some other group may send an observer. The ICRC has on occasion also observed trials, primarily with regard to prisoners of war or other victims of war covered by the Geneva Conventions or Protocols, but sometimes with regard to political prisoners. (Governments may also engage in trial observation, as the U.S. did in Czechoslovakia in 1988, or as the Inter-Parliamentary Union, an inter-governmental group, did in 1987 in Kenya.)

The greatest hope is that the mere presence of such observers will restrain violations of due process and substantive miscarriages of justice. The lesser hope is that accurate information will be obtained for reports and other action. There are occasions when a noticeably lenient sentence has been widely attributed to an international presence in the courtroom, but in general no one really knows why a court decides what it does. In the case of an impartial court, the underlying reasons for decision are not public knowledge. In the case of a politically instructed court, precisely the same situation obtains.

5. Prison Visits

Especially the ICRC but also AI make visits to places of detention to ascertain and help improve conditions. Aside from situations of international armed conflict, wherein the ICRC has a legal right to visit detainees, all such missions are by voluntary grant of the ruling authority. Only the ICRC has received widespread permissions for systematic visits. This is partly because the ICRC gives details privately to the controlling authorities only, and partly because the ICRC does not directly question the reason for detention but only the conditions. Even so, the ICRC has not been allowed to make systematic visits to so-called political prisoners in certain places, notably communist Eastern Europe and East Asia. (The ICRC made visits in Poland in 1982 when leaders of the Solidarity movement were detained under martial law.)

Since so much of what the ICRC does concerning prisons is not public knowledge, it is almost impossible to evaluate its effectiveness. Some Red Cross prison reports have been made public, because the ICRC practices the policy that if a government publishes incomplete or erroneous reports about its work, the ICRC is entitled to publish the entire series of reports in question. At the start of 1980 the ICRC did just this with regard to its visits to Iranian prisons, since the new Islamic Republic of Iran had previously allowed the publication of self-serving portions of ICRC prison reports submitted to governments under the Shah. From the full Red Cross reports one could document an improvement of detention conditions and treatment over time, after the start of Red Cross visits.[10] In other places, such as South Vietnam and Mozambique under Portuguese rule, the ICRC itself stopped prison visits.[11]

If one can project from those few cases where we do have some public knowledge, it would appear that the ICRC has been vigorous in working for improved detention conditions. It may be particularly effective in places like the Shah's Iran, where top officials are actually not well informed about what is happening in their own country.

A moral dilemma confronts both the ICRC and those who would evaluate it. Suppose some improvements are achieved, but violations of rights continue. The ICRC was active in territories occupied by Israel after the 1967 war in the Middle East. It eventually became known in 1987–88 that Israel had used pressure and coercion to secure confessions from Arab detainees, and that Israeli authorities had then committed perjury by denying in court that they had done so. There was a period in 1988 when Israeli authorities intentionally mistreated detainees. Should the ICRC have withdrawn from that situation in protest, or should the ICRC stay, as it did, in order to do whatever good it could in behalf of detainees? It is because of such dilemmas that some critique the entire process in which some conditions of detention are improved while basic rights are still violated—and in which some would say that detention should not exist at all.

The ICRC was not the only agency to visit prisons, although it had the most experience. Cuba in the late 1980s invited not only the ICRC and the U.N. Human Rights Commission to make prison visits, but also officials from America's Watch and other private groups. For a time it seemed that there were so many groups trekking to Havana for prison visits that they had to line up and take a number. (Cuban officials were denied a visa for the purpose of visiting American jails.) A new European draft convention on torture provided for prison visits on demand by the monitoring agency, whenever that agreement should come into legal force. A Boston-based group, Physicians for Human Rights, made some prison visits to check on health conditions.

6. Relief

The provision of goods and services in response to the need to fulfill basic economic and social rights is carried out by a huge number of private or unofficial organizations. These exist primarily in Western societies, for it is here that the private, nonprofit sector is most affluent and vigorous. In fact, more goods and services are transmitted by American private agencies to developing countries than are transmitted through U.S. official developmental assistance.[12]

In many situations the public and private sectors are intertwined, as in providing food to Kampuchea in 1979 and 1980 or in Ethiopia in the mid-1980s. Much of the money and some of the material originated with governments and intergovernmental organizations, but delivery was not only by these public organizations but also by such private agencies as CARITAS, Oxfam, Church World Service, the International Red Cross, and others. It is perhaps a reflection of the underdeveloped nature of the international society that certain vital jobs, such as responding to disasters, are left largely to the private sector. It is not that private agencies are incompetent; it is that the job seems too important not to have a complete public policy on the issue in question. The situation is as if fire protection in large cities were left to each private neighborhood association to organize voluntarily.[13] Hence there has arisen one of the third generation claims for recognition as a universal human rights: the right to humanitarian assistance.

In many situations this complex combination of official and unofficial actors works reasonably well in providing food, clothing, shelter, and health care to especially those affected by natural or man-made disasters. (One should note in passing the argument that all disasters are man-made in the sense that man has the capacity to plan for, and warn about, natural disasters; when he does not take such action, he transforms a natural phenomenon into a man-made disaster.) This provision of humanitarian assistance, which is actually a response to demands for fulfillment of basic economic and social rights, although not always referred to in the language of rights, is much too large and complex for simple description, much less general analysis, here.[14]

It is important to observe that access to humanitarian relief is not yet recognized by states as a human right, even though they have recognized the rights to food, shelter, and health care, and that provision of such assistance is still frequently tenuous because of political situations. In Ethiopia in the late 1980s, the ICRC withdrew from relief actions in the northern provinces because it could not guarantee, due to governmental policies, that relief would be distributed in an impartial, humanitarian manner.

FURTHER REFLECTIONS

It may prove useful to use, as we did in the preceding chapter, a conception of different types of states in order to gain further insights into unofficial action for international human rights.

Democratic First World

The unofficial means for protecting human rights are more developed in the democratic First World than elsewhere because of many reasons, but none more important than the tradition of pluralism (many centers of power). Amnesty International, for example, had a global membership in the 1980s of over two hundred thousand with the bulk of that located in West Germany and Scandinavia. In the United States in the mid-1970s AI's rolls had jumped dramatically from a paltry three thousand to over fifty thousand in about eighteen months. Part of this increase in membership was brought about by AI's mobilization of young people via rock concerts and other appeals to the tastes of the young. Means aside, it was clear that Amnesty was a Western-based organization.

In general, it can be said that it is in the West and from the West that: private letters are sent regarding political prisoners; private food is sent to those whose rights to life and health are most deprived; and private legal assistance is provided without charge. Activity per se cannot be equated with impact. But activity is a precursor to effectiveness. And it is clearly the democratic First World that shows the most activity concerning unofficial means of protecting human rights. Sometimes the unofficial steps may be unexpected in origin and impact: the Italian Communist party perhaps played an effective role in protecting some workers' and consumers' rights in Poland in the mid-1970s; [15] and the French, Spanish, and Italian Communist parties condemned the arrest and internal exile of the Russian dissident, Andrei Sakharov, in the early 1980s.

There is something of a chicken-and-egg problem in analysis here. For private agencies to be active in support of internationally recognized human rights, the ruling authorities must themselves acknowledge at least civil if not political rights. There must be a civil society, rather than totalitarianism, for private groups to have the legal and political space necessary for human rights activity. There can only be unofficial action for human rights if the government, speaking for the state, does not insist on total control of society.

Authoritarian Second World

As for unofficial activity to implement human rights in the authoritarian Second World, it is noteworthy that the international human rights concern has mobilized private responses across most of Eastern Europe. Groups were formed to monitor compliance with the Helsinki Accord and to press for implementation of other rights. In the Soviet Union and Czechoslovakia in particular these groups were at first harassed by the ruling authorities and largely suppressed through arrests, internal exile, harsh prison terms, and loss of professional work. Similar steps were taken in Romania and Bulgaria.

In other places and times other groups met with more success—at least temporarily. The Catholic church and Solidarity in Poland were clearly powerful actors meriting delicate treatment by the party-state apparatus until martial law was declared. Catholic and Protestant churches in East Germany were proving more assertive in challenging party-state policies. By the late 1980s there was, under the influence of the Gorbachev reforms, increasingly large and open demands for increased civil and political rights. It was estimated that as many as 50,000 Hungarians, the largest meeting since the 1956 uprising, demonstrated for political rights in the spring of 1988. Similar meetings were held in Poland. And the transnational movement to have conscientious objection to military service recognized as a human right grew stronger throughout most of Eastern Europe. (In 1987 the U.N. Human Rights Commission voted, in a non-binding resolution, to declare conscientious objection to military service as a universal human right.)

As mentioned earlier, for there to be effective private action for human rights, ruling authorities must recognize some basic civil rights: freedom of expression and association, above all, but also some increased freedom of the press. One way to look at the Gorbachev reforms was to see them as an effort to carve out a truly civil society in the Soviet Union—a "space" not under the control of the party-state. To the extent that such a civil society emerges, it would be in keeping with international human rights standards and would set the stage for further private—and eventually official—attention to other human rights. The Gorbachev reforms thus constituted steps of immense human rights significance, however they evolved.

It has been widely assumed that if Gorbachev retains power and is able to implement and institutionalize some civil and political liberalization or openness (glasnost), this will have a tremendous influence on Soviet allies. Most likely this is true, although each socialist country operates within the influence of its own culture and history. The party-state leadership in both Czechoslovakia and East Germany, for example, was extremely cautious in the late 1980s about following the Gorbachev reforms. They cracked down hard on groups such as the Helsinki watch groups which demanded many civil rights from their governments. Thus private groups in states linked to the Soviet Union still faced considerable harassment at the time of writing.

In Prague, political leaders had much to fear from an open review of their policies, while closet reformers had much to fear from endorsing reform before their leaders did so. The reformers of the Prague Spring of 1968, by 1988, were living abroad, in prison, or shovelling coal. Czech closet reformers in the contemporary period did not want the same fate. In Berlin, similar factors were complicated by a Prussian culture long supportive of authoritarianism. On the other hand, some Hungarian reforms had preceded the Soviet ones. But even in Budapest the effects of changed Soviet policies could be seen in street demonstrations, some of which were met by repression.

It is probably true that Soviet glasnost, if it continues, will impact on the East European states, but it may take longer in some states than others, depending on culture, history, and the nature of existing political leadership.

Authoritarian Third World

Unofficial activity to implement human rights in these authoritarian Third World states is greater than in Eastern Europe but less than in the democratic First World. In Latin America in particular, but also in places like the Philippines and South Korea, elements of the Catholic church have been dynamic in demanding implementation of all types of rights in places like Chile and El Salvador. Another relatively new feature of Latin American politics was the rise of women's groups demanding human rights and less murderous politics; these groups like the Mothers of the Plaza del Mayo in Argentina frequently arose because of brutal attacks on relatives.[16]

Unions also continued to press for implementation of the right to freedom of association, and specifically rights-oriented groups arose in most Third World states in response to obvious violations. All of these unofficial movements frequently meet with repression, including murder or "disappearances." Amnesty International formed an urgent network to try to protect human rights activists, on the belief that international support of such persons could help shield them from abuse. Many of the targets of attempted Amnesty protection were to be found in the authoritarian Third World.

It is important to observe that human rights and other private groups demanding rights are a feature of local politics across the authoritarian Third World. Thus an international movement, historically Western and sometimes criticized for being culture bound or ethnocentric, showed great appeal throughout the non-western world.

This phenomenon could be seen clearly in the Peoples Republic of China, for example, where indigenous students and others demanded implementation of internationally recognized human rights. The government there, as elsewhere, showed a varied record in responding to such rights demands. Sometimes there was some liberalization, but periodically there was a crackdown on private groups. Repression was sometimes more uniform, as in the Iranian Islamic Republic, where groups advocating womens' rights met difficulty from Ayatollah Khomeini.[17]

Democratic Third World

Unofficial activity for human rights in this part of the world seems to be growing. Threats to rights appear to stimulate rights organizations and movements. This was clearly the case in India. Mrs. Gandhi's period of emergency rule, leading to considerable despotism, political detention, and torture, was rolled back by internal citizen backlash; several human rights groups remain in existence in a continuing effort to monitor political behavior.[18] The same was largely true in the Philippines, where the Marcos period of martial law was overturned through "people power" in the streets (plus the impact of sectors of the military), and where numerous private groups have remained in existence

to continue the fight to implement various types of rights.[19] In the Philippine case, unlike the Indian one, transnational action for human rights was important in returning the country to rights standards. Such transnational forces included private ones like Western journalists, as well as public ones like the U.S. government.

A number of initiatives are underway to promote and protect human rights in all of the Third World but especially its democratic part. The U.S. government has an aid program to promote civil and political rights (there is also a special fund for ending apartheid in South Africa), as well as the National Endowment for Democracy which gives aid to undergird democratic processes. Both U.S. programs seek to identify private groups worthy of support in the interests of promoting and protecting rights. The International Commission of Jurists has long sought to promote a humane rule of law in many African and other lesser developed countries; it provides seminars for human rights lawyers, among other activities. The ICRC does something similar with National Red Cross Societies, and the U.N. provides some technical assistance in the human rights field.

Thus much transnational action for human rights is not just reactive to crises and deteriorating situations, but is also anticipatory and long range. Yet in the final analysis it seems clear that the best guarantee of implementing rights is an informed and concerned citizenry. Absent that commitment to rights by especially the elite but also at least part of the masses in a country, it is difficult if not impossible to make sustained progress in rights implementation. We shall return to many of these themes, briefly treated in this chapter, in the final chapter.

CONCLUSIONS

The protection of human rights through formal and informal means is still in its infancy. While the U.N. Human Rights Commission and its subcommission have been "at work" for over thirty years, and while the ILO goes back even further, efforts by others are more recent. The Inter-American Commission dates from 1959; its companion Inter-American Court only started handing down cases in the 1980s. The U.N. Human Rights Committee under the Political Covenant only got underway in 1977; the revised Committee of Experts under the Economic Covenant first met in the spring of 1987. Likewise on the informal side, while the ICRC has existed in more docile form since the 1860s, other NGOs are more recent, and AI dates from only 1961.

In historical terms these public and private protection efforts transcend a relatively small span of time compared with the hundreds of years in which most persons assumed that what a government does in "its" territory is of no concern to outsiders. We have accepted the principle of national sovereignty as a controlling general principle for over three hundred years (with a few exceptions such as Napoleonic and Nazi attempts at world empire), while we have been trying to implement most human rights according to global standards for less than fifty years. (In chapter 1 we saw that some rights have a longer history of serious attempts at implementation—e.g., in war, under slavery, for minorities and labor.)

The central, superficial deficiency in formal protection is that governments insist on controlling the process of implementation, refusing to permit enforcement by independent courts. Thus a majority of governments in the world insist on implementation either through majority politics (viz., state voting of political but non-binding resolutions) or through uninstructed individuals (as rapporteurs, members of working groups and committees and commissions) who lack the authority to have the last say about what should be done. (The regional human rights law and monitoring machinery in Western Europe is an illustrious exception to the general rule.)

The majority of states in the U.N. General Assembly is willing to create special committees to seek implementation of self-determination for the blacks of southern Africa or of human rights in territory occupied by Israel. But that same majority is unwilling to create similar bodies on forced labor or political psychiatry. And that majority is unwilling to systematically utilize supranational authority by uninstructed individuals under the human rights treaties. It will not even allow the creation of a U.N. commissioner for human rights who might function as an international ombudsman, and some of the more assertive private human rights lobbies are blocked by states from obtaining consultative status with the United Nations.

Underlying these superficial developments is the subject of political attitudes—especially on the part of elites who control governments and thus speak for states. From elite perspectives, it is in some ways rational for them to retard the development of international standards, both as law on the books and law in action—viz., implemented law. The international law of human rights restricts their free-

*"We are a watchdog committee, gentlemen, but it will facilitate our
work if everyone here remembers that we have no teeth."*

Drawing by Handelsman; © *1977 The New Yorker Magazine, Inc.*

dom of maneuver. Yet especially from 1945 to 1990 one can see a fundamental shift in world politics. Universal human rights have been accepted in law, and numerous efforts are made by inter-governmental
institutions (and states acting unilaterally) to have them implemented. States accept human rights standards and some, usually
weak, monitoring agencies because they think they can direct a given
human rights regime toward others, not themselves. But these hypo-
critical state policies actually advance the cause of international human rights over time. A core international regime of human rights is
created, as well as additional specialized human rights regimes, which
no one state can fully control.

If elite attitudes are the obvious key to this process, one should not
overlook the vigorous efforts by private groups to push and even badger
governmental elites into accepting human rights standards and incor-
porating them into state practice. Human rights NGOs, and other unofficial groups not defined as rights groups but who work for similar objectives, have increased in numbers, funding, and activity. They have
become a regular fixture in world politics. Given the reluctance of
many ruling interests to really accept international standards which
limit their policy choices, it is probably essential that the private
groups continue their lobbying in various ways for human rights.

One cannot proceed very far, certainly not in peaceful ways, without elite cooperation for human rights values. But there is considerable evidence that private activity reminds elites of what they should be doing, and embarrasses elites when they fail to meet international standards. For example, during 1987 Amnesty International publicly criticized the government of Kenya for its harassment of domestic critics, whereupon the governments of Norway, Sweden, and the United States picked up the story and also put pressure on Kenya.[20] It is the dialectic of elite-NGO interaction that explains much progress on international human rights.

In sum, the international law of human rights, as an ideology, provides sweeping but still ambiguous standards for evaluating governmental policies in the civil-political and socioeconomic areas. As such, the law is an important factor in the mobilization of concerned individuals and groups who desire more freedom, or more socioeconomic justice, or both. This mobilization has occurred everywhere, even in totalitarian and authoritarian societies. The resulting unofficial human rights groups help to informally implement human rights primarily through persuading elites to change official policies and practices.

International human rights law may sometimes help to formally and directly control behavior through governmental and IGO action. International law occasionally is a command given by the World Court, the U.N. Security Council, or a national court. Most of the time, however, international law functions as an agent of political socialization, "educating" elite and citizen into a new view of individual and society. In the present and for the near future, the international human rights agreements, as soft law rather than hard law, will probably make their most important contribution through mobilizing informal protection efforts. International enforcement will be rare, with international public and private efforts focusing on nudging states into more rights-oriented policies.

One of the difficulties with all these attempts at generalizations is that they are so general. In trying to cover the world and discuss many of the relevant factors at once, much of the "real stuff" involved in the politics of protecting human rights seems to get lost. In the following two chapters we try to correct this distortion by looking at official and unofficial efforts to protect human rights via United States foreign policy during the late 1970s and 1980s.

Chapter Five

United States Foreign Policy and Human Rights

Rhetoric and Reality

We need to be an example to other nations—both
of strength and prosperity—and of our vibrant
democratic institutions. For we cannot call on others
to meet high human rights standards unless we do so
ourselves. President Reagan has captured this concept
clearly in speaking of the United States as a city
upon a hill.
Walter J. Stoessel, Jr. Undersecretary of State for
Political Affairs, in *Current Policy No. 293*,
Department of State, 14 July 1981.

INTRODUCTION

"The United States was founded on the proclamation of 'unalienable' rights, and human rights ever since had a peculiar resonance in the American tradition."[1] So wrote the well-known historian Arthur Schlesinger, Jr. Both historians and political scientists have observed an ethical or moral strain in U.S. foreign policy, at least rhetorically. The contemporary emphasis on global human rights fits well with this American tradition. Yet there are numerous problems in specifying a place for human rights in U.S. foreign policy.

For some, U.S. foreign policy should give attention to human rights largely by passive example. U.S. leaders in the eighteenth century warned about too deep an involvement in behalf of such moral principles, fearing that the U.S. would become an imperial power. George Washington in his farewell address warned against such dangers. Later in the twentieth century moral isolationism tried to point policy in the same direction of restraint (Old World politics was an evil struggle for power and thus the U.S. should stay out). If the U.S. was pictured as a shining city on a hill, which it was to many of those who made the American revolution and led the country thereafter, it was to lead in the world by example at home, not by an activist rights policy abroad.

Yet progressively another strain in the American tradition of emphasizing the rhetoric of morality and rights competed for control of foreign policy. Around the turn of this century U.S. leaders justified American involvement in, and ultimately control over, Cuba and the Philippines in terms of supporting the right to liberation from Spanish colonialism. And Woodrow Wilson certainly created the image of an active, not passive, defense of democratic rights and self-determination through his self-styled crusade to make the world safe for democracy (however much such a "crusade" went unimplemented in U.S. practical diplomacy pertaining to Mexico and elsewhere). American ideological anti-communism in the 1950s fit well with this activist tradition of opposing "evil" around the world in the name of rights.

Thus a U.S. fondness for the rhetoric of morality and rights in foreign policy has been accompanied by a continuing debate over how much detailed attention that policy should give to specific rights in foreign countries. Complicating the picture still further is that considerations of self-interest (viz., expediential interests) have cut across this two-branched concern for rights. Chief among these expediential concerns has been the security of the U.S. Second only to concern for U.S. power has been concern for U.S. profit.

Hence in a world of nation-states, where there is no centralized monopoly of the use of force, and thus where each state must protect its own security as its overriding priority (else it will cease to exit), how much serious attention can the U.S. or any state give to protecting human rights abroad through its foreign policy? Moreover, economics reinforces politics. The global economy is basically a laissez-faire economic system. Should the U.S. engage in economic embargoes as sanctions for human rights violations, if this leads to the capturing of markets by others? In 1987 Japan replaced the U.S. as the leading trading partner with South Africa, at least partly because of U.S. (and other western) economic sanctions against South African apartheid. (Exchange rates in favor of a strong yen also had something to do with the value of Japanese trade with South Africa, compared to American trade evaluated in terms of the weak dollar.)

If we become more specific, and if we focus on U.S. foreign policy since 1945, one way to view matters is to say that starting with the Eisenhower Administration the American concern for morality and rights was collapsed into the U.S. strategic policy of opposing communism. Whereas the Truman Administration tried to consider international human rights as a distinct issue on the U.S. foreign policy agenda, and therefore supported human rights language in the U.N. Charter, the Universal Declaration of Human Rights, and the two basic U.N. human rights Covenants, it was forced to abandon this policy of limited support for internationally recognized human rights. Brickerism and McCarthyism in the Congress caused the Eisenhower Administration to back away from Truman's policies.[2] The result was that U.S. human rights policy was collapsed into its anti-communist policy. The rhetoric of rights became the icing on the cake of anti-communism. Or, while U.S. anti-communism had its roots both in morality and expediency, over time containment of communism became a basically strategic policy. What became primary was containing Soviet power.

That this was so can be seen in the fact that the U.S. rationalized its support for all sorts of repressive allies in the name of anti-communism. The U.S.-led "free world" was composed not only of industrialized democracies but also of dictatorships in Portugal and countries in the Third World too numerous to list. For example, unlike the other Western democracies, the U.S. accepted the Greek junta 1967–1974, along with its political detention and torture. The U.S. provided that authoritarian government with military assistance in the name of NATO solidarity while the West Europeans debated economic sanctions and did apply diplomatic pressure in behalf of democracy and other rights.

Global containment of communism necessitated an alliance with all sorts of unfree polities in places like South Korea, Morocco, Nicaragua, and above all in Vietnam. Specific concern for the recognized rights of persons took a back seat to insuring that a government was not communist. Repressive governments were not only accepted where they arose through domestic politics, but were even installed by the U.S. in places like Iran and Guatemala. The U.S. polity tolerated this contradiction until the Vietnam war, when a sizable number of American deaths and a deteriorating American economy led to a painful re-evaluation of U.S. foreign policy.

Because of growing American dissatisfaction with the general orientation of U.S. foreign policy under the impact of the Vietnam war, an orientation started by Eisenhower but continued by Presidents Kennedy and Johnson, a fundamental re-evaluation of policy started during the Nixon Administration. Or, to put it another way, the cornerstone of U.S. foreign policy collapsed during the Nixon period; global containment of communism was no longer automatically accepted as the basic rationale of U.S. foreign policy. This collapse allowed human rights to re-emerge as a distinct issue in U.S. foreign policy. Thus a major debate was re-opened in the 1970s about the place of internationally recognized human rights on the U.S. foreign policy agenda. By the late 1980s the debate was continuing. Hence it is important to examine more closely the place of human rights in the foreign policy of recent Administrations. At the same time, as will become clear, the role of Congress cannot be ignored.

KISSINGER RHETORIC AND REALITY

Because Henry Kissinger was a principal architect of U.S. foreign policy 1969–1976 and because he has left a relatively clear record of his views, we focus on him as representative of the Nixon and Ford Administrations. In so doing we do not try to answer the intriguing question of whether it was Nixon or Kissinger, or some symbiotic combination of the two, which was responsible for the major drift of U.S. policy. On the other hand it was fairly clear that Kissinger had great influence on the inexperienced Ford.

Under Kissinger's key role as both national security advisor and later Secretary of State, the major goal of U.S. foreign policy was to contain Soviet power by co-opting the USSR into a concert of great powers. This restyled Congress of Vienna (1815), about which Kissinger wrote his dissertation, was to bring both the Soviet Union and the Peoples Republic of China fully into the international system, and therefore give them a vested interest in stabilizing, not overturning, that system. Detente, or the reduction of great power tensions, was the means to this end. Increased east-west trade and reduced inflammatory rhetoric was part of the new process directed to the traditional goal of limiting Soviet (and PRC) power. The Vietnam war was not seen as a moral crusade to stem the evils of communism and to defend democratic rights, but rather as part of the power struggle with the Soviet Union. North Vietnam, as a Soviet client, must not be allowed to capture the south, as this would destabilize the configuration of power that Kissinger was trying to solidify as a basis for great power relations.

When seen against this background, Kissinger should not have been expected to emphasize individual rights—and he did not. As an academic he had written that human rights belonged within the domestic structure of states. To introduce considerations of democracy and authoritarianism into foreign policy was to complicate unnecessarily the calculus of geo-strategy.[3] Kissinger was also in the "realist" school of thought about U.S. foreign policy, and was thus critical of U.S. emphasis on moral and legal principles compared to calculations of power relations.[4]

Throughout the first Nixon Administration there was little attention to internationally recognized human rights except where they could be made to fit with strategies of containment. The U.S. government might emphasize North Vietnam's violation of the Geneva Conventions concerning treatment of captured American pilots. But Kissinger tried to de-emphasize Soviet treatment of dissidents and refuseniks (those, largely Jewish, denied permission to emigrate), not wanting human rights questions to interfere with larger Soviet-American relations. For the same reasons Basket Three of the Helsinki Accord originated with the West Europeans, not the U.S.; only the West Europeans originally wanted to pressure the USSR for human rights concessions in return for strategic and economic public goods from the

Copyright, 1975, Jules Feiffer. Reprinted with permission of Universal Press Syndicate. All rights reserved.

West. There was little if any pressure on U.S. strategic allies to improve their human rights records.

It was in this context that an important movement was launched in the Congress to get internationally recognized human rights back on the U.S. foreign policy agenda after an absence of about twenty years. Don Fraser (D., Minn.) began systematic hearings in the House Foreign Affairs Committee, Subcommittee on International Organizations and Movements, later renamed the Subcommittee on Human Rights and International Organizations. His attempt to consider internationally defined human rights as an important component of U.S. foreign policy, rather than just as part of anti-communism, obviously struck a responsive cord in the Congress. A bipartisan coalition supported his efforts in a backlash against twenty-five years of global containment of communism which had led into the swamp (figuratively and literally) of Vietnam. This coalition was joined by others who were looking for any reason to cut foreign assistance, or any reason to attack the party controlling the White House, or any reason to reduce U.S. commitments abroad.[5]

This congressional movement, really a patchwork of different factions, succeeded during 1974–1978 in putting a great deal of legislation on the books that ostensibly had to do with international human rights. There was general legislation linking human rights to security assistance, economic assistance, and U.S. voting in the multilateral development institutions, sometimes called the international financial institutions. All three were to be affected by a consistent pattern of gross violations of internationally recognized human rights in recipient nations. Furthermore, trade with communist countries, treatment of refugees, and the U.S. Export-Import Bank were supposed to be affected by international provisions on human rights.

In addition to this general legislation on human rights, Congress passed human rights legislation on specific countries. This started in about 1973 when the focus was on General Pinochet in Chile who took over in a coup from the elected Marxist President, Salvadore Allende. Subsequently the Congress passed country-specific legislation for a disparate list of countries which over time included El Salvador, Guatemala, Nicaragua, Haiti, Argentina, Chile, Paraguay, South Africa, Zaire, Liberia, Uganda, the Philippines, Laos, Vietnam, Cambodia, South Korea, Pakistan, Romania, and others. The exact import of each country-specific law varied. Sometimes the language was vague, placing no effective restrictions on the Executive. Sometimes the Execu-

tive was required to certify an improvement in human rights conditions before U.S. foreign assistance could be provided. Sometimes U.S.
military assistance was prohibited until certain human rights improvements were made. Sometimes U.S. economic assistance was to
be administered by private, not governmental, agencies in a country
because of human rights problems.

Moreover Congress adopted function-specific human rights legislation. For example, the State Department was instructed, through the
congressionally created Bureau of Human Rights and Humanitarian
Affairs, to compile public annual reports on the human rights conditions in all countries which were members of the United Nations. Em-
bassies were required by Congress to report on the steps they had
taken to oppose torture in the countries to which they were accred-
ited. Funds were voted to support civil and political rights in developing countries. Other funds were voted specifically to promote democracy. Still other funds were approved for particular organizations like
the International Committee of the Red Cross. U.S. training of foreign
police and intelligence forces was barred, with several exceptions.

Thus Congress reacted to the Vietnam war and the Nixon-Kissinger
Administration not only by legislating an end to that war, but also by
trying to restructure the foreign policy that had led to the war over four
Administrations. If the particular cause of congressional action was
the machtpolitik, or raw power struggle, personified by Nixon and
Kissinger, the more general dissatisfaction stemmed from what was
perceived as the moral bankruptcy of that policy. A pure power struggle with the Soviet Union, with China as a sideshow, did not fit very
well with an America used to the rhetoric of morality and rights.

When this congressional movement erupted in 1973–74, ironically
some twenty years after Congress had compelled the removal of international human rights from the U.S. agenda, Kissinger tried to employ
the rhetoric of rights to placate his critics. In 1976, his last full year in
office, Kissinger went to a meeting of the Organization of American
States and talked about the importance of human rights:

> [B]asic human rights must be preserved, cherished, and de-
> fended if peace and prosperity are to be more than hollow tech-
> nical achievements . . . Human rights are the very essence of a
> meaningful life, and human dignity is the ultimate purpose of
> government . . . Respect for the dignity of man is declining in
> too many countries of the hemisphere. There are several states

where fundamental standards of humane behavior are not ob-
served . . . The condition of human rights as assessed by the OAS
Human Rights Commission has impaired our relationship with
Chile and will continue to do so.[6]

In that same year Kissinger also said, "This Administration has believed that we must bend every effort to enhance respect for human
rights."[7]

Careful research would eventually show, however, that behind this
belated use of the rhetoric of rights lay a continuing disdain for the
subject by Kissinger.[8] This reservation surfaced on occasion, as when
Kissinger said, "There are certain experiments that cannot be tried,
not because the goals are undesirable but because the consequences of
failure would be so severe that not even the most elevated goal can justify the risk . . . Will we have served moral ends if we thereby jeopardize our own security?"[9] Meaning: if the U.S. pushes for human rights
in a friendly country, and winds up with an anti-American government, will we be better off morally—or politically? It was a question
that would become highly relevant to the Carter Administration and
its policies in places like Nicaragua.

Whatever the merits of Kissinger's view, it eventually became clear
that his rhetorical support for human rights was quite different from
the reality of U.S. foreign policy. According to published reports, at the
time of his Santiago speech to the OAS, Kissinger told the Pinochet government that it was meant for American domestic consumption and
was not to be taken as a genuine guide to U.S. policy.[10] He also instructed the U.S. Ambassador to Chile, who had raised human rights
issues in quiet diplomacy, to "drop the political science lectures."[11]
And in the face of U.S. law requiring country reports on human rights
conditions, Kissinger refused to allow those reports to be released to
the Congress, until just before leaving office in 1977 when several superficial ones were handed over.

Kissinger was nothing if not duplicitous (who else could have attacked Nixon so harshly when working for Nelson Rockefeller, then
worked so closely with Nixon, then criticized Nixon so harshly into a
live microphone after Nixon had resigned the presidency). Perception
of this trait on top of the Watergate scandal fueled the congressional
push to legislate a human rights concern into U.S. foreign policy. That
movement was as much an effort by a reassertive Congress to check
the Imperial presidency as it was anything else, for in the early- to

mid-1970s Congress was also passing the War Powers Act and other legislation designed to make the presidency share power with the Congress. Thus congressional legislation on human rights was founded partly on negative reactions to Nixon and Kissinger, representing the Imperial Presidency, as well as on negative reactions to global containment of communism in Vietnam.

It was in this context that Jimmy Carter appeared on the national political scene, emphasizing human rights, and calling for a government as good as the American people. If the Kissinger era represented the triumph of power calculations over consideration of specific rights, Jimmy Carter symbolized what Congress was already demanding: an activist policy on human rights.

CARTER RHETORIC AND REALITY

Given the widespread concern in American politics about morality and rights in U.S. foreign policy in the mid-1970s, it is not surprising that the Carter campaign of 1976 discovered that the human rights issue played well in Peoria.[12] The country wanted to hear about morality and rights, and Carter—the Baptist Sunday School teacher—was personally inclined to respond in kind. It is now apparent that the Carter Administration started in January 1977 without knowing what it was getting into and how complicated a human rights orientation would turn out to be.[13] It is also clear that a coherent human rights policy never emerged during the Carter Administration.[14]

The one point that is beyond doubt about Carter's human rights policy is that his Administration gave more rhetorical saliency to the subject than any other Administration in U.S. political history. On various occasions human rights were said to be the "cornerstone" and "soul" of U.S. foreign policy. The U.S. commitment to rights was said to be "absolute." The President, the Secretary of State, the first Assistant Secretary for Human Rights, Patricia Derian, as well as other high officials spoke repeatedly in behalf of international human rights. Cyrus Vance, the Secretary of State, gave a much quoted speech at the University of Georgia stressing U.S. acceptance of international human rights of three types: 1) rights of the integrity of the person such as protection from murder, summary execution, torture, and mistreatment; 2) certain socioeconomic rights which comprise basic human needs such as food, shelter, health care and education; and 3) other civil and political rights.[15]

Of particular importance was the rhetorical support for social and economic rights, which are not well established in the American political tradition. According to Anthony Lake, director of the Policy Planning Staff of the State Department: "Human rights include not just the basic rights of due process, together with political freedoms, but also the right of each human being to a just share of the fruits of one country's production." (These words seemed crafted to make clear that someone in, say, Algeria did not have a right to the fruits of economic production in the U.S.) Likewise did Arthur Goldberg, head of the American delegation to the Belgrade Conference on the Helsinki Accord, say: "In the United States, we also realize that human rights encompass economic and social rights as well as political and civil liberties." And Secretary of State Cyrus Vance said in June of 1978: "We recognize that people have economic as well as political rights."[16]

Beyond all the speech-making on rights, what was the Carter record in actually taking concrete steps to implement rights through U.S. foreign policy? First of all, the speech-making itself *was* concrete action. It helped (for better or worse) to raise expectations at home and abroad that rights would be seriously considered. For the U.S. President and other high officials to emphasize rights was to give support to individuals and groups around the world struggling for protection of rights.

Second, while there was rhetorical support for socioeconomic rights, little was done in concrete fashion by the Carter team to improve their implementation.[17] The U.N. Socio-Economic Covenant was signed by Carter, along with the Civil-Political Covenant, and submitted to the Senate for consent to ratification, but with extensive reservations and understandings which would have limited their impact on the U.S. if and when ratified. And after submission, Carter did not press vigorously for consent. The Covenant has never been ratified, nor have companion treaties such as the American Convention on Human Rights or the Treaty on Racial Discrimination. Abroad, the Carter Administration did not seek to realign economic relationships to implement better the rights to food, shelter, clothing, and adequate medical care. In Latin America, for example, it was business as usual.[18] With regard to introducing human rights considerations into the international financial institutions such as the World Bank and the Inter-American Bank, the Carter team resisted congressional pressures in

that direction, albeit unsuccessfully. The level of U.S. foreign economic assistance dropped under Carter. And in general Carter did not
want to interrupt business and economic relations for reasons of human rights;[19] he had to be pushed by Congress into an economic embargo on Idi Amin's Uganda.[20]

Third, in directing most of its attention to civil and political rights,
the Carter Administration had no clear conception or strategy for linking human rights to other security and economic interests. It professed
an even-handed approach and a case-by-case analysis of human rights
situations. But it was criticized for great inconsistency, and especially
the Reagan forces criticized it for undermining friendly authoritarian
regimes while directing insufficient attention to communist human
rights violations.

It was certainly the case that the Carter team manifested inconsistency. That Administration directed more criticism to the USSR than to
the PRC over rights violations; the U.S. was of course in the late 1970s
moving toward formal recognition of the Chinese communist
government—a movement inconvenienced by focusing on rights.
While Carter worked diligently to remove Somoza from power in
Nicaragua because of an atrocious rights record, the President deferred
to significant rights abuses in Saudi Arabia (the reason being fairly
clear: American cars do not run on bananas!). U.S. security assistance
was terminated to a number of Latin authoritarian governments; the
U.S. has no such security assistance to manipulate vis-a-vis Eastern
European regimes, several of whom were granted Most Favored Nation status in trade during the Carter years.

It may be the case that no state can achieve much consistency in
working for human rights in foreign policy.[21] However that may be, it
seems clear in retrospect that the Carter Administration wound up in-
advertently emphasizing rights violations in countries devoid of significant U.S. security and economic interests. Thus the U.S. under
Carter wound up focusing on certain regimes of the Western Hemisphere like Nicaragua, Uruguay, Guatemala, Chile, Argentina, and the
Dominican Republic. Its overall policy toward other countries like
Iran, Saudi Arabia, and Morocco, which manifested serious human
rights abuses, was much more mixed—which is to say that rights violations were not clearly elevated over other interests. (Some cartoon-
ists thought Carter had emphasized human rights in Iran, only to
abandon the concern under threat of political revolution.) And the
President appeared to have no difficulty in keeping a straight face

Bill Mauldin

By permission of Bill Mauldin and Wil-Jo Associates, Inc.

while he made speeches praising the protection of human rights and constitutional government in communist Poland and Ferdinand Marcos' Philippines.

During Carter's last two years in office, after the Soviet invasion of Afghanistan and the seizure of the U.S. embassy in Tehran, his foreign policy in general tilted away from the cooperative internationalism of Secretary of State Vance, who resigned over the Iranian hostage raid, and toward the militant internationalism of national security advisor Zbigniew Brzezinski. This resulted in a downgrading in general of human rights, and an upgrading in power competition with the Soviet Union. In fact, the mood of the entire country shifted, albeit incompletely, away from the Vietnam syndrome (a reluctance to become involved in foreign armed conflict), and toward an emphasis on more military spending, which is not totally incompatible with a weakened Vietnam syndrome (one can want to be better prepared, but still reluctant to become involved). In broad terms, the country as a whole wanted to focus on power, not so much on rights, and on economics, given stagflation (low economic growth combined with high inflation).

It was precisely in this context that Ronald Reagan captured the Republican nomination, and ultimately of course the Presidency, emphasizing national greatness in the past, and calling for a renewed commitment to anti-communism and laissez-faire economics. Just as Carter and his rights rhetoric had been a reaction to his predecessors, especially Nixon and Kissinger, so Reagan was a reaction to Carter. It should not have been surprising that initially Reagan rights policy was profoundly different from Carter's.

REAGAN RHETORIC AND REALITY

The first Reagan Administration believed strongly in American exceptionalism.[22] The President repeatedly made speeches referring to the U.S. as a city on a hill, to be emulated by others. When applied to rights, this meant that the American version of rights, emphasizing only civil and political rights, would guide policy, not the international version that also contained social, economic, and cultural rights. The first of the annual State Department country reports on human rights conditions in foreign states compiled by the Reagan team contained an introduction clarifying such matters; only civil and political rights would be considered as rights, the international version being so broad as to allow communist countries to cover up civil and political rights violations by emphasizing other "rights."[23] Reagan's Ambassador to the U.N., Jeane Kirkpatrick, was equally clear in her denunciation of socioeconomic rights, and in her criticism of U.N. treatment of rights issues.[24] Reagan's first nominee to be Assistant Secretary of State for Human Rights, Ernest W. Lefever, was on record criticizing Carter for trivializing human rights through his broad approach which did not focus solely on communist violations, and he wanted to remove U.S. legislation on human rights in foreign policy for the same sin of being so broad as to make trouble for authoritarian friends of the U.S. (The institute which Lefever headed had also accepted money from the Republic of South Africa to circulate views favorable to that regime.)[25]

The Secretary of State, Alexander Haig, like the President himself, made speeches emphasizing the threat to the U.S. of Soviet-led communism. In a statement less than crystal clear (but not unusual), Haig said that human rights would not be emphasized as much as counter-

terrorism, but then added that this was because terrorism violated human rights (which still made human rights the key element). In general (no pun intended), Haig reflected faithfully the Reagan emphasis on international communism rather than violations of human rights per se. In situations like El Salvador, the Reagan team attributed the problem to communist intervention from outside, not to violations of rights and denial of justice internally.

After Eliott Abrams was confirmed as head of the human rights bureau in the State Department, (Lefever withdrew his name after the Senate Foreign Relations Committee, despite its Republican majority, voted 13–1 against confirming his nomination), U.S. policy was fashioned in a manner largely consistent with the basic rhetoric of the Administration. That is to say that, after much confusion from January 1981 to about that October over what kind of rights policy the Reagan team would pursue, Abrams played a leading role in fashioning a policy that emphasized communist violations while downplaying noncommunist violations. The so-called Kirkpatrick Doctrine became a guide to human rights policy: authoritarian violations of rights were not as bad as totalitarian violations, and authoritarians could evolve in more humane directions whereas totalitarians could not.[26] In effect, U.S. human rights policy was collapsed into, or made an appendage of, strategic policy. The overriding concern of the Reagan team was contesting Soviet power; while seen as a moral crusade as well as a strategic necessity, it meant that rights violations in non-communist countries would not receive great attention.

That this was so can be seen in any number of concrete situations. An early visitor to the Reagan White House was the repressive leader of South Korea, who was given a red carpet reception. Ambassador Kirkpatrick met with leaders of repressive Argentina as well as with South African officials. At the U.N. she tried to block investigations and resolutions dealing with rights violations in countries like Chile, El Salvador, and Guatemala. The Reagan team repeatedly requested expanded foreign assistance from Congress for all sorts of authoritarian regimes with major violations of human rights; it explicitly refused to link human rights violations with either security or economic assistance as required by U.S. law. The Administration also refused to link human rights concerns with U.S. votes in the multilateral banks, also required by U.S. law, but rather voted against loan applications only from leftist regimes.[27]

Reagan and his lieutenants were harsh in their denunciations of especially Soviet and Cuban violations of human rights. The President
made a speech referring to the USSR as the "evil empire," and Cuba became a special target of the U.S. in the U.N. Human Rights Commission and the General Assembly. The issue of forced abortions and
other coercive family planning measures was raised with special vigor
with regard to the PRC, and U.S. funding for international family planning agencies was eventually terminated. The Administration was
also shrill in its denunciations of human rights violations in Nicaragua.

There were three, perhaps four areas of foreign policy in which the Reagan Administration had a rights policy which went beyond the Kirkpatrick Doctrine. First, the Administration did involve itself to protect certain individuals being repressed in authoritarian regimes; it intervened, for example, in behalf of Kim Dae Jung, an opposition political leader in South Korea. Second, it did restrict, as required by U.S. law, the transfer of some crime control equipment, which can be used for repressive purposes, to certain authoritarian regimes with a poor record on human rights. In this respect it followed in the steps of Carter precedents, although electric shock batons were still approved for both South Africa and South Korea, at least until the press and Congress forced a change in policy. Third, it did, through the Agency for International Development, and as required by U.S. law, redirect some economic assistance away from general development projects and toward basic human needs, and did implement special supervisory procedures, because of human rights violations in some countries. Again, the Carter Administration had done the same. Fourth, the Administration claimed that it engaged in quiet diplomacy to persuade authoritarians to correct rights violations; the extent that it did so in fact is not clear, nor is the impact of such demarches, if they occurred, given expanded foreign assistance to such regimes. If the aid is flowing, why should authoritarians listen seriously to such overtures?

Overall, it is fair to say that the human rights reality of the first Reagan Administration was consistent with its rhetoric. Human rights policy in rhetoric and reality was reasonably clear, but clearly narrow.[28] The focus was on communist violations. Toward authoritarians the Reagan team was supportive, believing in "constructive engagement" not just toward South Africa but toward Guatemala and other authoritarians. The long term intentions may have been good, but the short term reality was that rights violations were ignored or deemphasized.

Into the second Reagan Administration it appeared that U.S. human rights policy underwent some changes.[29] Ironically but predictably the Reagan team, having de-emphasized authoritarian violations of rights in the name of strategic competition, found itself confronted with a series of rebellions—some of which jeopardized U.S. security interests. In South Africa, the Philippines, Haiti, Panama, South Korea, and Chile, domestic rebellions erupted or intensified against repression, oppression, and corruption. Events outpaced a U.S. policy wedded to the status quo in places like South Africa, Haiti, and the Philippines. Particularly in places like the Philippines where the U.S. relied heavily on a port and an air base, the President tried to explain away the problems of the Marcos regime and only at the eleventh hour came to support democratic and human rights movements led by Corazon Aquino. In places like Haiti, U.S. attention was so belated that the U.S. role was limited to providing a plane on which "Baby Doc" Duvalier could flee to France in the face of a popular insurrection. Despite congressional attempts to get the Reagan Administration to focus on human rights abuses there, the Administration had drifted with the status quo because of the absence of any communist threat.

Stung by these events, the Administration began to re-evaluate the tactics of its strategic policy, with human rights policy as an appendage. This was less a shift in human rights policy per se in most places, and more a shift in how to protect security interests which secondarily necessitated a shift in human rights thinking. This was most clear in places like Chile. Continued repression by the Pinochet dictatorship had led to a resurgence of the violent left. Against the background of events in places like South Africa, the Philippines, and Haiti, the Administration increased its public pressure on Pinochet to institute political reforms and limit repression. The U.S. even sponsored a critical resolution at the U.N. Human Rights Commission. The Reagan team, however, could not (at the time of writing) bring itself to vote against Chilean loan applications in the international financial institutions.

In South Korea the Reagan forces intervened on the side of striking workers, demonstrating students, and democratic politicians as the rebellion there threatened power relations on the Korean peninsular. And in Panama where popular discontent with General Noreiga manifested itself, which raised questions about the security of the Panama Canal, Washington terminated bilateral assistance and engaged in public criticism of the regime.

In a few places, like Paraguay, which were of little strategic or security significance, there was a genuine shift in human rights policy independently considered. The U.S. embassy in General Stroessner's Paraguay associated itself with democratic political forces, for which it was harassed, leading to more U.S. criticism of denial of civil and political rights there.

But as a rule what triggered greater U.S. attention to authoritarian rights violations in the second Reagan Administration was political instability in strategic places. Absent that instability, there was still a strong inclination to ignore rights violations. This was clear not only in Haiti, but also in Liberia, for example, where a coup had resulted in a large increase in U.S. foreign assistance, and where Secretary of State George Shultz tried to sweep human rights abuses under the diplomatic carpet despite congressional pressures.[30] As a scholar of Latin America has noted, the U.S. is historically more interested in human rights affecting perceived security interests than human rights per se.[31]

Thus by the end of the second Reagan Administration, U.S. policy on rights abroad was similar in some ways to the Carter period. Authoritarians as well as totalitarians had become targets of U.S. concern and even pressure. Indeed, the Soviet Union and its allies were no longer special targets of U.S. public criticism, especially as Washington moved toward a serious disarmament agreement with Moscow (although the Administration continued its diplomatic attacks on Cuba and Nicaragua). Bilateral assistance was being manipulated on a slight basis in the name of rights, although there was still a general reluctance to do this.

A full accounting for the reasons behind this shift after 1985 has yet to be provided. No doubt the force of democratic and human rights movements abroad was primary; U.S. relations with the ancient regime were swept away by facts in the Philippines and Haiti. The prospect of more of the same was evident in places like South Korea, Chile, and Panama. But other factors were also at work. Some ultra-conservatives like Kirkpatrick had left the government, and others like Abrams had left the Human Rights Bureau where the more moderate Richard Schifter had taken over. Then too congressional pressures had continued for a more balanced human rights policy. Economic sanctions, weak but symbolically important, had been voted on South Africa. Large amounts of military assistance had been denied to authoritarian Guatemala. Concern was evident about atrocities committed by the "contras" fighting against the Sandinistas. Members of Congress like Senator Richard Lugar and Representative Stephen Solarz had played high-profile roles in trying to get the U.S. distanced from Marcos. Hearings had been held about how the Administration was using the Endowment for Democracy to support conservative groups in France, and maybe even anti-democratic parties in Panama.

For whatever exact combination of reasons, there were significant differences in the two Reagan Administrations over the treatment of human rights violations abroad. At least superficially, the second Reagan Administration seemed closer to the Carter Administration than to the first Reagan Administration. And whatever the rhetoric of any Administration, it seemed that Washington would have to take human rights seriously in the reality of its foreign policy. The early Reagan team had clearly wanted to downgrade human rights as a distinct issue area, for the purpose of emphasizing the struggle against communism. In its later manifestations that team had to give human rights matters high priority in many places around the world.

CONCLUSIONS

It is indeed clear that in U.S. politics there is a fondness for rhetoric about morality and rights. But it is also clear that fondness for rhetoric is not the same as carefully fashioned policy. In recent U.S. foreign policy, that is, from about 1973, Kissinger, Carter, and Reagan all used the rhetoric of rights. Each, and their policy teams, meant something different. During this period a tendency was evident for the passive approach to human rights in foreign policy to lose out or be rejected. The lack of an activist policy by Kissinger and Nixon helped galvanize the Congress into assertiveness. Both Carter and Reagan wound up with an activist orientation, the former by design and the latter largely by force of events. But given an activist inclination, questions must still be answered about the relationship between concern for human rights and concern for expediential interests like security and economic well-fare.

With regard to security, it is clear from the Carter period that Washington needs to address this relationship explicitly. Otherwise the government will be charged with inconsistency or, what is worse, with neglecting U.S. security needs. But it is equally clear from the Reagan period that Washington does not guard its long-term security needs by ignoring human rights violations in friendly countries. In this regard there is a long list of examples from which the U.S. could profit were it so inclined. Greek anti-Americanism in the 1980s, which is strong and which jeopardizes NATO solidarity, can be traced directly to U.S. support for the Greek junta 1967–74. Iranian anti-Americanism, which is stronger to put it mildly, can be traced even more directly to U.S. blanket support for the Shah's rule. Argentinian anti-Americanism, which is not as strong and which has cultural roots, is nevertheless present in the 1980s and was not reduced by the Reagan Administration's embrace of the junta there until the Falklands/Malvinas war. The future

Black government of South Africa, when it arrives in power, is not likely to be terribly friendly to the U.S., given the U.S. track record in realistically rather than rhetorically seeking an end to apartheid.

One should not pretend that the subject is simple. In terms of abstract principles, the Reagan team had a point. One may not advance either the cause of human rights or U.S. security if one replaces a repressive government with a repressive government hostile to the U.S. The governments in Iran and Nicaragua are usually cited in this regard (although in fact the Sandinistas are clearly better in human rights terms than the Somoza dynasty). The subject is particularly difficult when one deals with a country in which there seems to be no moderates in the political spectrum. Given a choice between the extreme left and the extreme right, Washington will rationally choose the extreme right every time: there will be no immediate security threat to the U.S.; and the regime will be sympathetic toward American businesses. More to the point, however, is that Washington has helped inflict this Hobbesian choice on itself. The U.S. has largely ignored gross violations of human rights in places like El Salvador and Guatemala; in the name of security the U.S. has looked the other way while right-wing governments literally exterminated moderate reformers. Those not killed were driven into further, frequently leftist, rebellion because of the absence of prospect for peaceful reform.

Thus the U.S., both for its own long term security and for the sake of supporting human rights, should oppose authoritarian violations of rights in the hopes of promoting moderate, gradual change. Properly considered, security interests are not only compatible with human rights; they are enhanced by human rights. This the Reagan Administration accepted rhetorically under the name of "constructive engagement," or the Kirkpatrick Doctrine, or the improvement doctrine. But in reality that Administration did not work effectively for such reforms, which is precisely why it was faced with political instability in so many friendly countries during 1985–88. One does not bring about an improvement in the human rights situation by loading up authoritarian regimes with foreign assistance, multilateral assistance, and saying publicly that there is nothing worse than communism—especially since such regimes label any progressive reform as communistic.

On the other side of the coin, or the other side of the Kirkpatrick Doctrine as it were, it is not historically clear that communist regimes can never evolve in a more humane direction. The Dubcek government in Czechoslovakia was clearly doing so before being crushed by the Soviet Union in 1968. Both Hungary and Yugoslavia have a different record on human rights broadly defined than the Soviet Union. Even the USSR itself under Gorbachev is experimenting with Glasnost, or openness in political, cultural, and other matters at the time of writing. Some of this experimentation goes beyond what Solidarity sought, and temporarily achieved, in Poland in the late 1970s and early 1980s. In some ways—i.e., competitive elections for local officials— Soviet Glasnost also goes beyond experiments in "liberalism" or loosening restrictions in China. Then there are other types of communist situations in places like Zimbabwe.

This is to say that a well considered human rights policy may produce desired results even in communist countries, which could also reduce security threats to the U.S. If U.S. human rights policy toward "totalitarians" is not shrill, if it emphasizes the expressed commitments of communist governments in documents such as the Helsinki accord or the U.N. Covenants (to which the USSR is a party), and if its seeks genuine improvement in internationally recognized rights rather than just a propaganda victory, over time desired changes may in fact occur. To the extent that they occur, such changes may alter the U.S. perception of an implacable, inherently aggressive enemy. To the extent that U.S. leaders still believe that totalitarians are inherently aggressive, then human rights reforms in those regimes should reduce U.S. security fears.[32]

It is likely, however, that any Administration's attempt to blend security and human rights concerns will manifest a great deal of inconsistency. Given the nation-state system, Washington, like other capitals, must give priority to security. This could rationally mean, for example, that the U.S. at times will properly choose to engage in only quiet diplomacy with the Soviet Union about human rights violations. Particularly in the light of prospects for serious arms control or even disarmament, this is arguably the correct course. If strategic nuclear war occurs, no one will have any human rights recognized or implemented. Yet at precisely the same time that the U.S. might choose quiet diplomacy with the USSR, it might rationally choose to go public about, or manipulate some relationship with, some other country. The lack of competing interests in that second country might justify such a tactical policy choice, as well as the prospect of beneficial change. Thus while the U.S. might profess, as indeed most Administrations have, a balanced or even-handed approach to human rights questions, its foreign policy on particular rights questions in particular countries at particular times is likely to manifest great variance. One should not realistically expect otherwise, despite the rhetoric.

The relationship between human rights and economic interests is equally problematical. The Carter and Reagan Administrations were similar, but not identical, when it came to public sector economics. As specified by Congress, official economic assistance was continued by both Administrations to even gross violators of internationally recognized human rights as long as that aid was directed to the most needy people or to basic human needs. There seems no reason to question this approach, although the concepts could be sharpened and there may be debate on what is, in a given situation, a BHN program. But in principle one should not punish a people for the sins of its government.

There has been more debate about introducing human rights considerations into the workings of the World Bank and other international financial institutions. Congress and the Carter team, but not the Reagan forces, accepted in principle the desirability of this. Certainly a strong defense can be made in support of U.S. law on this issue. First, U.N. resolutions stress that economic development is to be ultimately for purposes of human dignity, not purely for economic growth. Thus an emphasis on blending human rights and economic development is consistent with international community standards.[33] Secondly, the IFIS are not purely economic institutions in the first place. Their decisions greatly affect politics in general and human rights in particular. In fact, politics is already introduced into their workings when they decide to loan to shaky right wing governments pursuing foolish economic policies, but decide not to loan to leftist governments.[34] Thus one is not corrupting purely economic institutions by interjecting human rights considerations. Along with Stanley Hoffmann, one can make a reasoned argument in behalf of what the Congress has required.[35]

Perhaps the most controversial part of this entire subject pertains to private sector economics. To what extent should the U.S. government restrict trade and other private transactions on human rights grounds? Given American belief in capitalism, and given the lobbying strength of the American business community, restrictions on private markets have never been popular in principle. Still, restrictions have been either voted by Congress or decreed by an Administration on a variety of countries, mostly communist, but also on Rhodesia, South Africa, Uganda, Panama, and others during contemporary times. There have been numerous inquiries into this subject, with most authors concluding that such economic sanctions do not control a situation, certainly not in the short run, but that such sanctions may be important as political symbolism—demonstrating real commitment on the part of sanctioning states.[36]

Another dimension of this subject requires equal attention. It seems fairly clear from the Carter period that if the U.S. government tries to manipulate only public sector economics, and leaves private markets alone, its human rights policies will have reduced impact. The Carter Administration, and Congress, tried to pressure economically Pinochet's Chile but did not interfere with private bank loans and other private transaction which strengthened that regime. U.S. withholding of economic assistance constituted no more than a slap on the wrist. Moreover, despite the Carter team's rhetoric in support of human rights, as long as private economic transactions continued to benefit only the elite, the overall human dignity of the masses continued unchanged. This was certainly the case in Latin America, where Carter pursued a "business as usual" approach economically, and where in many countries as much as three-quarters of the population remained outside the official economy.[37] In such situations, which existed in other Third World countries, real question can be raised about emphasizing only civil and political rights without attention to grinding poverty and illiteracy.

It may be uncomfortable, but it seems to be true that a serious attention to human rights requires manipulation of private economic transactions. This the U.S. has been willing to accept vis-a-vis communist governments. The Congress has voted, and three Administrations have implemented, the Jackson-Vanik Amendment denying Most Favored Nation status in trade to communist countries denying reasonable emigration. The Congress has even extended this requirement to cover religious freedom in addition to emigration. Some American firms have been hurt economically, losing business that otherwise would have occurred. Whether the American society will accept a broader application of this approach remains to be seen. In moral terms, it is not difficult to argue that American profit should not occur from situations of gross violations of human rights. Getting this argument accepted in the American business community is made easier if competitors do not take American business—that is, if collective restrictions can be organized by the OECD, the U.N., or some other international organization.

If this essay demonstrates one fundamental truth, it is that human rights in foreign policy is no less complicated a subject than arms control and disarmament or any other part of foreign affairs. According to two serious students of U.S. human rights policy, that policy became "possibly the most tangled web in American foreign policy."[37] As the second Assistant Secretary for Human Rights and Humanitarian Affairs said, "The human rights problem is so complex that mistakes will inevitably be made."[38] In the late 1980s Washington was still struggling to devise a bipartisan human rights policy. It was clear that the subject would not disappear, however problematical it might be.

Chapter Six

Humanizing American Foreign Policy

Nonprofit Lobbying and Human Rights

When the Reagan administration entered office in January 1981, its human rights policy was at its nadir. The administration's policy has advanced considerably since that time . . . Much of the turnabout has come because of the congressional stewardship of our American human rights foreign policy, the work of non-governmental organizations and voices of the media.
Jerome Shestack, President, International League for Human Rights, "Status of U.S. Human Rights Policy, 1987," *Hearing*, Subcommittee on Human Rights, House Committee on Foreign Affairs (February 19, 1987), p. 85.

INTRODUCTION

The International League for Human Rights is one of the more active nonprofit, non-governmental groups active in the struggle to make human rights policy, both in Washington and at the United Nations. Its President, Jerome Shestack, has also served as a U.S. representative at several human rights conferences. In his opinion private groups such as the League played an important role, in conjunction with other actors, in influencing U.S. human rights policy abroad—as the quote above indicates. This chapter seeks to examine whether that claim is true.

Could it be that the zigs and zags of Carter's policy on human rights noted in the previous chapter, and its failure to fully mesh human rights with security and economic concerns, were the result of pressure from lobbies? And, what was the impact of these same lobbies during the ReaganPresidency? The literature in political science suggests that, in general, public opinion and lobbying are weak influences on officials especially on foreign policy matters; the personal views of officials are supposedly the chief determinant of policy.[1]

But from the 1960s there was an increase in the number of nonprofit interest groups active to influence American foreign policy. One source listed over 500 groups active on human rights in North America, most of them in the United States.[2] In other issue-areas, such as consumer protection, environmental protection, and civil protection (protecting the citizen from bad government), "the lobbying achievements of public interest groups have sometimes been striking."[3]

In this chapter we are concerned with the impact of nonprofit lobbying on American foreign policy during the period from renewed concern for human rights through the Reagan Presidency (1973–88). To what extent was this attempt to reintroduce human rights into American foreign policy the product of noneconomic, nongovernmental organizations (NGOs)? To what extent have their lobbyists been influential in defining, implementing, and maintaining human rights standards in American foreign policy? Has there been a fundamental change toward more effective lobbying and toward more influence for "public interest" lobbies in the foreign policy field, and, if so, is this likely to last? What effect did the change from Carter to Reagan have on human rights groups?

In an effort to answer these questions interviews were conducted in Washington and New York between September 1979 and March 1987 with three types of persons: staff members of nonprofit organizations interested in human rights and American foreign policy; congressional personal aides or staff members of congressional committees; and State Department officials (a list of offices in which interviews were held and a discussion of methodology will be found in the Addendum to the Bibliography).

The approach of this chapter is as follows. First comes a clarification of lobbying and lobbying for human rights in foreign policy. Next is an analytical description of that lobbying. Then there is a survey of attitudes about NGO influence. Finally, the conclusion tries to analyze the exact significance of private or unofficial groups working for human rights.

Lobbying, defined as the conscious and relatively short-run effort to influence governmental policy whether by direct or grass-roots means, has traditionally been dominated in the foreign policy field by for-profit organizations joined by a few "ethnic," "church," and "peace" groups.[4] More recently, as already mentioned, nonprofit organizations concerned with foreign policy have become more numerous. There has been more activity in pursuit of public goods—viz., those benefits not limited to or especially favorable to the material or other gain of the members of the organization.

Whatever the definitional problems of distinguishing on paper Mobil Oil from Common Cause, the latter seeks and obtains no particular and especially no material gain from its policy objectives.[5] When American labor unions lobby not for their particular and material benefit but to oppose, say, governmental repression of labor rights such as freedom of association in Chile or the Soviet Union, then in that role they are public interest groups acting in the foreign policy field.[6] It is in this sense that we say that public interest groups have proliferated to work for human rights standards in American foreign policy. Whether their descriptive title be union, church, ethnic organization, registered human rights lobbyist, or otherwise, they are engaged in lobbying.

There are in fact two types of public interest lobbies: registered and unregistered.[7] In the first group are those organizations which declare themselves lobbies and register as such under law. An example in the human rights area is the Friends Committee on National Legislation—the Quaker lobby. In the latter group are those educational, informational, cultural, religious, and professional organizations which in fact consciously seek to influence governmental policy in the relative short run but maintain the legal fiction that they are only informing governmental officials or perhaps raising questions for their own information. For example, the Washington office of Amnesty International may write the State Department to ask what is the department's policy on disappeared persons in Latin America. Through such procedure Amnesty hopes to get the department to rethink its policy toward such states as Guatemala and Chile (while also hoping to maintain nonlobbying status with the Internal Revenue Service). Or the International Commission of Jurists may arrange to have itself asked by a member of Congress to testify at a congressional hearing.

Many organizations lobby without being registered as a lobby, and this is certainly true for human rights. In interviews, a spokesman for Freedom House spent considerable time explaining that his organization was educational. He subsequently spent considerable time also explaining why he thought Freedom House played a crucial role during the summer and fall of 1979 in congressional decisions not to lift economic sanctions against the illegal Rhodesian regime. He proudly attributed great weight to Freedom House testimony and personal conversations with senators and representatives.[8]

Lobbying for human rights may relate to foreign or domestic politics. A party to a treaty has an obligation to put its domestic legislation and policy in accord with treaty provisions. A treaty member equally has the right to put forth its view about foreign behavior covered by the treaty. President Carter acknowledged this duality. While speaking of human rights violations abroad, he indicated that the U.S. government had to respond to foreign comments about its record at home.[9] An important study would be the domestic effect of U.S. rhetoric about internationally recognized human rights. The present chapter, however, is concerned with human rights as an issue in American foreign policy; I inquire about only those groups which seek to influence American policy toward foreign actors and events.[10]

LOBBYING FOR HUMAN RIGHTS

Lobbying for human rights is not a precisely defined subject. The nature of both the issue-area and the groups accounts for this complexity. Lobbying in general, however, is well known.

As should be clear by now, this study defines the issue-area of human rights in relation to international documents. If a subject is found in human rights legal instruments, it is an issue of human rights. As indicated in chapter one, these instruments are not only numerous but also lengthy, vague, and sometimes conflicting. Human rights is a broad and still amorphous term. Court decisions are mostly lacking which could provide clarity and precision. For example, the right to peace can be derived from the legally stated right to life. The right to organize for union purposes is generally stated in several treaties. Religious freedom is broadly defined. Self-determination is listed as the first right in the two 1966 U.N. treaties. Therefore any group interested in peace, arms control, or disarmament; workers' rights; church activity; or national freedom and independence can—with considerable reason—claim to be working for human rights. It is true, as noted in a previous chapter, that one can draw a distinction between groups which base their activities strictly on rights listed in international documents and groups which do not. But also as noted previously, frequently rights-based groups and other groups working for the same ends are both active in the policy process.

Working for human rights is synonymous with working for a "progressive" foreign policy in which individuals are at the center of policy. Working for human rights is synonymous with humanizing policy. The goal of human rights advocacy is to insist that the power, security, and economic well-being of states and their ruling elites be accompanied by concern for the average citizen and/or the least well-off in political and economic terms.[11]

This necessarily broad conception of the human rights issue area, stemming as it does from an accurate awareness of treaty provisions, when added to the global scope of the subject means that a tremendous variety of advocacy groups can be active. As noted briefly in chapter four the mix is indeed untidy,[12] as a look at several such groups, selected almost at random, suggests.

(1) Members of Congress for Peace through Law is an organization with a private staff whose activities are funded by private contributions and grants. It is a quasi-private lobby made up principally of governmental officials. (2) The Ad Hoc Committee on the Human Rights and Genocide Treaties advocates certain steps which in its view should be taken by the United States. It is a classic public interest lobby. (3) The American Association for the Advancement of Science had been marginally concerned for some time with the persecution of foreign scientists. In the 1970s it created a committee on Scientific Freedom and Responsibility and a "clearinghouse" on human rights with a full-time staff member. The objective of the clearing house is to create a human rights program in each of the professional associations that are members of the AAAS. The member associations or the central staff may contact government officials with regard to human rights abroad. For example, the American Psychiatric Association has undertaken investigative missions to establish the facts about psychiatric abuse in foreign countries and has organized letter-writing campaigns aimed at Congress. (4) The American Civil Liberties Union, long considered a domestic public interest lobby, currently describes itself as also working for the "cause of human rights and individual civil liberties overseas," and advocates that the United States "should refrain

from supporting or financing specific operations of any foreign government which involve a denial of civil liberties to the governed." (5) The Amalgamated Meat Cutters and Butcher Workmen Union has a director for human rights. (6) Paraguay Watch consists of ecumenical church groups, human rights organizations, and individuals in the United States, Europe, and Latin America "who are concerned about the human rights situation in Paraguay."

By comparison with the confusing mix of different lobbying groups, the process of lobbying is reasonably well understood. Lobbying can be directed at legislators, administrators, courts, the attentive or mass publics. The resources of the lobbyists include first and foremost the quality of the information they seek to impart; second, the legitimacy of the lobby within the context of societal values; and then in no particular order money, membership, organization, and leadership. The tactics of lobbying include knowing who the appropriate decision makers are, how to make and keep open channels of communication, when a certain stage of decision making has been reached in the policy process, and how best to make a presentation.[13]

Using these conceptions, and keeping in mind the diverse nature of the groups active in the untidy issue-area of human rights, we can describe the activities of nonprofit lobbies as follows.

The primary target of nonprofit lobbying for human rights is Congress—linked to public opinion. Thus the human rights lobbies fit the conventional pattern on this point.[14] The dominant approach by those lobbyists is summed up by a spokesperson for the United Church of Christ: "We like to approach particular congresspersons in the context of constituent mail and media exposure." According to a respondent at Amnesty International, getting a congressperson to make a personal appeal (in behalf of political prisoners) is "perhaps the most important thing we do." A staff member at New Directions reflected the same theme: "We concentrate on Congress, but we're unimportant when [the President] is on the phone unless we can mobilize some public opinion—and we can only do that once or twice a year." The primary goal of the Network is said to be "changing public awareness and consciousness;" the Network has organized to do this by creating sections of its membership along the lines of congressional districts so as to try to influence especially the House. Said a staffer at the Coalition: "Our clout comes from our linkage to public opinion." The Washington Office on Latin America concentrates on Congress and "elite public opinion in the D.C. area."

Nonprofit groups were somewhat reluctant to lobby the executive branch, especially from 1973 to 1976, and again 1981–88. Said a spokesman for the Washington Office on Africa (woa): "The State Department and National Security Council have their own momentum. "According to a New Directions respondent: "Decision making in the executive branch is too nebulous—who knows where and when decisions are made, and frequently executive branch types are resentful of our intrusion." According to a Coalition interviewee: "When the executive branch is unified on an issue we have no influence, so why bother; anyway, there was no point under the Republicans."

Some change was perceived by lobbyists after creation in the State Department of a Bureau for Human Rights and Humanitarian Affairs (HA), and when Carter was president. Said the woa's staffer: "We had some access to the White House through the office of Andy Young and when we tagged along with TransAfrica [a black lobby for improved U.S. relations with black Africa]." The pattern, however, was that while contacts had improved, especially when focused on HA at State, no overall change had occurred in nonprofit relations with the executive as a whole. Lobbying on State, the Treasury, or the White House was relatively infrequent and perceived to be without great promise for influence.[15] There was a slight difference in self-described influence or at least access during the Carter Presidency.

An exception was the International Human Rights Law Group (IHRLG). Its direct, legal lobbying was aimed about 50 percent of the time to the State and Justice departments. This group, for example, made representations to the assistant secretary of state for HA about why someone should not be deported or should be granted political asylum (in the United States decisions about refugee status result from a combined political and legal process; decisions about political asylum are made at the discretion of the Justice Department, but as advised by the State Department).

A number of State Department officials believed that the focus of nonprofit lobbying should indeed be Congress—even if the nonprofits wanted something from the executive. One remarked that nonprofits have "little leverage by themselves; they must get Congress and individuals there to act in some way." Said another: "The State Department responds to politics; nonprofits should get a congressperson to ask us to do something, based on one hundred percent accurate facts." Said a third: "The nonprofits are taken seriously here because they have developed a congressional constituency—especially in the House."

Judicial lobbying does occur, principally—as expected—by the lawyers' groups. Other groups may become involved. WOA was a plaintiff in the *Diggs* v. *Shultz* cases concerning U.S. sanctions on Rhodesia. The Washington Office on Latin America (WOLA) cooperated in a 1979 action by the IHRLG. Such judicial lobbying may become more prevalent if and when the United States ratifies more human rights treaties.[16] As of 1988, however, most lobbying was clearly directed toward Congress and the public.

As for the resources of human rights groups, the quality of their information about prisoners, the judicial process, and other human rights subjects seemed highly regarded. An assistant secretary of state observed that his department relied heavily on their information, and that they probably had more "legal knowledge" than any sector of the government. Said a deputy assistant secretary of state: "We use them extensively in compiling information for our human rights reports." According to a congressional aide: "They are very useful in parading people through for us to meet; they know a lot." Knowledge of personal contacts seemed to be one of WOLA's chief resources. That group was widely reputed to know most of the important democratic politicians of Latin America. It hosted an important reception for the Nicaraguan leadership after the overthrow of President Somoza. In image-conscious Washington, hosting an important event is a symbol of acceptance, and, according to one interviewee, "WOLA has arrived."

There was no doubt that the access and influence of human rights lobbies vis-a-vis the executive branch declined during the Reagan Presidency—especially during his first administration. Consistent with the analysis presented in chapter three, Elliott Abrams as Assistant Secretary of State for Human Rights and Humanitarian Affairs, 1981–1985, carried on a public argument with many of the groups. He accused them of myopia and bias, arguing that they paid insufficient attention to communist violations of rights and threats to the United States. At times during his tenure as head of the human rights bureau, the State Department tried to discredit information from organizations like Amnesty International—information that turned out to be accurate.[17] While the situation improved, from the point of view of the human rights lobbies, after Richard Schifter became Assistant Secretary, still as a generalization it can be said that NGO access to and influence in the executive branch was relatively low during the Reagan Presidency.

The Reagan period apart, executive and legislative officials contacted nonprofits with some regularity to request facts and policy ideas—mostly the former.[18] "Mainstream" groups such as Amnesty were contacted more than supposed "radical" groups such as the American Committee on Africa. Research groups such as the Institute for Policy Studies were contacted less than the more active lobbyists such as ADA. Critical research groups such as the Center for International Policy were contacted least of all. The Coalition, however, which originated as an antiwar group, said it received about fifteen calls a month from governmental officials. According to a spokesman for the International League for Human Rights, it averaged one call a week requesting information during congressional hearings on human rights. During my interview with that spokesperson, an assistant secretary of state (not from HA) phoned for information.

In general the evaluation of NGO information on human rights followed ideological lines. Many political appointees in the Reagan administration disparaged the information communicated by human rights lobbies. Even among pragmatic foreign service and civil service personnel in the executive branch, some disenchantment was recorded about the quality of information provided by the nonprofits. One State Department official claimed they provided nothing not already known in his geographical bureau. Another found Amnesty's information good in general but "sloppy" on the Middle East. A Senate staffer said he would never rely only on nonprofit information but would use their input along with that of the CIA, State, and Defense.

Especially among liberal members of Congress and officials of HA during the Carter administration, nonprofit information was highly regarded.

Nonprofits in the human rights area were almost universally regarded as legitimate participants in policy making—especially from the congressional viewpoint (insofar as it is reflected in the current sample). In the past one of the factors mitigating against "ideological," "peace," and "church" groups was that they were perceived to be naive, idealistic, without political acumen—and therefore out of the mainstream of American politics.[19] Perceived as "fringe" groups, they lacked political legitimacy. From the mid-1970s until at least 1981 human rights advocacy found a new image. President Carter and the Congress both emphasized furthering human rights as a goal of American policy. The American public supported the idea—at least relatively so, as long as the subject remained amorphous.[20] Amnesty shared the Nobel Peace Prize in 1977. The result was a new legitimacy for human rights groups. Even Congressman Charles Wilson (D., Tex.),

"The vote is now fifteen to one that we deplore Mussolini's attitude. I think it would be nice if we could go on record as unanimously deploring Mussolini's attitude."

Drawing by Helen E. Hokinson; © 1935, 1963 The New Yorker Magazine, Inc.

who had done battle with certain nonprofits over Nicaraguan issues, referred to them as "worthy adversaries" who had a right to be heard.

It seems clear that human rights lobbies retained a basic legitimacy despite their difficulties with the first Reagan administration. Indeed, as noted in chapter three, even the Reagan Presidency performed something of a "turnaround" on human rights in its second manifestation, pressing for human rights changes in several friendly authoritarian regimes. Reagan's rhetorical support for an even-handed human rights policy, unlike his earlier fondness for the Kirkpatrick doctrine, worked to the long-term advantage of the human rights groups and their general acceptance or legitimacy.

Some State Department officials who were interested in greater attention to human rights saw such legitimacy for nonprofits that they expressed concerns to them and tried to use nonprofits to further their policy goals. Sometimes this effort was overt and formal. In August of 1978 the administrator of the Agency for International Development (an independent agency attached to the State Department) wrote to the Inter-religious Taskforce on U.S. Food Policy asking for support for the foreign aid appropriations bill in Congress, indicating AID's priorities and alerting that nonprofit group as to when the Senate Appropriations Committee was going to take up the bill. Sometimes the effort was covert and informal. In another 1978 incident, certain officials at State (not in HA) believed that the language of part of the Foreign Assistance Act should be altered to make the act more legally binding on the executive. These officials explained their position to the ADA, which then in collaboration with other nonprofits successfully lobbied the matter through Congress. High officials at HA, however, claimed they did not do such things. "We are a new bureau, suspect by others, and so we have to play the game by the rules; we can't leak to the nonprofits, no matter how legitimate they are."

While most if not all human rights nonprofits were seen as legitimate, some had a better image than others. The transnationals seemed to have a better image than the strictly American groups. Amnesty, the International League for Human Rights, the International Commission of Jurists were reputed generally to have better information and more impartiality than strictly national groups. And there seemed to be no charges of "foreign" interference in American politics, even though, for example, the Washington office of Amnesty was headed in the late 1970s by a British national. However, the nonprofit group mentioned most frequently as most effective was a strictly American one—WOLA. But even oft-criticized groups such as the Center for International Policy or the Council on Hemispheric Affairs were generally seen as legitimate actors.

As for the financial resources of human rights nonprofits, with the exception of certain ethnic and labor groups which became secondary human rights groups, their budgets were decidedly not large. But neither were their budgets shrinking by the 1980s. The WOA had started with $25,000 in 1972 and was up to $65,000 by 1979. WOLA had started with only $5,000 in 1974 and was spending $60,000 to $80,000 by the end of the 1970s. The Coalition was directing about $50,000 to human rights, the International League about $100,000, and Amnesty's Washington office about $60,000. With the exception of Freedom House, which spent $585,000 in 1979, it was clear that the human rights groups lacked the financial resources to compete at the dollar level with firms like Allis-Chalmers, which reportedly spent a considerable sum in an effort to unblock an Export-Import Bank loan to Argentina in 1979 that would result in Argentine purchases from that firm. The nonprofit groups obviously lacked the financial resources of those foreign governments who reportedly paid large sums to prestigious Washington law firms to lobby in their behalf on human rights issues.[21]

Yet the human rights nonprofits continued their efforts without financial collapse during the period under study, and the collective total of their expectations was not tiny. Some church groups had guaranteed incomes from their congregations. Other groups obtained grants from private foundations. Sales of publications and small membership dues provided further funding. Educational and professional groups increased their (slight) spending for human rights. And relatively well-financed groups such as the Zionist-Jewish lobbying coalition or the United Auto Workers moved into the area for selected issues. Occasionally there was a modest windfall, as when the WOA received an individual contribution of $40,000 to be used for lobbying to keep U.S. sanctions on Rhodesia and was able, for a year, to hire four more staffers to work the Hill on the issue.

Once again the Reagan period merits some differentiation. One of the effects of the Reagan era was to give some legitimacy to certain groups which had previously been regarded as ultra-right fringe groups. One of the better examples was the extremely well financed Heritage Foundation, which peppered U. S. officials with reports—on human rights as on other subjects—from a far-right or ultra-conservative point of view. Thus in the first half of the 1980s especially, a number of well-financed groups joined the policy fray in Washington in order to push an ultra-nationalist, ultra-unilateralist view of human rights in U.S. foreign policy. In general they espoused the Kirkpatrick doctrine that the human rights issue should be directed toward the Soviet Union and its allies, and Kirkpatrick found a place in the American Enterprise Institute (AEI) after she left the government (in addition to her position at Georgetown University). It was difficult to measure the precise influence on policy of groups like Heritage and the somewhat more centrist AEI, but the conventional wisdom was that groups like the Heritage Foundation had considerable influence on the first Reagan administration, but not so much on the Congress or the second Reagan administration.

The membership of most—if not all—human rights nonprofits was politically insignificant in the sense that electoral damage or reward could not be credibly linked to human rights votes in Congress. No group, save the Jewish or labor lobbies, seemed able, or was believed able, to mobilize voters on human rights questions. (Certain State Department officials, and at least one congressional aide, were sensitive to nonprofit connections with the *Washington Post* and other sources of media pressure on governmental officials.) The membership of most human rights groups could be described as politically weak, small, white, middle-class, and concentrated in the northeast and California—with some strength in the industrial Midwest.[22]

Amnesty as an unregistered lobby never threatened to mobilize its American membership vis-a-vis Congress; under Amnesty's operating procedures its American members were to write directly to foreign officials about prisoners in foreign countries. American members of AI were occasionally asked to write U.S. and state officials in opposition to the death penalty for any prisoner in the U.S. Conversely, the ADA's membership was primarily interested in domestic issues; its foreign policy lobbyist was therefore largely cut off from direct grass-roots support.

Neither WOA (and its parent American Committee on Africa) nor WOLA had gone in for a mass-membership organization. The same was true for Freedom House. The International League did have American registered lobbies as affiliates, but league staffers saw themselves more as expert witnesses rather than organizers of lobbying based on public opinion. The Friends Committee on National Legislation had a mailing list of 7,000 but a membership of only 200. The Coalition's Working Group had no individual members at all. Even the nonprofit groups which placed some emphasis on indirect lobbying through public opinion, such as New Directions, the United Church of Christ, and the Network, had memberships that ran only into the low thousands. For example, New Directions had never reached its goal of 100,000 members, had some 14,000 on its rolls, no doubt had even fewer active members, and had not especially emphasized human rights issues except as related to foreign aid.

The organization and leadership of human rights nonprofits seemed an important resource. The number of full-time staffers in Washington was very small. Sickness or other problems to half-a-dozen (or fewer) persons could possibly have crippled much of the direct lobbying effort. But the leaders seemed generally hard-working and dedicated. Many of the groups had engaged in alliance building in order to husband resources, avoid duplication and overlap, and maximize impact. The Human Rights Working Group of the Coalition was a major effort in this direction, and much time was spent by the leaders of such groups as the Quakers, the ADA, the United Church of Christ, and others to coordinate strategy into an effective lobbying program. A number of groups remained outside this Working Group of some forty to eighty nonprofits. Nevertheless, there was clearly a major effort at coordination among the Washington-based nonprofits. Leaders seem to have engaged in a minimum of institutional infighting. Said an assistant secretary of state: "The idea of human rights is still serviced by the nonprofits; they are not just servicing their own institutions."[23]

As for tactical expertise, which may be a continuation of the above subject, there seemed to be a tremendous variety of styles at work. Groups such as the Quakers, WOA, WOLA, ADA, and the Coalition were regarded as knowing well the legislative calendar and who the key decision makers were. A problem resided in the relative obscurity of executive decision making. Said an assistant secretary of state: "The nonprofits can't bring their leverage to bear over here or at Treasury because they don't know the timing of decisions." Some very few groups, such as the Council on Hemispheric Affairs, were regarded rather widely as abrasive and counterproductive. One State Department official thought the nonprofits wrote too many indiscriminate letters. A Senate aide thought the human rights groups had concentrated too much on the liberal Democrats and had ignored moderate, reasonable, swing votes. The general picture, however, and one that will be reinforced by the discussion on influence, is that human rights nonprofits are widely regarded as knowing who sympathetic officials are and how to maneuver in Washington.[24]

BELIEFS ABOUT INFLUENCE

Understanding the influence exerted by groups on public policy is one of the "most critical and difficult" issues of political analysis.[25] The difficulty of factoring out of multiple causations the single, supposedly independent role of groups is widely recognized.[26] Moreover, to evaluate influence, one must make a judgment about "success" or "victory." To analyze how much human rights nonprofits have achieved, one must have a clear notion about achievement. This is not so simple. If the goal of some groups is to raise public and elite awareness about human rights so that policy may be changed eventually, how is this progression to be evaluated at a given point in time? Or, if the United States reduces economic assistance to the Philippines because of human rights violations (as transpired in 1978), is this a victory? Was the cut token, thus reflecting victory for the "hard-liners"? Would real victory be reflected only by a larger cut?

Perhaps the central problem in analyzing group influence is that rarely does a lobby completely "turn around" an official on a given issue. It is widely known that most lobbyists try to work with sympathetic officials rather than to convert opponents.[27] One of the principal human rights lobbyists has written: "Much of what a human rights lobbyist does is to suggest to a Member of Congress what the Member would have done had the Member had time to think about it. What a lobbyist suggests is the logical product of the values the Member already holds."[28] Said another lobbyist in an interview: "I don't expect to have the clout of the DOD [Department of Defense]. I can support progressive members of Congress. I can let him know the public is interested. I can help him sell an idea on the Hill."

Thus there is usually a convergence between a lobbyist's and an official's influence. Group influence therefore does not usually exist independently but is merged with other factors. For example, WOLA's executive director was on the phone to the White House in 1978 when the army of the Dominican Republic threatened to interrupt voting in the presidential election. President Carter eventually made a statement to the effect that military intrusion into the electoral process would adversely affect U.S.-Dominican relations, which was the policy position recommended by WOLA and associated groups. But it is virtually impossible to ascertain the exact influence of nonprofit groups in this U.S. policy-making process.

What do human rights nonprofits think about their influence? Many staffers initially profess not to know. Some take credit for having started the modern U.S. concern for human rights. Most feel they are weak and opponents strong. Most, however, claim specific victories.

Many of those interviewed had apparently not thought analytically about wins and losses in the policy struggle. Not a few staffers seemed to be religiously, ideologically, or ethically committed to their activities. They were active because it seemed the right thing to do, not consciously because they believed they had been or could be influential. Also, some appeared so busy they had not reflected upon an overview of their impact. A very few were reflective and analytical, at least when asked to respond to specific questions.

Nonprofit groups have been given little credit for originating the modern U.S. concern for human rights. Professor David Weisbrodt suggested the complete absence of group influence on Congressman Donald Fraser when he decided to hold hearings in 1973.[29] The journalist Elizabeth Drew wrote about the origins of Jimmy Carter's interest in human rights without mentioning the groups a single time.[30] A broader view, however, seems in order.

Several nonprofit staffers argued that it had been their groups which had "defined the background" against which Fraser and later Carter had acted. They believed their focus on the moral, human, and human rights issues in Vietnam and in American foreign policy in general had helped create a climate of opinion in which certain officials had then taken specific initiatives. For example, individuals associated with the National Council of Churches argued that it was their concern with torture in Brazil and American funding for foreign police training which, with the support of Senators Church, Abourezk, and others, had really started the renewed U.S. concern for human rights between 1969 and 1971.

Fraser does seem to have taken independent initiative in 1973; his chief staff aide of the time said when interviewed that nonprofits had "no specific influence" on the hearings or on resulting legislation. As for Carter and 1976, the Friends Committee on National Legislation, representing six additional groups, met with Carter staffers on 2 October and presented certain human rights concerns to them, verbally and on paper. The International League of Human Rights presented certain views to the new administration in February 1977. And the HA Bureau solicited ideas directly and personally from such people as staff members of the Carnegie Endowment. Thus, without denigrating the importance of official actions, it seems accurate to recall the extensive group activity about such issues as political prisoners in South Vietnam and U.S. funding for foreign police and interrogation officials, and to note for the first time the nonprofit contacts with Carter's staff and appointees in 1976 and 1977.

To recount nonprofit reminders about their activity at the start of the period under study is not to say that nonprofits are megalomaniacs. Indeed, as is true for other lobbies, they see themselves as weak and their adversaries as powerful.[31] Said a spokesman for the Quakers: "We lose whenever the executive trots out the national security argument." Said an Amnesty spokesperson: "The human rights lobbies are so weak that if you pulled out one of the key lobbyists the movement would be seriously hurt." Almost all interviewees from the nonprofit sector cited a core set of defeats: failure to limit military spending, failure to get strong sanctions on the Republic of South Africa, failure to achieve U.S. compliance with U.N. sanctions on Rhodesia from 1971 to 1977. Some saw their victories as more the product of unique events than of nonprofit power. According to one respondent: "As long as the issue was napalming kids in Vietnam we could get some action; aid to dictators during peacetime is different." Said another: "After [Steve] Biko's death in South Africa the House was interested in doing something, but that interest faded quickly." A researcher at the Center for International Policy summed up the pervasive pessimism by saying simply: "We lose all the time."

Yet, human rights nonprofits believe they have accomplished a number of specific gains. Certain examples seem especially interesting in that the group role can be identified and the claimed influence does not appear to be contradicted by interview data or other evidence.

1. The Harkin Amendment, or Section 116(a) of the Foreign Assistance Act, restricting U.S. economic assistance to regimes in gross violation of internationally recognized human rights unless such aid reaches needy people, was first drafted in 1975 by staffers of the Quakers and WOLA, and was then lobbied to successful passage with the help of the ADA. Obviously, Congressman [later Senator] Tom Harkin (D., Iowa) and the members of Congress who supported the measure—especially Congressman Steven Solarz (D., N.Y.) and Senators McGovern and Abourezk—played roles of varying influence. But nonprofits initiated the idea, found sympathetic members to push it, and provided supporting information. Senate drafting was also done by the Quakers.[32]

2. The Washington Office on Africa, in 1977 and 1978, sought to stop U.S. Export-Import Bank loans to South Africa. Congressman Paul Tsongas (D., Mass.) agreed to sponsor such a bill, but most of the other members of the Subcommittee on International Trade, Investment, and Monetary Policy seemed initially unsympathetic to the idea. The WOA then enlisted the help of the NAACP Task Force on Southern Africa, the Washington representatives of the United Church of Christ, and the Catholic Conference to persuade Congressman Stephen Neal (D., N.C.), chairman of the subcommittee, that such a cutoff would assist the struggle of blacks for racial justice in South Africa. With the centrist chairman persuaded, a number of other members were prepared to follow his lead. The cutoff proposal was adopted on a vote of ten to five. In the full committee an even larger vote resulted after a debate which featured strong advocacy by Congressman Parren Mitchell (D., Md.), chairman of the Black Caucus.

But when the issue reached the floor, a crippling amendment that had been overwhelmingly rejected in full committee was narrowly defeated. With this signal that passage of the Tsongas language was in doubt, the chief sponsor met with WOA and recommended that a compromise proposed by Congressman Thomas Evans (R., Del.) would be worth considering. WOA agreed to the compromise after Evans agreed to certain clarifications and improvements. In essence, the compromise legislation would deny Ex-Im credits for exports that would enable South Africa to maintain or enforce apartheid, to the South African government and its agencies, or to other purchasers unless they had endorsed and were proceeding to implement the so-called Sullivan principles of fair employment practices (including willingness to engage in collective bargaining with labor unions).

This revised version passed the House easily and slipped through the Senate without debate as it moved toward adjournment in mid-October. At the time of writing, no Ex-Im credits, guarantees, or insurance have gone to support exports to South Africa since the passage of the legislation. The State Department has prepared a questionnaire which prospective purchasers must fill out in order to assure the Secretary of State that fair employment practices are being implemented. But no prospective purchaser has so far been willing to fill out such a questionnaire as the price of getting Ex-Im Bank support.[33]

3. The ADA in 1976 was one actor among many who sought to deny U.S. assistance to the Pinochet regime in Chile. The ADA not only supplied factual information to members of Congress, but also, when it appeared, on 4 May, that a proposal for aid reduction would lose in the House Committee on International Relations, lobbied four members who had missed earlier votes. The ADA lobbyist walked one of the representatives to a key afternoon vote. The committee passed the aid limit measure, which subsequently survived the rest of the legislative process.[34]

4. In 1978 certain officials in the State Department told the ADA's lobbyist that more pressure could be put on the executive if Congress would alter the opening wording of Section 502B (2) of the Security Assistance Act. This landmark piece of legislation required reduction or termination of U.S. security assistance to regimes grossly violating internationally recognized human rights, unless the president certified to Congress that U.S. national security required continuation. The original wording stated: "It is the policy of the United States that. . . ." The argument was that this was a policy statement rather than a legally compelling mandate to the executive. ADA lobbied the argument with certain members of Congress. After some infighting within the House International Relations Committee, the original wording was struck. This left a legally stronger statement which read: "Except un-

der circumstances specified . . ., no security assistance may be provided. . . ." This language eventually became law (along with some other language also changed in 1978 which was also partially the product of nonprofit efforts).[35]

5. Amnesty International contacted the attorney general's office in 1979 in quest of a more liberal parole policy for Latin American aliens detained in the United States. Amnesty appeared to be the only group interested in this issue. A more liberal policy was adopted by the Justice Department. Also in 1978–79, Amnesty sought revisions in the U.S. laws defining and governing refugees. The law was changed, with Amnesty, the administration officials responsible, and the offices of Senator Ted Kennedy (D., Mass.) and Congresswoman Elizabeth Holtzman (D., N.Y.) coordinating their efforts. (The Office of the U.N. High Commissioner for Refugees was also making suggestions independently to members of Congress, which shows among other things the difficulty of specifying exact influence among domestic and transnational lobbies.)

Other examples could be cited in which nonprofits claim, without contradiction thus far, to have played some clearly identifiable role of influence in conjunction with other actors.

In addition, there is influence claimed which cannot be quite so precisely identified and cross-checked. The quality of State Department annual human rights reports is viewed as much improved by many sources. Several nonprofits attribute this progression to nonprofit criticisms of previous reports (this view tends to be confirmed by certain State Department officials). Of course it is members of Congress who schedule the hearings concerning the annual country reports and control who testifies, but it seems fairly clear that the private human rights groups—with their own sources of information—have played an influential role, in tandem with Congress, in giving effective oversight to State Department reporting.[36]

A number of nonprofit interviewees believed that nonprofit support for the HA Bureau gave that bureau added "leverage" in State Department internal proceedings—at least during the Carter Presidency. Also, several nonprofits claimed that their overtures to members of Congress had resulted in hearings being held on various subjects— such as disappeared persons in Latin America or violations of human rights in East Timor. Furthermore, some groups were not sure of their impact but had advocated wording that was said to be close to the wording finally found in policy—such as President Carter's statement in the early fall of 1979 indicating a continuation of U.S. sanctions on Rhodesia.

There were still other nonprofit claims that were clearly contentious. A Freedom House spokesman attributed "central influence" to the organization in U.S. deliberations during 1979 about Rhodesian sanctions. Freedom House had sent a team to supervise the 1979 elections in order to make a judgment about whether they were "fair and free." After those elections Freedom House first urged the lifting of U.S. sanctions "in such a manner as will encourage . . . further democratization," then criticized President Carter for not lifting sanctions, and later sought to block a Senate effort to lift sanctions immediately. Freedom House claimed that it had been told it was influential with the Thatcher government in the United Kingdom. But the U.S. administration refused to lift sanctions during most of 1979, thus going against Freedom House's position. Several interviewees in Congress did not attribute much influence to Freedom House, even with its use of former Senator Clifford Case to reach members of Congress. Other interviewees seemed confused by that organization's nuanced advocacy over time. A State Department official said flatly: "Freedom House lost on Rhodesia."

What do congressional respondents think about nonprofit impact on U.S. human rights policy?

One pattern in congressional attitudes, and the one that fits with much conventional wisdom, is that nonprofit lobbying on American foreign policy and human rights is insignificant as a dominant pressure. Said an aide to [then] Congressman Harkin: "We are never taken where we don't want to go." Similarly, an aide to Senator Lawton Chiles (D., Fla.) remarked: "Lobbies can't get us to do something we don't want to do or can't do. Chiles is from a conservative state; he can't get out front on human rights; a positive rating from ADA is the kiss of death." According to former congressman Whalen (R., Ohio), now a nonprofit staffer: "Lobbyists generally don't sway votes; they provide ammunition for set positions." An aide to Congressman Hyde (R., Ill.) said lobbying Hyde would be a waste of time; she saw no nonprofit influence on the House Banking Committee. A foreign policy aide to [the late] Senator Zorinsky (D., Neb.), who was widely viewed as highly individualistic, ranked nonprofits last in influence on that senator in comparison with: personal convictions of the senator, the administration's position, constituency factors, and press reports. A House committee staffer said he could think of no human rights issue where nonprofits had been "decisive" or "highly influential." A senate committee staffer made the same point somewhat more colorfully: "Listen, I know that the Latinos have been beating the shit out of each other for years; what are WOLA and those groups going to tell me that I don't already know."

The same respondent, however, went on to say the following: "While nonprofits are 'nondecisive' they have raised the saliency of human rights issues. Human rights is now big politics, and senators cannot yield easily to for-profit lobbying." The House committee staffer who had also viewed nonprofits as without decisive influence said something very similar: "Representative Bonker (D., Wash.) has voted against Boeing on some human rights issues despite the fact that his constituency would be economically hurt by a military cutoff for human rights reasons. The nonprofits have had a secondary role in this sort of thing. And they have shaped the tone of hearings of Bonker's subcommittee." (Donald Bonker took over the House Subcommittee on International Organizations when Donald Fraser resigned to run for a Senate seat. Bonker later decided to change sub-committees, at which point Gus Yatron [D., Pa.] took over the chair of the renamed Subcommittee on Human Rights and International Organizations.)

According to Senator Chiles's aide: "Personal inclinations are affected by exposure to issues, and nonprofits give a certain exposure that helps shape votes." Former congressman Whalen, having downgraded lobbying, went on to say: "Where information is scarce or a congressman's mind is not made up, nonprofits can be effective." Several respondents spoke of their need to be "prodded." The thrust of remarks was, in composite form, as follows: "I don't have much time for this issue; nonprofits remind us to do things; they have the facts; they urge us to hold hearings or move in a certain direction; I welcome that; it helps me." One of Senator Donald Stewart's (D., Ala.) aides said she had never been contacted by the HA Bureau. A staffer working with Congressman Bonker said the State Department was "not helpful" in meeting foreign politicians. These aides and others looked to nonprofits for facts and policy ideas. Therefore nonprofit lobbying is accorded secondary influence by a number of congressional interviewees.

Occasionally nonprofit influence is given great weight in this secondary role. Said an aide to Senator Paul Sarbanes (D., Md.): "Look, those human rights groups helped elect Sarbanes, and he knows it." In general, however, human rights nonprofits were described as not being

able to play "hardball politics" on the basis of grass-roots support—
with the exception of Jewish groups. The groups were said to have
other ways of generating secondary but significant influence. An aide
to Congressman Harkin was most emphatic: "What happened on the
Harkin Amendment happens all the time; that is but the most dramatic example. Nonprofits draft stuff all the time and bring it to us.
The group called Bread for the World was very important in getting human rights language into the bill on supplementary funding for the IMF
[International Monetary Fund] in 1978. They tied funding to meeting
basic needs. It was their idea; we helped—and then they helped us get
it through.[37] And ADA got us interested in human rights in East Timor
[seized by Indonesian armed forces]."[38]

According to Senator Stewart's aide: "The WOA was very influential
in the senator's vote on keeping sanctions on Rhodesia. He leaned that
way. After all, he is for civil rights in Alabama. But WOA countered
other lobbying and also countered Senator Helms [R., N.C.]. WOA reinforced Stewart and gave him important facts." Said an aide to Senator
McGovern (D., S.D.): "We develop ideas with the nonprofits all the
time. At the request of those groups we write letters and raise questions with the State Department and foreign governments."

Congressional liberals seemed most inclined to attribute more influence to human rights nonprofits, but conservative Congressman
Henry Hyde used information from Freedom House in submitting a
proposal to restrict foreign assistance to some seventy countries. And
Congressman Wilson thought WOLA and others had been "very influential" in hearings on Nicaragua. Another conservative respondent
said: "After the nonprofits testified on Argentina, there was a general
feeling in the Congress that those sadistic bastards down there were
not going to get one more cent from us." And an aide to a conservative
member of Congress saw nonprofit influence in the following:
"Harkin gets those groups a room, they have a hearing and invite the
Washington Post, and pretty soon the bill goes through."

What do State Department officials think about nonprofit influence
on human rights?

The first level of response was glowingly positive during the Carter
administration, and somewhat surprisingly this was true for respondents in both HA and ARA (whose initials inexplicably date from a time
before the bureau was renamed the Bureau of Inter-American affairs;
the name changed but not the initials).[39] A sample of views makes

clear at this first stage that nonprofits were viewed as influential on a large variety of issues. Almost all Carter officials in HA were interviewed; here are some comments.

A very senior official: "The nonprofits have great influence. Amnesty, along with the *New York Times*, kept alive the issue of political prisoners in Indonesia. We disagree with their numbers on that one, but they really did refuse to let us forget about that problem. At every turn nonprofits confront the State Department with generally accurate information. They have contacts with foreign opposition forces that the U.S. government can't easily get. They are very influential on the Hill, and they have caused a big shift in our policy on Latin America; they have moved us away from simply supporting stable dictatorships."

An official responsible for contacts with nonprofits: "They shaped the creation and functioning of this bureau. In 1977 the International League gave us a report that helped us get going. We use nonprofit information all the time. I am in charge of liaison with the groups—that's how important they are; we're the only bureau in the department to have that kind of official. I make tours to get their critiques and ideas. They were especially effective in opposing Somoza and getting a tough U.S. position toward the USSR concerning the trial of Orlov."

A middle-level official: "Before Carter went to Korea the nonprofits enhanced our sensitivity to human rights issues there. It was impossible for us to ignore human rights with all their activity, especially that of the North American Coalition on Korea. Nonprofit criticism of our performance at the Belgrade meeting under the Helsinki Accord is going to make the United States tougher at the Madrid meeting. Some of the nonprofits have personal ties to Vance; on Korea, Uruguay, Argentina—they can reach the top. And after they testify on the Hill we can't just go over there and take the same position as the department's regional bureaus that everything is getting better; we'd lose our credibility with the groups and their supporters in Congress. They will be out in front of us, but we'll have to follow. Look at their impact on our country reports. They generate pressure on bureaucratic laziness. Lots of foreign service types don't want new, complicating factors. Nonprofits make those types take human rights into account—via Congress and public opinion."

A lower official: "Nonprofit testimony at congressional hearings

"Here's the record, Chief. He's a member of the Sons of Democracy, the American Friends of Worldwide Democracy, the Guardians of the American Heritage, the People's League for Good Citizenship, the Friends of Freedom, the Conference for the Furtherance of Constitutional Government, the League for the Preservation of American Freedom, the Sentinels of Democracy, the Golden Rule Association, the Society for the Support of the Constitution of the United States, the International Congress for the Furtherance of Democracy, the Conference for the Observance of the Ten Commandments, and the Society for the Preservation of North American Wild Life. We think he's a Commie."

Drawing by Alan Dunn; © 1947, 1975 The New Yorker Magazine, Inc.

pressures us too; we can't ignore it—especially if we can't refute it. ADA, WOLA, Amnesty—they all have influence on the Hill, and therefore over here too. The UAW is also effective on human rights."

An official with regional responsibilities: "The nonprofits are not stunningly effective, but they push us all the same. They critique us, and they have influence; but they don't turn policy around completely."

Another regional official: "We used Amnesty and International

Commission of Jurists information when we pushed for, and got, a U.S. abstaining vote on IFI [International Financial Institutions] loans to Guatemala in 1979. And the nonprofits make us think very, very carefully. They have a huge impact here if they can get a member of Congress to write us. U.S. policy would not be the same without them; it's important that they make loud and consistent noises. They got the administration to back off from Somoza, and they've been effective on Argentina, Chile, El Salvador, and Guatemala."

A functional official: "Embassy reports and internal department memos are always making reference to nonprofit reports. Their influence is secondary but important, especially in providing information."

A very brief effort to cross-check these interviews with ARA personnel did not initially change the pattern of responses.

According to a deputy assistant secretary of state: "The nonprofits now have more influence in my bureau than any other of the private groups. They have supplanted the Chambers of Commerce. Sometimes they work via Kennedy's office, and that has clout over here. Human rights is now part of the decision-making process; the groups can go to HA and even directly to Vance. U.S. policy on Latin America is changed drastically; look at Chile, Argentina, Uruguay, Nicaragua, and so on—and that is because of the groups and their work on the Hill."

He continued, "In other places, like Korea and the Philippines, the groups are not so effective because of U.S. security interests. It's said that Allis-Chalmers and other American firms can out-lobby the human rights groups. That's not true. Firms spend more money and get higher access, but that doesn't mean they affect policy. Policy frequently is unaffected by any lobbying. On the Allis-Chalmers thing, they did not win [by unblocking an Ex-Im loan in 1979]. We decided to unblock because that government was going to allow the Inter-American Commission on Human Rights to enter the country. If you list the nonprofits' top fifteen goals in Latin America, they have got 75 percent of each of them. They even affect the naming of our ambassadors."

Said a middle-level official: "The nonprofits have had a significant impact on Latin America. The department is piss-poor at being in touch with unofficial opinion, and nonprofits really help there. In 1975 an ARA spokesman gave really lousy testimony on Uruguay. The nonprofits wiped him out. Fraser, Harkin, Koch (D., N.Y.) all went after him. Kennedy's office joined in. The nonprofits had the facts. After that, ARA began to take human rights seriously. Nonprofits are the key—they give facts to members of Congress. And the nonprofits have been able to bust open the department's routine, especially when they act through Congress. We'll ignore the mail, but not congressional mail. The nonprofits have reoriented American foreign policy back to democratic principles, and this is enormously important for U.S.–Latin American relations."

Said a lower ARA official: "The nonprofits kept the pressure on us to get Timerman out of Argentina [the well-known Jewish newspaperman was finally allowed to emigrate], and even small, unknown groups have gotten us to raise questions with Paraguay. Groups have also gotten the United States to vote negatively or abstain in the IFIS. We don't ignore their views."

A spot-check with an AID official concerned with Latin America confirmed the emerging picture: "In 1978–79, WOLA met with us concerning aid to Nicaragua and Latin America. There were no dramatic policy shifts, but the result was a more critical bureaucratic process within AID. We started looking at new factors. At about this time, three loans were suspended to Chile because of human rights factors, and AID concurred in those decisions. AID and ARA really don't want to change, but the nonprofits together with HA push for change—and sometimes they win. If AID wants a program funded now, it has to evaluate its relationship to human rights. That's really a big change. The [Carter] administration is of course primarily responsible in the narrow view. It would not be the same with Reagan. But the nonprofit groups started the push, set the agenda, and kept the heat on. The big change is in Latin America, and the groups get some of the credit."

It would be misleading, however, to view nonprofit influence on the State Department and executive branch as consistently significant, even when giving unbalanced attention to Latin America where the groups have been very active. One factor lessening nonprofit impact is their lack of knowledge of the timing of executive decisions (discussed previously). Other debilitating factors emerged from continuing HA and ARA interviews.

According to a very high HA official: "There are plenty of losses in the human rights cause. Nonprofits lack money and manpower to press the department all the time, whereas firms can lobby consistently. There is an intricately connected opposition to human rights groups—and to HA—made up of business and the DOD. We can't attack the American way of business, or national security. Opponents have captured these slogans. We and the groups are at a disadvantage. That's why the United States has such a spotty and erratic record on human rights. The department has changed some. But the DOD, Treasury, Commerce, and the NSC [National Security Council] still want business and politics as usual. [National Security Adviser] Brzezinski makes fine speeches but he's no help, and his staffer on human rights is just collecting another line for his academic vita. So the groups can accomplish some things, but they're weak except on the Hill and with regard to Latin America."

Said a middle-range HA official: "Nonprofits are too absolutist. They don't like compromise, and sometimes they're naive and simplistic." Another HA official said the work of nonprofits in the human rights area was tied too much to ethnic pressures: "They scream about Jews emigrating from Russia and Rumania, but who's screaming about disfigurement of female genitalia in North Africa which is maybe being paid for indirectly by AID and their medical clinics?" Another in HA said she did not need to be prodded by nonprofits, and still another said nonprofits had no direct impact on his desk.

The more the ARA respondents talked, the more they cast some doubt on the glowing reports given earlier of nonprofit political acumen and influence. Said a senior official: "Although they are influential on the Hill, they are not directly influential at State on the nuances of policy made under congressional statute. Also, some of the groups misuse or misrepresent the facts, and this will do them in over time. Furthermore, they're absolutist—won't compromise."

A lower-ranking official was, in the final analysis, generally prone to discount nonprofit influence, despite his earlier remarks: "We listen to the groups, but their influence always falls short of the final decision. They've got a one-track mind, and we have to have an overview that takes many things into account. Generally, we supported their principles, but we disagreed with their suggested means and actually with the whole notion that pushing human rights—beyond verbal pronouncements—could be effective. It's very difficult to get constructive, practical steps toward human rights. The Latin governments increasingly discounted our negative position on bank loans. So there was not much we could do. We listened to the groups but went our own way. It has to be recognized that pushing human rights interferes with military and economic interests."

Extensive interviewing has not yet been done in the State Department for the period of the Reagan administration. Spot interviewing, as well as public information already noted, made clear that nonprofit influence declined after 1981. This was to be expected, if one keeps in mind the fundamental point about lobbying: lobbyists cannot take officials where they don't want to go, but rather must find sympathetic officials to work with.

The Human Rights bureau under the leadership of Elliott Abrams, normally the natural ally of the human rights groups, was distinctly unsympathetic to most of the groups active on human rights in Washington. The leadership of the HA bureau, including an assistant to Abrams drawn from ultra-right wing academic circles whose wife worked for the ultra-conservative Heritage Foundation, displayed a clear tendency to ideologically discount representations that did not focus on communist violations of rights. The geographical bureaus, never very warm to an emphasis on human rights even under Carter,[40] were even less so under Reagan—at least until about 1986 and growing political instability in places like Haiti, the Philippines, and South Korea. There was no human rights specialist on the National Security staff.

In general, as has been much noted, the entire subject of *internationally* recognized human rights, in a balanced approach, was downgraded 1981–85. In this general political atmosphere in the executive branch, the private human rights groups were at a distinct disadvantage and had to concentrate on Congress.

CONCLUSIONS

A simple view of interest group influence, one which sees interest groups as capable by themselves of directly affecting policy, has not stood up very well to empirical testing.[41] Lobbies rarely convert the opposed or constitute an independent and dominant force in policy making.[42] Nothing in the present study indicates that human rights nonprofits can "turn around" policy or take State Department officials or members of Congress where "they don't want to go" on foreign policy.[43] Moreover, human rights lobbies, like other public interest lobbies and many for-profit lobbies, lack the raw materials of "hardball politics"—namely, money and votes.[44]

Paradoxically, this chapter suggests the not-insignificant influence of human rights nonprofits on American foreign policy especially during 1973–81, but also to lesser degree thereafter, especially through Congress. Indeed, one can now question much of the conventional wisdom about lobbying and foreign policy. In particular, one can question whether foreign policy lobbying is necessarily less—and less important—than lobbying on domestic issues; whether "ideological," "church," and "peace" groups consistently lack influence; and whether the State Department possesses greater information on certain issues than Congress and interest groups.[45]

It remains very difficult to be precise about the influence of particular groups. Different participants in the political process—and different observers—have different perspectives. Some interviewees may be aligned from the outset with certain groups. Some may have a bias toward church groups, others toward secular ones. This chapter has attempted to obtain an overview of the way the process worked from the mid-1970s and to arrive at a summary of the impact of the human rights groups in general. Some groups may have been slighted—e.g., the Friends of the Filipino People, who seemed effective at times on the House side. Further interviewing with a broader sample of respondents could, no doubt, improve the picture drawn thus far.

But it does appear that in the 1970s and 1980s nonprofit lobbies in the issue-area of human rights significantly affected both legislation and State Department operating considerations. There is no scientific test for "significance" as used here, and certainly much remains to be researched (e.g., nonprofit influence on a broader range of congressional and State Department officials, on other executive departments and the White House, on the press and vice versa, and on various publics). But the evidence thus far collected suggests that nonprofit lobbying has had an incrementally significant impact on policy, particularly through the provision of information to Congress, setting agendas for policy making by requesting hearings, and focusing on problems and monitoring the performance of executive agencies.[46]

It is as if certain members of Congress were provided with a research and lobbying institute for human rights, covering most of the globe's human rights issues, with a research staff of dozens, with a budget of several hundred thousand dollars, and with a lobbying force of fifteen full-time staffers. Seen in this caricatured way, and keeping in mind the supposed lack of detailed information on the part of Congress compared to the executive, one can appreciate the significance of the nonprofit effort. This picture is without nuances, for the various groups were not always united on goals, strategy, or tactics. It is worth noting, however, that other public interest coalitions have also been fractured but effective.[47]

The following formula seems to capture best nonprofit influence. The first order of significance goes to the temper of the time or climate of opinion and the type of official internalizing that dominant mood. The second order of significance goes to the nonprofits: their leadership, their quality of information, their image of legitimacy (which was itself partly a product of the temper of the times). Causal relationships cannot be scientifically established, but it seems clear that these factors converged to produce a major change in American foreign policy on human rights between 1973 and 1979.[48]

There was undoubtedly a "cyclical upswing" in public interest in ethics and human rights after the Vietnam war and the Watergate affair.[49] A result of this was the election and/or reinforcement of members of Congress like Don Fraser, Tom Harkin, Ed Koch, Ted Kennedy, Paul Tsongas, etc. It is apparently normal for public interest lobbies to find a meeting of minds with liberal politicians, and human rights nonprofits had a number of sympathetic members of Congress to work with especially in the 1970s.[50] Likewise did human rights lobbyists find sympathetic ears in the person of Jimmy Carter—and through him Cyrus Vance, Warren Christopher, and Patricia Derian, to name only the most prominent. Increasingly many conservative members of Congress became interested in some version of human rights, and in a number of cases a bipartisan coalition pushed for attention to human rights.

Moreover, many members of Congress were assertive in foreign policy matters. They were distrustful of the imperial presidency, its secrecy, and its tradition of power politics. This, too, was part of the temper of the times, and it was a crucial element in congressional willingness to legislate both generalities and specifics concerning human rights in order to affect executive action in foreign policy. Therefore the nature of governmental officials is an importance of the very first order. Since lobbies must attach themselves to, or work with, sympathetic officials, it is the nature of the regnant officialdom—and the public mood from which it stems—that is the principal control on the influence of a lobby.[51]

But the resources and leadership of human rights lobbies themselves constitute a distinct importance of the second order. If the nonprofits were largely handed a new legitimacy because of the temper of the times, it was they who capitalized on it and maximized it. Most of them were careful about their image and information. Amnesty in particular went to great lengths to project an image of neutrality, refusing money from the Ford Foundation and refusing to provide the State Department with certain information if a foreign government had not commented on Amnesty's findings. WOLA, perhaps less neutral in a policy sense but equally concerned about the validity of its information, made sure that members of Congress heard directly and thus without distortion from opposition leaders and victims of repression in Latin America.

If information was the true currency of lobbying, then the nonprofits had a legal tender that they protected, through image management particularly, from the perils of depreciation.[52] Furthermore, nonprofit leadership knew well the legislative calendar and congressional personnel, and that leadership apparently recognized that the monitoring of executive agencies—with the opportunity to criticize reports and embarrass officials—generated considerable influence.[53]

Most fundamentally, what gave human rights lobbying a second-order significance were the same forces that made other public interest lobbying sometimes effective: a new middle-class politics based on affluence and leisure time, interest in reform, distrust of established traditions and procedures, and a focus on single-issue areas. Human rights lobbying was thus part of a broader phenomenon in American politics that led to new activity by previously weak groups which demanded new legislation and new agencies to represent their concerns.[54]

There were even some close observers of the Washington scene who were prone to give the human rights lobbies a first-order significance. According to Sandy Vogelgesang, a State Department official, the network of nonprofit agencies was "often" a "decisive factor propelling recent U.S. promotion of human rights." She goes on to quote Patt Derian, the first assistant secretary of state for human rights, as saying that the human rights lobbies were as important at times as the Jewish lobbies.[55]

It is now clear that the public mood begin to shift as early as 1978–79, affected by such things as growing economic problems in the U.S., the Soviet invasion of Afghanistan, and the seizure of U.S. nationals in Iran. An increasing concern with economic and security issues caused the human rights question to recede somewhat, relatively speaking. The election of Ronald Reagan, and his appointment of a large number of ultra-conservative ideologues, especially to positions in the State Department, certainly affected U.S. foreign policy on human rights.

This is not the place for an extended treatment of the Reagan administration and human rights, a subject briefly noted in the preceding chapter. What should be stressed here is that while executive views changed considerably on human rights in foreign policy from 1981, and while private human rights groups found themselves with less access and influence in that quarter, congressional views did not shift so drastically. Thus human rights nonprofits still had allies on the hill.

From 1981 the nonprofit human rights lobbies, whether registered as such or not, tended to re-emphasize by necessity what they had emphasized less exclusively before. There were more sympathetic officials, more accessible, in a continuingly assertive Congress. Thus the groups participated heavily in the hearings on the nomination of Ernest W. Lefever, named by Reagan to be assistant secretary of state for human rights, and played some role—difficult to measure exactly—in the withdrawal of that nomination after crushing bipartisan defeat in the Senate Foreign Relations Committee.

There followed for much of the Reagan Presidency a continuing clash over human rights, with various and varying members of Congress aligned with different nonprofit lobbies, struggling with the Reagan team for control of policy.[56] There was continuing congressional legislation and oversight, and the private groups were deeply involved in both aspects of a seamless process. While the Reagan team, especially until 1986, was able to reorient much foreign policy on human rights, Congress in tandem with the private groups won some legislative victories, frequently involving the power of the purse, concerning such states as Guatemala, Chile, and to lesser degree El Salvador and Nicaragua.

Especially among House Democrats, the private human rights groups found willing allies for the oversight of Reagan policies, as on the subject of the annual human rights reports. In other ways the groups remained active in the Washington policy making process. If it be true that Reagan really intended to downgrade the human rights issue except when applied to communist countries, then it can be said that Congress, with secondary but significant support from the groups studied here, prevented that from happening—as the Reagan team found out in South Africa, the Philippines, South Korea, Haiti, Liberia, and other states around the world. While Reagan appointees did take human rights initiatives themselves, of course, an assertive Congress and a vigorous nonprofit sector were an important part of the Washington policy making process—as was coverage of human rights in the elite media such as *The New York Times* and *The Washington Post*.

In summary, much new information and many new ideas had been introduced by human rights nonprofit groups between 1973 and 1988. Like other nonprofit groups in other issue-areas, the human rights nonprofits had been creative and helped produce changes in American public policy. It is certainly possible that, whereas most for-profit interest groups seem to have had a reputation for influence that exceeded reality, nonprofit lobbying for human rights may have had a second-order influence that exceeded a reputation for weakness. Persuasion may be accomplished secondarily through provision of information, but it is still persuasion.[57] Future studies may indicate whether this secondary-but-significant influence for nonprofit lobbies is reasonably permanent, even though subject to normal ups and downs, and, especially, whether nonprofit indirect lobbying (perhaps combined with educational processes) can produce the kind of public opinion that will sustain direct human rights lobbying over time.[58]

Chapter Seven

The Political Philosophy of Human Rights

What is discriminatory in terms of the claims of individuals becomes justifiable in terms of the claims of groups.
Vernon Van Dyke, "Human Rights without Distinction as to Language," *International Studies Quarterly* 20, no. 1 (March 1976), p. 34.

INTRODUCTION

Underlying human rights agreements, efforts to implement them, and related U.S. policies are views of political man and public authority. These philosophical views have been deferred until now, primarily to show that much international action can be taken on behalf of human rights despite theoretical differences over rights. It is also evident that much legislation can be adopted within one state like the United States despite disagreement between Democrats and Republicans, American liberals and conservatives. Any approach which emphasizes the philosophy of rights will magnify disagreements and ambiguity, because philosophers within one nation, much less in a multicultural world society, have never agreed on where rights come from and what are rights properly speaking. But it remains true that for many actors in world politics, the philosophy of rights does matter. Therefore it is time we tried to clarify the complex subject of philosophy of rights which lies just beneath, and sometimes on, the surface of internationally recognized human rights.

In this chapter I suggest first of all that contemporary views toward human rights stem from three general philosophical orientations: conservatism, liberalism, and communalism. Conservatism, as a philosophy of unequal rights, dominates in the practice of some states, but it is rarely endorsed openly as pure conservatism because of the late twentieth-century rhetorical emphasis on equality. The U.N. Charter's Article 55 speaks of human rights "without distinction." The Universal Declaration speaks of "equal and inalienable rights of all members of the human family." Thus however much some elites may view themselves as divinely or otherwise entitled to rule over others, they are unlikely to admit this openly in a century semantically committed to equal rights. Not since the fascism of the 1930s and 1940s have claims to permanent superior status been articulated openly. Communist claims to the need for a dictatorship of the proletariat are seen as an intermediate measure leading to full equality in the ultimate classless society. Yet conservatism defined as unequal rights does exist in practice, as we shall see.

Another philosophical basis for human rights is liberalism. This philosophy is known for its central emphasis on the equal worth and autonomy of the individual. Liberalism has come to mean many things, including the belief in the beneficial nature of change. (This meaning has little evident relation to human rights.) When applied to rights, liberalism is a philosophy interpreted in different ways, especially on the subject of whether equality extends to the right to equal material benefit or only covers equality of civil and political rights. Some of the states which have been most interested in international human rights reflect a basically liberal philosophy in their approach to rights, but they do not always have the same definition of liberalism. One can contrast here the United States and the Scandinavian countries.

Another philosophical basis for human rights is communalism. This philosophy is known for its central emphasis on some group, such as a class or a national people. It has been frequently said that whereas liberalism emphasizes the autonomy of the individual, communalism emphasizes that the individual is always found in groups and individual welfare is always bound up with the fate of the group. Communalism, like liberalism, has come to mean various things. A basic division among communalists occurs over the question of which group should be the unit of analysis and action: the Marxists say socioeconomic class, while some non-Marxists say a national people. Obvi-

ously, the group orientation of Marxist states and of certain Third World states affects their approach to implementation human rights.

I readily admit that this tripartite approach, as well as other ideas presented in this chapter, will not answer all questions about a philosophy of rights. Indeed, were I to construct the perfect treatise on theories of rights I would belong on some mountaintop as guru to all. As noted previously, philosophers and theorists of rights have never agreed on fundamentals; they are unlikely to agree on the basis of this synthetic chapter here. I merely suggest that this tripartite approach, as well as other ideas offered, provides some understanding of the theoretical debate over human rights. Moreover, I do not pretend that all political philosophies can be neatly wrapped up in my three packages. I only suggest that it is useful to speak of three major philosophies as benchmarks along the wide spectrum of opinion. Indeed, I will suggest that elements of one philosophical tradition can show up in another school of thought.

One other point bears stressing, even at the risk of some redundancy. By taking up the question of philosophies of rights only now in our inquiry, the present approach—as it has from the opening pages— implicitly agrees with Stanley Hoffmann and his analysis of philosophies in relation to rights. That is, rights arise in response to particular situations; rights lead to claims or demands on specific institutions that certain objectionable threats and deprivations be eliminated. Hence there can be a recognition of universal rights at the very time that there is disagreement on the philosophical foundations of those rights.[1] Rights arise out of social practice, at least in an empirical sense. And thus the most important point is to emphasize the recognition of rights in the contemporary social (viz., political and legal) practice of states and other actors in world politics. In inquiring into philosophies of rights, we should not emphasize metaphysical debate at the expense of empirical practice.

THREE POLITICAL PHILOSOPHIES

One can gain some initial understanding about the philosophy of rights through the chart represented in table 4.1. The chart represents rationales for rule. It shows two variations on each of three principal philosophies. In essence, it presents elite claims seeking to justify national political-legal regimes. Such claims entail views toward human rights. While the chart is organized as a spectrum with a "left" and a "right," fitting with political rhetoric, this organization should not be carried too far. Elements of conservatism, for example, could show up in other schools of thought. And it has been suggested at times that the Soviet model of communism is essentially a version of conservatism—a continuation of many elements of Czarist Russia under the facade of a communalist ideology. The reader should keep in mind that this presentation is based on three ideal types or models, (hopefully) useful for understanding, but not to be confused with the complexity of political reality.

Conservatism

Our first political philosophy entailing a view about rights is conservatism. Extreme conservatism is called fascism, although this labeling is problematical. (In fact, this entire subject is problematical—viz., full of problems.) Fascism proved such an amalgam of disparate ideas and contained so much emphasis on emotion rather than clear thinking that it has never led to clear definition widely accepted. Nevertheless, and skipping all the complexities of the real world, fascism represents an extreme philosophy of unequal rights on two counts. Some peoples or races are said to be superior, to have more rights, than others (and thus fascism contains communalist elements). And within fascism a ruling group has more rights than others.

Only the strongest, the most powerful are entitled to have rights. This process eliminates the weak, the bad. Thus Jews in Hitler's Germany did not even merit the right to life. Nor today do certain South American Indians have this right in General Stroessner's Paraguay, de-

TABLE 4
Spectrum of Main Ideas about Rights, with Prevalent Images of States

LABEL	Communalism		Liberalism		Conservatism	
	Marxist Communalism	National Communalism	Egalitarian Liberalism	Classical Liberalism	Classical Conservatism	Fascism
RHETORICAL EMPHASIS	right of especially worker class to material equality	right of national group to welfare based on equal material benefit	right to material equality and political freedom for individuals	right to equal freedom for individuals	unequal rights	rights only for the most powerful
IMAGE	USSR	Algeria	Sweden	U.S.A.	Brazil	Paraguay

spite that state's facade of liberalism. Behind the facade of elections and democratic rights operates a political regime dominated by ideas of racial superiority and unequal rights. Other regimes in Latin America, influenced by Iberian culture which itself was sometimes characterized by fascism (eg., Franco in Spain), have shown these same traits of extreme unequal rights—eg., Argentina under military rule.[2]

Classical conservatism, which from one point of view has nothing at all in common with fascism, is associated, at least in the West, with Edmund Burke. Its roots, however, go back to Plato and *The Republic*, where the best system of rule was said to be by philosopher-king, unchecked by law or popular will.[3] For Plato men were not equal; there was to be no equal freedom and certainly no attempt to produce equal material conditions.[4] Later conservatives such as Burke developed the theme that this truth had been demonstrated by the past. What existed at present was good because it had survived from the past. It was not good to try to change things for the better in the future, because the past showed that could not succeed. Thus inequality—of happiness, freedom, material condition—was an immutable historical fact. It followed that some were destined to have more rights than others. (From this point of view conservatism was diametrically opposed to fascism, the latter espousing a notion of permanent revolution and radical change.)

Who are the modern conservatives? Initially they are hard to find if one looks at rhetoric, because the twentieth century is—superficially at least—an egalitarian age. Most elites claim to rule in the interests of popular equality, not of privileged position. Even the military in Latin America, which has historically claimed a special privilege to save the various Latin nations from themselves, couches its rhetoric in egalitarian terms. In the 1970s it added human rights language as well. Typical was the statement by the military leader of Argentina in 1978. President Jorge Videla said that military rule was temporary, that it would restore democratic rule, and that its basic purpose was "to recover the national dignity and human rights that were affronted by terrorist aggression."[5] Even the South African elite described apartheid not as racial separation producing gross inequality and denial of freedom but as separation permitting equal human development according to different ethnic values.

Some modern conservatives do, however, openly deny equal rights. Elements in Brazil openly say that only the middle and upper classes should have the right to benefit from national progress. An American author has noted the difference in this regard between liberals and conservative Brazilians. In liberal Europe and North America, he writes, "One no longer thinks of the lower classes as having few, primitive needs, of the poor as enjoying their poverty, of the social order as a divine given. But in Brazil I found these attitudes still prevalent, still untroubled—in the raw, so to speak. If anyone wants to know what callous capitalism can sound like, a visit to the elegant boardrooms of rich Brazilians would prove revealing."[6]

More generally, one of the bastions of modern conservatism is constituted by certain Western financial circles. Their philosophy is one of mass deprivation so that the banking and monetary systems, run by and for an unelected elite, can continue in an uninterrupted and profitable way. Political, civil, and social rights are an impediment to wise decision-making by this economic elite. The key right is the right of economic freedom. Democratically elected governments are a nuisance to these circles, as are the rights of the underlings. Said a professional financier in 1978: "Switzerland has a government like all governments in that it does silly things. But there is an absence in Switzerland of some of the prime causes of economic problems such as labor laws, minimum-wage laws, union powers. Thus, Switzerland can adapt to changing circumstances better than other governments."[7]

(A number of figures known in the West as conservatives are not Burkean conservatives but are really liberals with a classical interpretation of liberalism. I will show this in the discussion of the liberal view. They believe in rights to political freedom and legal equality of opportunity, and they believe that the freedom of economic competition produces the most for the most—albeit distributed unequally— that an overall good system can achieve. These figures, from Adam Smith to Milton Friedman to F. A. Hayek are really the classical variety of liberal, although they are called conservative in many circles.)[8]

Who are the critics of conservatism? They are legion. In an egalitarian age unequal rights are said to be unfair, unjust, unacceptable (the philosophical grounds for this stand will be analyzed subsequently). In practical (utilitarian) terms, conservatism is criticized for what it does to society. Consider military rule and its support by the extremist conservatives (fascists?) in Argentina:

> The Argentinian radical Right consists of desperate men, sniffing weakness, treason, "Reds" everywhere, and certain that only their toughness—which is another word for brutality—

can secure survival. They see themselves as patriots, who can easily become killers with a sense of destiny . . . They even have a French ideoloque to inspire them: the ideas of Charles Maurras—whose Action Francaise combined royalism, authoritarianism and anti-Semitism.[9]

Quotes could be collected endlessly, both about how privileged rule—whether military or not—was to be better than other rules, and about why conservatism was not better but infinitely worse. Either way conservatism was clearly a model of unequal human rights.

Liberalism

The word liberalism has certainly been used in more ways than can be described here. But its central and historical meaning is a belief that the highest good or value is individual well-being, and that personal well-being is found through freedom and equality. Liberals believe that moral man and moral society can be developed—or at least a better man and society. Politics, in the words of the liberal T. H. Green, is "essentially an agency for creating social conditions that make moral development possible."[10]

There are two primary foundations for the liberal school. Each has had an impact on modern human rights. The first of these is the natural law school, which the British scholar Hersch Lauterpacht saw as the "inspiration" for human rights.[11] Natural law thinking posits that humankind is naturally free and equal, is naturally worthy of highest concern. Why? Answers vary. One line of thought finds this to be true because people exist in the image of god(s). In this vein one finds some Greek thinking, as well as that of Catholics like Thomas Aquinas. Whether or not a deity figures in, natural law thinkers see people as possessing rights because of the natural order of things. Humans have certain "inalienable rights," in the Jeffersonian phrase, because they exist in a larger order, one governed by metaphysical rules which establish that they have rights.

On the one hand, natural law thinking has had great appeal, from the Greeks and Romans, through the Christian Middle Ages, and on through Locke and Rousseau to the American and French revolutions of the eighteenth century. Momentous political events occurred in the West in the name of the natural rights of man. On the other hand, other serious thinkers found the idea of natural rights foolish; Jeremy Bentham referred to natural rights as "nonsense on stilts."

The second foundation of liberalism is utilitarian thinking, classically represented by the works of John Stuart Mill. Pursuit of human happiness and welfare through freedom and equality is the highest value or good because that is what proves useful. Useful to what? To society. A liberal society is said to be a stable and productive one. The highly egoistic thinking of the early utilitarian Jeremy Bentham gradually gave way to an emphasis on individual happiness because that was good for, or in the interest of, the larger group. Utilitarianism became group welfare through individualism, with the group determining what is good for the individual. Majority rules. To counteract tyranny by the majority, individual freedom and equality became valued in and of themselves even though they limited majority rule. Freedom and equality thus have equal standing with group welfare, either because freedom and equality contribute supremely to human happiness or because natural law thinking invaded utilitarianism.[12] In any event, individual freedom and equality supposedly led to "the greatest good for the greatest number." This became the rule and test for goodness.

Around this standard rallied a large number of thinkers, from Adam Smith and David Ricardo on the right of the classical utilitarian wing to Mill, and Green, and Sidney Webb on the left. Obviously, if Adam Smith and Sidney Webb are both utilitarian liberals, much separates the ends of the utilitarian spectrum.[13] As we shall see shortly, much separates many liberals of whichever wing. Nonetheless, many have supported the core utilitarian notion that progress—a better society— is achieved through the free exercise of individual equality. On the other hand, Edmund Burke found the primary idea of equality a "monstrous fiction."

The two versions of liberalism provide much support for the human rights movement. Natural law thinking argues from first principles. It has been as persuasive as it has been unprovable. Jimmy Carter was quoted as saying he would push for human rights because it was the right thing to do. That is natural law thinking. A modern and careful analysis of political philosophy reaches the same conclusion. Human rights stem from natural law, not social organization.[14]

Equally modern and careful analysis reaches a utilitarian conclusion. In an oft-quoted book, Maurice Cranston argues ultimately:

> To claim the traditional rights of man is to claim, among other
> things, both security *and* liberty. Security is not something

which is at odds with human rights, because it is itself a human
right; it is nothing other than the right to life restated. The security of the individual is bound up with the security of the
community; the private enjoyment of the right depends upon
the common enjoyment of the right. The demand for liberty
and security is not the demand for two things which can only
with difficulty be balanced or reconciled; it is a demand for two
things which naturally belong together. Part of the traditional
Western faith in freedom is a belief that a free country is *safer*
than an unfree country. History gives us good ground for continuing to think that this belief is true. [15]

Hence both foundations of liberalism continue to attract adherents.
And both continue to attract critics. The most fundamental criticism
of natural law thinking is that frequently what seems like an absolute
right based on the natural order of things turns out to be a relative and
changing belief reflecting culture, time, place. What was once seen by
some as an absolute right to freely manage and dispose of property is
now seen by some as either a limited right or no right at all. The fundamental criticism of utilitarian thinking is that there are no intrinsic
values save group welfare, and that thus almost anything can be justified as good in the name of the group. The majority, acting on the basis
of free and equal votes, can require the individual's death if that is
deemed good for society.

Two further observations on liberalism, whether of the natural law
or utilitarian variety, are important. First, liberals have rarely agreed
on how freedom is to be meshed with equality. Classical liberals emphasize freedom and relegate equality to the equal opportunity to
compete freely. The results of this formula are verifiable and thus predictable: inequality of men's socioeconomic conditions *and* civil-political influence. Free competition, economically and politically, is obviously to the advantage of those who start the competition with the
advantages produced by race, nationality, education, wealth, family
contacts, and so forth. The mass of those less advantaged wind up with
a lower intake of food and a lower level of political influence.

The United States has historically chosen this classical liberalism,
only slightly modified by a limited welfare state. A provocative critique by the British novelist John Fowles is worth noting:

The American myth is of free will in its simple, primary sense.
One can choose oneself and will oneself; and this absurdly opti-

mistic assumption so dominates the Republic that it has bred
all its gross social injustices. Failure to succeed proves a moral,
not a genetic, fault . . . The myth becomes so pervasive that it
even ends up as the credo of those, the underprivileged, who
most need to disbelieve it. I have seen it in even the most intel-
ligent liberals there . . . impeccably sympathetic in their attitude to things like Medicare, Black anger, environmental
control and all the rest; yet still they hanker after the old and
other American dream of freedom to cash in on other people's
inequality . . . Americans came to America to escape two
things; political tyranny and fixed odds in the struggle for life,
and they have never realized that the two aims are profoundly
hostile to each other—that the genetic injustice of life is just as
great as the old European economic injustice. Their system
dealt with the latter by assuming an equal dispensation of energy, talent and good luck to all men: and now they are smashed
hard on the reef of the far deeper injustice.[16]

The same point can be made in more conventional—and boring—
political science terms and logic. In the United States in the 1970s, the
bottom 20 percent of wage earners received but 5.6 percent of the total
national income.[17] What is the welfare and happiness, not to mention
the equality, of this group in Harlem, downtown Detroit, and the rural
South? And in this context, how important is equality of voting rights?

Unlike classical liberals, other liberals emphasize equality and
sharply limit freedom. In Denmark, parents do not have the freedom
to name their children as they wish. Certain names have been pro-
scribed by the democratically elected government in the interest of

protecting all children equally. The intent is to protect a child from the adverse consequences of having to go through life with the name of, say, Tarzan. This requires restriction of personal freedom (it is not clear what the authorities would say if the child were named Hans Christian Tarzan Petersen!). Also in Denmark, a shop-owner is not permitted to remain open for business after 2:30 P.M. on Saturday, or to be open on Sundays. Unions have succeeded in getting such a national law passed in order to guarantee freedom from (in their view) excessive work. Even the small shop-owner, who may not have union laborers, must comply. But can it be liberalism if individual freedom is so progressively restricted?

Hence liberalism manifests a general inability to present an agreed-upon understanding of how its twin pillars of freedom and equality are to be combined. That is why William Ebenstein has written that "in practice it is not easy to ascertain when equals are still equal and when they become unequal."[18] Classical liberals fear loss of individual freedom through group decisions on principally socioeconomic equality. Egalitarian liberals fear the "predatory democracy" of the freedom to compete, with unequal results. The differing evaluations of liberalism are reflected in a comment by a professor who is non-Marxist, non-radical, non-minority, and from the establishment of tenured Harvard: "Now it is quite true that liberalism in practice has often been a cloak for oppression."[19] But whose oppression? Does implementing the right of freedom deny equality, and vice versa? Do rights for some mean denial of rights for others?

Only partly in jest do I say that this entire debate about liberalism is summed up via seatbelt laws. In most of Western Europe citizens accept the law requiring use of seat belts in the front seat of private cars, and in some nations small children are not legally permitted to ride in the front seat at all. Community interest in equal safety for all so re-

By permission of Johnny Hart and Field Enterprises, Inc.

quires, as processed by democratic law-making. In the United States, by comparison, Nebraska and Massachusetts repealed seatbelt laws, and other states never passed them, in deference to individual free-dom—even at the expense of equal safety as determined by the orga-nized community.

For now it suffices to recapitulate our criticism of the liberal model. Liberalism is divided on (1) the origins of and reasons for freedom and equality, and (2) how to combine these two values. Yet liberalism has been one of the major philosophical foundations for the modern focus on human rights. Indeed, Jack Donnelly has suggested that serious at-tention to human rights requires a liberal state.[20] Philosophers cer-tainly care whether these beliefs are true philosophically, or whether they can be made to fit logically and consistently with other beliefs. What is politically important is that these values have exerted consid-erable appeal. However interpreted, they have affected the exercise of power and have shaped international public policy.

Communalism

One might think that since liberals so disagree among themselves on various points other views would not be needed. Such, of course, is not the case. There is a third philosophy which affects human rights: the communal or solidarity school. Rights stem from membership in a community or group. Individuals form solid groups. It is that fact which governs their rights. What is the ultimate source of these com-munal human rights? Answers vary. Indeed, the extent of disagree-ment among the communalists makes the liberals look unified.

One wing of the communal school of thought is Marxist. Now, not only have books been written but also libraries have been filled with interpretations of Marxism. There is wide agreement, however, on tra-ditional Marxist views of man and his rights. This agreement can be briefly summarized.

In the Marxist view of history, the central problem in the capitalis-tic stage is precisely that man is seen from the liberal point of view. He is seen as an individual, with rights, set apart from other men and from society as a whole. Marx is critical of liberal views of human rights. "Security is the supreme social concept of [liberal] society, the concept of the police. The whole society exists only in order to guarantee for each of its members the preservation of his person, his rights and his property." To Marx reality was otherwise. Man was controlled by eco-nomic forces rather than being independent. He was not really an individual but had real existence only as a member of an economic group. For Marx society did not consist of "relations between individual and individual, but between worker and capitalist, between farmer and landlord, etc. . . ."[21]

Marx saw the result of the liberal, individualistic view of man as being man's alienation from other men because of exploitation. The solution was to recognize "historical truth:" that the supreme good was labor, the best class was made up by workers. Thus the true view was that, while other groups might have rights at a given stage of history, workers' rights were superior and destined by history to triumph. In the early writings of Marx this was the ostensible meaning of the dictatorship of the proletariat; the rights of one class were superior to others. (In this sense, and in the light of our earlier discussion, we can see that there is an element of conservatism in Marxism, and especially in Marxism-Leninism.)

Paradoxically, the Marxist view of future communism—when classes have been eliminated, exploitation has ceased, government has withered away—is "deeply individualistic." Under communism man can emerge "as an individual, developing fully, freely and in an all around way, which presupposes life in a genuine community." Thus it was the nature of the community that determined the rights and fate of man. In a communistic community man could be a true individual; in a capitalistic one he could only be alienated and exploited under bourgeois rights. Ironically, Marx depicted "communism as a fulfillment of the individualistic goals which liberalism had proclaimed but had been unable to realize."[22]

Therefore, Marxist thought sees the present dominated by groups. Socioeconomic classes define man. Man struggles in class conflict. The worker class will triumph. Its rights are superior. Only its victory will lead to the communistic society capable of liberating man and allowing him to be a true individual.

The Marxist view of human rights can be extended almost ad infinitum and certainly ad nauseum. Rather than quoting further Marx, Engels, Lenin, and others, I find it more relevant to quote contemporary but traditional Marxist elites. Their views reflect an emphasis on groups rather than individuals, on material rather than procedural rights, and on class rights that can be easily blended with national rights. Georgi Arbatov, adviser to Leonid Brezhnev, said: "Each people has the right to set up its own prime priorities of human rights. Here the rights that were the main driving force in our own revolution were very essential human rights. One was peace, another the right to live,

bread, to have something to eat, not to starve."[23] And a Soviet specialist in human rights said in 1978: "Priority should be given to the study
of the so-called communal rights (rights of solidarity)—the right to
peace, the right to self-determination, the right to development and
the right to a healthy environment."[24]

Against this traditional Marxist-Leninist background one can better understand the meaning of the Soviet Constitution of 1977. It contains guarantees of human rights, but all such rights are to be exercised
within the bounds of group solidarity and welfare. Freedom of speech
and opinion, for example, are guaranteed so long as such speech and
opinion are consistent with the needs of the revolution of the proletariat and the security of the Soviet state within which the revolution
lives.[25] History and its economic forces have determined that the
working class, and those nations where it has come to power, are ethical groups. No individual has the right to hurt this class and those nations. Singular action cannot be allowed that would set back progressive realization of full freedom and equality and happiness in the
complete communism of the future.

Thus, as a leading authority on communist law has noted, in the Soviet Union, "rights are protected only insofar as their exercise con-
forms to the function for which the right was granted."[26] This is as traditional Marxist theory specifies.

But there is other Marxist theory, for example, as represented by the
Socialism with a Human Face that the Czech Marxists sought to implement in the mid- and late-1960s. And the rise to power of Gorbachev after 1984 in the Soviet Union greatly complicated the picture
of Marxist theory on human rights. Gorbachev, like Dubcek in
Czechoslovakia, permitted some dissent within establishment circles, some freedom of speech and association not controlled by the
party-state, and other elements of apparently "liberal" rights even
though they entailed criticism of what otherwise passed for "scientific
truth." Gorbachev even spoke on occasion of competitive elections for
lower positions.[27]

At the time of writing, this author was invited to lecture on human
rights in Prague, and his Czech host wrote a paper stressing "the problem of the limitation of human rights by the State, which a) must not
contradict international law, b) must not result in the liquidation of
these rights in their practical implementation, c) must apply to all persons without any discrimination." The subject of Marxist theory of
rights was obviously problematical—and in a great state of flux.

A second version of communalism and solidarity is non-Marxist. Rights ultimately derive from national experience and needs. It is the national group which promotes and protects rights. In the Hegelian version, man has the freedom to follow the higher good established by the national spirit.[28] In more modern versions, man has the right first and foremost to national self-determination and national economic development, from which all other rights derive and depend.

Thus Jahangir Amuzegar, an Iranian, has argued that Western views place too much emphasis on the individual. This is said to be especially true of the United States and is seen as a reflection of American history. At the time of the American Revolution, the individual could be "a much stronger master of his own economic destiny" and so he developed individualistic political views. But in modern times "world production and exchange is still colonial." The individual in the Third World has no chance to counteract this corporate power. So a national response is required. Hence what is needed is national equality and independence, leading to national plans of economic development and national education. It is nation-state action which will allow the people to have rights. Perhaps later there can be attention to individual rights. But now what matters are the rights of a national people.[29]

There are so many variations on this theme that a consensus on human rights derived from national communities must remain somewhat amorphous. Yet out of the cacophony of non-Marxist communalists emerges a set of rights which was articulated at a meeting of nongovernmental representatives in Algiers in 1976. Said this group (made up largely of non-Marxists from the Third World):

> Convinced that the effective respect for human rights necessarily implies respect for the rights of peoples, we have adopted the Universal Declaration of the rights of peoples. . . :

> Articles
>   1. Every people has the right to existence.
>   2. Every people has the right to the respect of its national and cultural identity.
>   3. Every people has the right to retain peaceful possession of its territory and to return to it if it is expelled.
>   4. None shall be subjected, because of his national or cultural identity, to massacre, torture, persecution, deportation,

expulsion or living conditions such as may compromise the
identity or integrity of the people to which he belongs.

5. Every people has an imprescriptible and inalienable right
to self-determination. It shall determine its political status
freely and without any foreign interference.

6. Every people has the right to break free from any colonial
or foreign domination, whether direct or indirect, and from any
racist regime.

7. Every people has the right to have a democratic government representing all the citizens without distinction as to
race, sex, belief or colour, and capable of ensuring effective respect for the human rights and fundamental freedoms for all.

8. Every people has an exclusive right over its natural wealth
and resources. It has the right to recover them if they have been
despoiled, as well as any unjustly paid indemnities.

9. Scientific and technical progress being part of the common
heritage of mankind, every people has the right to participate
in it.

10. Every people has the right to a fair evaluation of its labor
and to equal and just terms in international trade.[30]

Critics of communal thinking about human rights are not few in
number. The principal criticism is that expressed by Senator Daniel
Patrick Moynihan, former American ambassador to the United
Nations—namely, that elites antagonistic to human rights have taken
the language of human rights for service in their own causes against
freedom.[31] This criticism is particularly directed against traditional
Marxism. Whatever the fate of human happiness and freedom and
equality under the projected communism of the future, the socialist
road to that future is characterized by dictatorship, privilege, and suppression of the rights—even for workers—supposedly guaranteed. Today's means gobble up the projected ends of tomorrow. Hence, said
Zbigniew Brzezinski, national security adviser to President Carter,
"the historical inevitability of our time is not some utopian revolution
but it is the increasing self-assertiveness of man on behalf of his own
human rights"[32] (rights belong to man himself, not to his group; and
Marxist promises are utopian anyway).

Non-Marxist communalists escape some of this cross fire, although
there has been ample criticism of the African Charter on Peoples and
Human Rights for weakening the latter concept in order to emphasize
the former—as represented by governments. One African leader, Tan-

zania's former President Julius Nyerere (a Roman Catholic), articulated a blend of liberalism and communalism. Nyerere has openly articulated a goal of socialism, and thus many liberals think of his philosophy as communalist. His philosophy, but not his practice entirely when he was president, is partly otherwise and worth noting. On a number of occasions Nyerere defended individual rights. He addressed the subject of human rights most fully in 1968, when he said:

> For what do we mean when we talk of freedom? First, there is national freedom; that is, the ability of the citizens of Tanzania to determine their own future, and to govern themselves without interference from non-Tanzanians. Second, there is freedom from hunger, disease, and poverty. And third, there is personal freedom for the individual; that is, his right to live in dignity and equality with all others, his right to freedom of speech, freedom to participate in the making of all decisions which affect his life, and freedom from arbitrary arrest because he happens to annoy someone in authority—and so on. All these things are aspects of freedom, and the citizens of Tanzania cannot be said to be truly free until all of them are assured.[33]

This was not a one-shot speech. Nyerere defended individual rights on a number of occasions, and at other times he warned of glorifying national grandeur. Yet a large part of his thinking was directed to communal, economic rights: "What, then, of socialism? . . . The important thing for us is the extent to which we succeed in preventing the exploitation of one man by another, and in spreading the concept of working together cooperatively for the common good instead of competitively for individual private gain."[34] This same orientation has guided a number of African elites, in particular, such as Robert Mugabe, elected Prime Minister of Zimbabwe, a Western educated Catholic Marxist and nationalist. Other orientations in the Third World are different, as in Arab socialism, which has proven both in theory and practice to be much less sympathetic to individual political and civil rights.

THE THREE VIEWS IN INTERNATIONAL SOCIETY

It is clear from this chapter that there are great differences over attitudes toward human rights. But the debate has been posed in abstract terms, or on the assumption that we are talking about a citizen in any national society. What happens when we transfer the debate to a situation of many societies, or to only the international society? There are three possible developments.

First, the attitudes may remain the same. For example, it is possible that Jimmy Carter became president with the idea that liberalism in America should govern U.S. foreign policy as well.

A second possibility is that liberals and communalists must become conservatives in their foreign policies. One may have one set of rights internally, but if world politics is thought to be ruled only by the law of the jungle then a foreign policy based on unequal rights or survival of the fittest may be necessary. The view is widespead that it is acceptable, and perhaps even ethical, to beggar thy neighbor. To protect the good society at home, it is argued, one is entitled to do all manner of mischief abroad including denying rights directly or indirectly.

A third possibility is that liberals and communalists may have to temper or qualify their attitudes toward rights in order to take account of the uniqueness of international society. For example, liberals may have to give up the original or national formulation of liberalism without completely becoming conservatives. This third possibility has in fact been addressed by a number of both liberals and Marxists.

Classical liberalism viewed the individual always as an end linked to freedom and equality, not as a means linked only to state security. At least paying lip service to this view, Kissinger said in 1976: "The precious common heritage of our Western Hemisphere is the conviction that human beings are the subjects, not the objects, of public policy; that citizens must not become mere instruments of the state."[35] Said Jimmy Carter in 1978: "There is one belief above all others that has made us what we are. This is the belief that the rights of the individual inherently stand higher than the claims or demands of the State."[36]

But even liberal states sometimes view the individual as a means to another end having little to do in the *immediate* sense with human equality and freedom. The extreme situation is found in war. Two examples suffice to make the point, and both examples are discussed in the readable book *A Man Called Intrepid* (which, naturally, was not written by a political scientist).[37] During World War Two the highest American authorities approved the murder of an American national on American soil; he was said to be helping Hitler. Also during that war, the Allies killed a number of children in Copenhagen during an air raid designed to liberate the leadership of Danish opposition to

Hitler. In both cases the ultimate denial of human rights—the right to life—was justified (at least by the author of the book) in the name of preserving the group (American and Danish national independence from Hitler).

Less extreme situations pose equally difficult choices. What does the liberal do when faced with a repressive, or partly repressive, regime which is important to the well-being of a liberal regime? This was the situation confronting the Carter administration in 1978–79 when Iran was racked by street violence and other opposition to the Shah. He had ruled in part through denial of certain political rights, detention of opponents, and torture. Yet women had been allowed to exercise some rights, and peasants had been given land. Moreover, the Shah was economically and diplomatically supportive of the United States.

Since Carter failed to renounce the Shah and fully distance the U.S. from his regime, at times Carter seemed to agree with Kissinger. The latter had previously asked rhetorically, "Will we have served moral ends if we . . . jeopardize our own security?"[38] Yet Carter did not fully endorse the Shah, either. In fact, the Carter administration vacillated over policy toward Iran. One of the reasons for this stance was the difficulty of predicting the future. In the opposition to the Shah were Western educated constitutionalists committed to implementing rights and to normal if nonaligned relations with the U.S. Also in opposition, as we know well in the 1980s, were Islamic fundamentalists opposed to many if not most internationally recognized human rights—and opposed to normal relations with the United States.

Kissinger agreed with the American philosopher Reinhold Niebuhr, who had argued that ethics in world politics could never be the same as personal ethics. According to Niebuhr, "group relations can never be as ethical as those which characterize individual relations." Moral man, and Niebuhr means liberal man, must—in world politics—combine liberal morality with power considerations. The result will be a situation judged partially unethical by the standard of individual liberalism. "Politics will, to the end of history, be an area where conscience and power meet, where the ethical and coercive factors of human life will interpenetrate and work out their tentative and uneasy compromise." Niebuhr could have been describing the central difficulty in Carter's policy toward Iran in 1978–79 when he wrote, in 1932: "The question which confronts society is, how it can eliminate social injustice by methods which offer some fair opportunity of abolishing what is evil in our present society, without destroying what is worth preserving in it, and without running the risk of substituting new abuses and injustices in the place of those abolished."[39]

It is a fact that in war as in many other situations, liberalism in world politics becomes qualified by the principle of making secure the power base of liberalism. One must protect the power of the liberal group, even if this means treating people as means rather than ends or supporting—in an intermediate sense—denial of rights.

A number of post-Marx Marxists have said something similar. They have said that the state cannot wither away—and it is indeed a dictatorial state—so long as capitalists are still trying to subvert the workers' revolution. These views constitute the Niebuhrism of Marxism. Just as Niebuhr saw the qualification of liberalism as necessary in world politics, so Lenin and similar political thinkers see the qualification of Marxism as necessary for (both domestic and) international reasons. Historically Marxist states have expanded rather than withered away, and this is at least rationalized as necessary to protect the progressive revolution from its enemies.

"Of course, if national security is involved,
disregard everything I've said."

Drawing by Dana Fradon; © 1977 *The New Yorker Magazine, Inc.*

This analysis leads to a crucial judgment between qualified liberalism and qualified Marxism. Each factually seeks to protect its power base and to suppress some rights of individuals for the sake of survival in world politics. The liberal view is that war is an exceptional event and also that liberal support for human rights in relative terms is a demonstrated fact. Thus the liberal view is that qualified liberalism is still preferable to Marxism, since the latter sees class war as very long-range and denial of many rights as consequently long-term. The liberal sees Marxist promises of rights as largely utopian. The Marxist reply is that liberal rights are a sham blocking true freedom and equality, and that future communistic rights are well worth sacrifices now.

THE PRACTICE OF RIGHTS AND VALUE SHARING

From the rhetoric about political philosophy and human rights we have noted three basic views: conservatism, liberalism, and communalism. Furthermore, we have noted that both liberalism and communalism may be qualified by their spokesmen in the interest of protecting the power base from which spring the philosophy and the related view of rights. Thus there is a tendency for both liberal and Marxist foreign policy to be conservative in fact, in the sense of at least deferring to unequal rights abroad or perhaps no (few) rights at all. Neither the United States nor the Soviet Union expressed great difficulty about being aligned with regimes that engaged in gross violations of internationally recognized human rights from 1947 to about 1977 (from this latter date U.S. policy became more troubled, if not completely different).

This leaves us with a dilemma. On the one hand, we have observed the reality of human rights treaties and of widespread efforts to implement them through international and national steps. On the other hand, we have just observed the variety of views underlying the human rights activities. It would therefore appear at first glance that the human rights norms stand little chance of being implemented because of differing conceptions of the philosophy of rights either in the abstract or when considered as applied ethics.

This contradiction may be real. On the one hand, it is clear that the human rights treaties reject conservatism as an official ideology for the world community. Conservatism is essentially a philosophy of imperfection[40] which hinges on the inequality of individuals and on the impossibility of changing man and society for the better. On the other hand the treaties stress some version of equality and seek to point the world community toward radical change for the better. The human rights movement may ultimately fail because states *practice* conservatism: they may practice foreign policies which pay little attention to rights in world politics, whatever their conception of rights at home. All too frequently it appears that each state does what it can do by force, subsequently claiming it has a defensive right to that action.

But it may also be true that the human rights treaties can be implemented to a significant degree because the *practice* of rights shows that some values are shared regardless of the fact that an abstract discussion of philosophy emphasizes differences. There is of course no denying that not only the philosophy but also the practice of rights is markedly different in the United States and the Soviet Union. And we have already noted that the vagueness and generality of some of the wording in the human rights treaties was an effort to paper over these real disagreements about philosophy and practice. But if we raise the question, "What is the practice of rights in Sweden, Yugoslavia, and Senegal," we may find that along with philosophical differences are similarities in the practice of rights. What we wish to know at this point is whether the national practice of rights offers any hope that the philosophical differences can be overcome—or at least bypassed.

One way to proceed is to examine national constitutions and national laws. This comparative law approach has been employed by others. What will be attempted here is a very limited examination of the practice of rights within the three major coalitions of contemporary world politics: Western, communist, and Third World. This point of view is less interested in the rights which are written down in national constitutions and more interested in the exercise of rights as practiced in national political systems. We want to know to what extent the philosophical differences are duplicated in political practice. We are still interested in practice or exercise of rights, not simply political power. Thus we are asking not whether man exercises power individually, in groups, equally, etc., but whether his rights stem from individual status, group status, equal status, etc.[41]

There is considerable truth in the notion that Western regimes practice liberalism while non-Western ones embody communalism. The truth, however, is only partial; it is significantly qualified by contrary evidence and sheer uncertainty. The following points seem worth noting.

Western Communalism

Parts of the West practice a considerable amount of communalism. The pioneering work of Vernon Van Dyke has made this clear.[42] A particular religious group—Catholicism—is guaranteed certain rights, especially concerning education, in Spain. Linguistic groups are guaranteed certain political and civil rights in Belgium. Linguistic-territorial groups in Switzerland determine the language of education and much more in that country.

In the highly individualistic United States, a great debate raged in the 1970s and 1980s about precisely this trade-off. The Bakke case handled by the Supreme Court centered on the question of whether a particular group (in this case the black minority) could be guaranteed a certain percentage of places in higher education (in this case, a professional school), even if this "affirmative action" meant limitation on equal and free competition among individuals (as the white male petitioner said it did). The Court reached a compromise decision and the debate continued. (It was significant, if typical, that the Reagan administration argued for total freedom and the removal of laws on affirmative action or "reverse discrimination." That administration, like most groups made up of the wealthy and otherwise privileged, usually argued for total freedom. It is only the poorer and less-privileged elements that have need of laws, and rights, which can counter unbridled power and wealth.)

The central point for present purposes is that the West practices more communalism than many have noticed. Individual freedom and equality is combined with group preference. The overall situation, in philosophical terms, is perhaps most appropriately labeled neo-utilitarianism, with group rights added to individual freedom and equality in order to produce the greatest good for the greatest number. As with all societies, there is a contradiction at work.

Vernon Van Dyke has noted it: "What is discriminatory in terms of the claims of individuals becomes justifiable in terms of the claims of the group."[43] This is as true in the liberal West as on the road to communism.

Marxist Liberalism

Parts of the Marxist camp allow at least some liberalism—or have allowed for a short time. One of the most interesting historical examples of this phenomenon was the liberalization of the Dubcek government in Czechoslovakia in the spring and summer of 1968. That Marxist government permitted individual and equal freedom of opinion and speech, and of emigration, before it was replaced through the armed intervention of the Soviet Union and certain other Warsaw Pact nations. Since this experiment in "Marxism with a human face" was not allowed to evolve by its own dynamics, we do not yet know a great deal about whether Marxist communalism must necessarily reject the basic elements of liberalism.

A second interesting example involved the trade union Solidarity in Poland. In some respects this development carried communist liberalism much farther than the Dubcek regime. Events took place in Poland in the early 1980s that were unprecedented in an Eastern European communist system. Although Solidarity claimed that it did not seek the role of party, much less of government, in effect Solidarity determined along with the party and the government the nature of Polish society. Solidarity finally defined itself at its 1981 National Congress as a "social movement."

Spokesmen for Solidarity demanded and got prime time on state-run television to contradict the government's version of news. For a time Solidarity determined the length of the work week, as well as official policy on other issues. From the popular support of this independent movement it was clear the Polish people wanted freedom of association, the right to strike, and real democracy in the form of secret ballots and a choice among candidates. This movement was terminated by the Polish military, which may have acted to forestall another Soviet invasion.

As noted in earlier pages, the Soviet model of Marxism was itself undergoing change at the time of writing, which led to renewed demands for rights in Czechoslovakia, Poland, and Hungary in particular, but also in other places like East Germany. At fundamental issue in all of these Marxist regimes was whether ruling elites would recognize that individual rights existed apart from conformity with the party line. Could Marxism be combined with rights to free speech, free association, and even to work apart from political allegiance? From a theoretical view these liberal developments were problematical, wherever they occurred. If Marxism were scientific truth, as claimed, how could there be various versions of truth? (There was also a more practical problem from especially the Soviet elites view; how could they maintain power at home and in Eastern Europe if they tolerated real rights?) On the other hand, could there not be tactical differences of opinion about how to achieve general goals?

In Yugoslavia, the so-called system of self-management presented a situation that might be termed limited liberal communalism. Consider this description by a Yugoslav political scientist:

> The first and most important idea is that of the emancipation and liberation of labor. This is a Marxist idea which we think to be . . . the humanistic essence of socialist transformation . . . Only if the worker obtains effective control over means, conditions, and results of his work, will he be able to control the social forces which are produced by his own collective work. He will be able to control the immediate direct political power in the society. The way to achieve such liberation is the transformation of state ownership into public social ownership . . . By developing self-management we overcome the situation in which government is the universal owner and universal manager of the whole economy, which always implies the danger that this enormous power might be transformed into political oppression. By transforming state ownership into public ownership under the control of the workers themselves, we deprive bureaucracy of the main source of its power . . . Self-management, in our view, implies more than decentralization in the economy and other spheres of life. It requires the abolishment of hierarchical structures in every single cell, in every working unit, in every institution of the society. This principle generates a revolutionary change in the pattern of interest articulation. It offers the possibility for direct expression of individual and personal interest at every level of social organization. In that way the ground is prepared for a revival of direct democracy.[44]

This favorable assessment of individualistic self-management is not shared by all. The U.S. State Department annually concludes in its human rights report on Yugoslavia that the regime strives to keep ultimate power in the hands of a few. The State Department view is certainly shared by those like Milovan Djilas, a Yugoslav former communist leader detained for disagreeing with President Tito. Indeed, in 1977 Djilas charged that, proportionally speaking, Yugoslavia had about as many political prisoners as the Soviet Union. But, and significantly, Djilas suggested this was a recent rather than inherent development. The debate about the potentialities for implementing human rights through individual self-management continued. The State Department noted that there were considerable individual rights in Yugoslavia based on freedom and equality.[45]

Thus, under Marxist regimes whose primary conception of rights was communal, some individual rights and real freedom and equality have existed—at least in some places and for some times. The argument should not be overstated. Yugoslavia was a long journey of rights from Albania and Bulgaria. And rights were so denied in Romania in the 1980s, especially for ethnic Hungarians, that many of these latter were fleeing to Hungary. But even in East Germany, not usually cited as a paradise of human rights, at least by liberals, individual rights existed. These individual rights existed usually in the economic sector as a spur to production. Some individual rights existed also in the social sector. And a more general right of individual dissent from governmental policy had been pushed in the late 1970s and 1980s over the issue of the introduction of military education into the public schools, although this right has not been formally acknowledged.[46]

Third World Melange

Different parts of the Third World practiced different conceptions of human rights. There were liberal regimes like Venezuela and Botswana. There were communal regimes like Mozambique and Vietnam. Significantly, there were regimes whose practice of rights reflected a mixed or hybrid philosophy. Tanzania had a basically socialistic economy, but the government there had finally shown reluctance to continue compelling individuals to move into collective farms. Thus there existed an uneasy mixture of communalism and liberalism, or collectivism and individualism.[47] Likewise, in Lebanon prior to its civil war there were individual voting rights and private property rights, but some rights were apportioned on the basis of the three most important religious groups: Christians, Sunni Moslems, and Shi'ite Moslems.

There was also extreme conservatism and extreme communalism. The spectrum was not a straight line but rather a curve: the left and right ends met. They met at that point where neither conservatism nor communalism could effectively justify or rationalize genocide or murder. Did ideological or philosophical differences matter concerning Democratic Kampuchea under Pol Pot and Uganda's dictatorship under Idi Amin?[48] And what was the difference between these two genocidal (autogenocide and near-genocide) regimes and the extremist conservatives in Chile after Allende's fall? People disappeared in the night never to be heard from again—or tortured bodies were later discovered.

Thus the Third World in its practice of rights was a melange of liberalism, communalism, liberal-communalism, and brutal conservatism (sometimes in the name of revolutionary communalism). Patterns were hard to distinguish: they may even be non-existent. Amin's genocide was accompanied by successful efforts to create an African human rights commission. The Latin American conservatives committed atrocities while the liberals of the hemisphere tried to utilize the American commission and court of human rights. Vietnam consolidated its military victory in the south with political re-education camps, and Sri Lanka degenerated into ethnic atrocities, while South Korea moved toward democracy.

Given the human rights actually practiced in the Third World, or in a few cases the total absence thereof, it was no wonder that a great debate continued about what human rights model was appropriate for the Third World. We will return to this subject in the next chapter.[49]

CONCLUSIONS

Competing views over human rights there are indeed, and an observer of the debate can be pessimistic. According to Harvard's Barrington Moore, it is "impossible" to get "assent among informed and thoughtful people with sharply contrasting political persuasions" about what to do to improve the human condition.[48] And we have seen that the pursuit of power in world politics makes it difficult for even the national liberal to be an international liberal, or for the Marxist interested in human emancipation to pursue that goal in world politics.

Yet we have also seen that there is, factually, some sharing of attitudes towards rights when we examine practices of rights in different nations. Some basically communal regimes tolerate some individualism, and vice versa.

A pessimist would, no doubt, emphasize first of all the extensive practice of conservatism on the part of many ruling elites. This widespread practice is reflected in the fact that about half the states of the world have yet to adhere to the two 1966 covenants. A pessimist would also emphasize the differences between Western liberalism and Marxist communalism, not to mention the attitudes toward rights entailed in a resurgent traditional Islam.

An optimist would, no doubt, emphasize the very fact of the existence of so many human rights norms; he or she would also emphasize how much the treaties had already overcome philosophical differences. After all, it could be argued, both liberalism and communalism—especially Marxism—were interested ultimately in the true freedom and equality of the individual. Perhaps the differences were tactical and temporary. Was not the West moving more toward communalism? And were not some versions of Marxism recognizing a domain for individualism, at least when allowed to evolve of their own dynamics? Were Sweden, Senegal, and Yugoslavia the common denominators of the future, being the imperfect models most in accord with the dictates of the international human rights norms? We will return to these questions in the final chapter.

Chapter Eight

The Future of Human Rights
in World Politics

All truth passes through three stages. First it is
ridiculed. Second, it is violently opposed. Third, it is
accepted as being self-evident.
Arthur Schopenhauer, quoted in Benjamin B. Ferencz,
Planethood (Coos Bay, OR: Vison Books, 1988).

INTRODUCTION

December 10 is Human Rights Day around the world, for it was on 10
December 1948 that the Universal Declaration of Human Rights was
adopted. On 10 December 1979 Soviet police broke up peaceful demonstrations designed to mark the occasion and detained some fifteen to
twenty persons. Yet later that same month the International Commission of Jurists called 1979 "remarkable" because of the toppling of dictators and progress on other human rights issues.[1] This was a typical
year, with both positive and negative developments.

By the 1990s should one be optimistic about human rights developments in the context of world politics? Or should one be pessimistic
about the condition and prognosis of human rights in the world? From
the very first pages of chapter 1 we have noted the mix between positive and negative developments concerning human rights. But still,
what are the proportions of ingredients in this mix? A balanced perspective on this question is aided by recognizing two fundamental
points about law, and specifically the international law of human
rights.

1. It is normal for there to be a tension, a difference between what is

ANDY CAPP by Reggie Smythe © 1978 Daily Mirror Newspapers Ltd. Dist. Field Newspaper Syndicate.

and what should be.[2] That is, legal rules are normally not the same as customary behavior or practice. The law is different from, and supposedly progressively ahead of, behavior. If law and behavior were the same, there would be no need for law. People would already be doing what was desired and thus would not need law to direct behavior. One uses law precisely because one wants to change what is to what should be. Because of this tension or difference, law is always violated. Thus it is misleading to overemphasize the question, "Is law violated?" It almost always is, because law and behavior are usually not the same.

It is important to raise the question "How *much* is law violated, and to what extent are violators compelled to adhere to the norms?" For if the norms are so far ahead of reality that there is extensive disobedience without effective compulsion in support of the rules, then the norms become discredited.

Precisely this phenomenon has occurred with regard to some resolutions adopted by the U.N. General Assembly. These norms (which are not directly binding as law) have been so at variance with international behavior that they have lost their credibility as shapers of reality. They are generally disregarded, if read in the first place. (Other U.N. resolutions do affect both diplomacy and law.)

Hence a problem for human rights law is that it may be so visionary as to become irrelevant as an influence on real behavior. The gap between what is endorsed as right and just and what is clearly the nature of the real world may be so great as to make human rights law a "dead letter" regardless of the fact that it exists as "law on the books." It may be either presumptuous or facile to say so, but the nature of the world is the first problem confronting implementation of human rights norms.

Ernst Haas has performed a useful service in giving us a partial overview of the situation. Haas observes that since human rights include both civil-political and socioeconomic rights, it is helpful to characterize states both politically and economically. Thus, in the context of human rights, political systems can be classified as competitive (fully democratic), semicompetitive (partly democratic), noncompetitive (simple authoritarian), or totalitarian (unlimited authoritarian).[3] In the same context, economic systems can be characterized as mixed-industrialized (advanced, with some private enterprise), mixed-developing (not advanced, with some private enterprise), command-industrialized (advanced, with almost no private enterprise), and command-developing (not advanced, with almost no private enterprise). Tables 5 and 6 represent world overviews according to these categories, with table 5 focusing on the economic situation for the year 1978 and table 6 comprising a political schematic for 1977. While the numbers would change slightly in a more recent year, the overall picture would not change in its broad outlines.

From these two tables, one can derive the preliminary judgment that many human rights norms are up against formidable odds. Almost half the population of the world lives in countries which deny meaningful political freedoms and participation. Almost three-quarters of the number of states in the world are authoritarian. Over one-third of the population of the world is generally denied the right to own property—a right claimed by the West and endorsed in the Universal Declaration. (Some private enterprise is tolerated even in command economies, and the trend by the 1980s was toward more such tolerance.)

Other tables give a comparable view about denial of other rights. As we have noted already, the Overseas Development Council (ODC) is a nongovernmental organization in Washington, D.C., that measures the physical quality of life according to infant mortality, life expectancy, and literacy rates. The first factor is one indicator of part of the commitment to protect the right to life, since medical care of infants is a basic component of the right to life. Life expectancy is a factor composed of many components. It is one useful, if incomplete, guide to overall quality of life—which is, of course, the result of attention or inattention to many fundamental rights. Literacy is a factor indicating the most basic commitment to the right of education. Many questions can be raised about the use of these three factors, but these statistics are available and generally reliable. One use of them leads to the view laid out in table 6. From such a table one can see that the physical quality of life, as defined, is about four times better in Japan than in much of black Africa and about twice as good in Eastern Europe as in the Islamic Middle East. While use of more recent indexes would show some progress by some countries over time, the relative differences among regions has not changed very much.

Still other tables tell of similar deficiencies in implementing socioeconomic rights. The right to life and to adequate health is predicated on access to drinkable water and to sanitary disposal systems. What is the world picture regarding this elementary need? WHO provides the disturbing view outlined in table 8. Fully one-half of the people of black Africa, Asia, and the Islamic Middle East do not have adequate sewerage. Over one-half in black Africa and Asia do not have safe water.

Most rights are meaningless unless there is adequate nutrition. Brain damage results from severe nutritional deficiencies, and even at higher levels of nutritional intake there can be mental and physical weaknesses if certain caloric requirements are denied. FAO and other agencies concerned with food have established those requirements and have surveyed the world. While food deficiencies can exist in the more affluent countries, it is in the poor countries, naturally enough, that the right to adequate health through adequate food is most denied. Chart 1 on page 197 provides one picture of the situation.

Even these limited overviews make clear the extent of repression and oppression in the world. In that the international law of human rights seeks to change the present reality into a more free and just world order, it faces a monumental challenge.

2. All law has trouble controlling powerful actors. This is true even in effective national legal systems. American law, which has provided order for over two hundred years (with the major exception of the American Civil War), has long had trouble effectively regulating corporations. Likewise does law have trouble regulating powerful unions, as is evident in places like the United Kingdom, where illegal strikes are sometimes common. Many examples could be chosen from modern events to demonstrate that even in stable legal systems powerful actors—whether corporations, unions, or the two together comprising a particular industry—have refused to accept law, have forced a change in the law, and sometimes have used illegal violence without penalty. The following is one such example.

In early 1974 the U.S. federal government passed a series of laws on gas for truckers. This tripartite legal policy essentially consisted of higher gas prices, lower speed limits, and fixed rates charged by truckers for delivering freight. A number of powerful trucking con-

TABLE 5
Percentage of World Population and Number of Countries by Economic System

Economic System	Industrialized Mixed Economy		Developing Mixed Economy		Industralized Command Economy		Developing Command Economy	
	Pop.	Countries	Pop.	Countries	Pop.	Countries	Pop.	Countries
Competitive	18%	23	18%	18		0		0
Semicompetitive	1%	5	16%	26		0		0
Noncompetitive		0	12%	39	9%	0	2%	9
Totalitarian		0		0		7	25%	13

TABLE 6
Percentage of World Population and Number of States
by Political System

Political System	% World Population	Number of States (1977)
Fully democratic	36	41
Partially democratic	17	31
Simple authoritarian	13	48
Unlimited authoritarian	34	20

cerns opposed this policy as unfair and detrimental to their interests. Certain of these trucking concerns used violence as well as nonviolent picketing, slowdowns, and curtailment of service to back their views. The U.S. government was unable to regulate the truckers under existing laws. After several small concessions the government made major changes in the rules: a lower ceiling on diesel fuel prices and higher freight rates through the Interstate Commerce Commission. The government thus tried to compensate the truckers for the higher regular fuel costs and increased delivery expenses brought about by lower speed limits. The old law was changed, at least two-thirds of it, in the face of the power of the truckers and their willingness to use illegal violence.[4]

When international law fails to regulate states we often speak of the collapse of the legal system. But in fact national legal systems may also fail to regulate powerful entities. Yet when this occurs we do not speak of collapse. We speak of adjusting the law to a closer relationship with reality and with the exercise of power.

The problem of regulating powerful entities is pronounced in international law. International law is called upon to regulate what is, in principle, the most powerful actor in the world: the nation-state. Regulating the state is similar to, but more difficult than, regulating powerful actors within the state. J. L. Brierly has summarized the situation well.

The fundamental difficulty of subjecting states to the rule of law is the fact that states possess power. The legal control of power is always difficult, and it is not only for international law

TABLE 7
Physical Quality of Life Index, 1978
(Scale of 100)

Selected Countries

Japan	96
Canada	95
U.S.A.	94
New Zealand	94
Australia	93
Israel	89
South Africa	48
Rhodesia	43
West European average[a]	92.7
East European average	88.4
South American average	72.5
Central American average[b]	65.5
Asian average[c]	55.7
Islamic Middle East average[d]	42.5
Black African average	25.7

[a]16 countries, not including Luxembourg and Monaco, but including Greece.
[b]11 countries, not including Belize, but including Cuba.
[c]15 countries, not including North Korea, Bhutan, and Mongolia.
[d]19 countries from Morocco to Pakistan, including Lebanon and Turkey. Islamic Indonesia is in the Asian group.

that it constitutes a problem. The domestic law of every state has the same problem, though usually . . . in a form less acute. In any decently governed state domestic law can normally deal effectively with the behavior of individuals, but that is because the individual is weak and society is relatively strong; but when men join together in associations or factions for the achievement of some purpose which members have in common the problem of the law becomes more difficult. Union always gives strength, and when the members of these bodies are numerous, when they can command powerful resources, and when they feel strongly that the interests which their combination exists to protect are vital to themselves, they often develop a tendency to pursue their purposes extralegally, or even illegally, without much regard to the legal nexus which nominally

TABLE 8

Percentage of Population with Access to Water Supply and Excreta Disposal: Regional Averages

Region	Access to water		Access to excreta disposal	
	Urban	Rural	Urban	Rural
Sub-Saharan Africa	66.3	10.4	70.3	14.2
North Africa, Middle East, and Southern Europe	74.3	64.4	94.0	93.0
South Asia	66.3	17.2	66.9	2.5
East Asia and Pacific	58.3	9.8	66.6	14.8
Latin America and Caribbean	78.0	34.9	80.3	25.4

NOTE: Estimates are based on information for years between 1973 and 1977, in accordance with availability of data.

SOURCE: World Bank estimates as of September 1978. Collated by Johannes F. Linn in *Cities in the Developing World: Policies for Their Equitable and Efficient Growth* (New York: Oxford University Press, 1982).

> binds them to the rest of the society of which they are a part. In fact, they behave inside the state in a way that is fundamentally similar to, though ordinarily it is less uncompromising than, the way in which sovereign states behave in the international society . . . The problem of subjecting states to law is more difficult than, but it is essentially similar to, that which confronts the state in its treatment of powerful associations within itself.[5]

International human rights law seeks to regulate primarily the behavior of powerful states (and through them, mainly, the behavior of associations and individuals). It seeks this on a sensitive subject, for most states are highly concerned about international inroads on their relationships with their own nationals. It is common, as Brierly noted

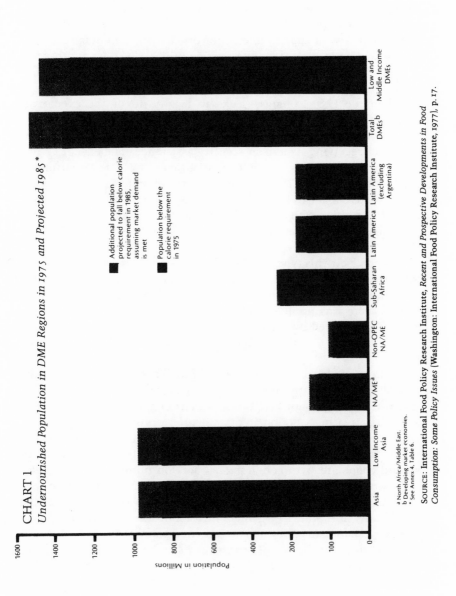

CHART 1
*Undernourished Population in DME Regions in 1975 and Projected 1985**

Population in Millions

1600
1400
1200
1000
800
600
400
200
100
0

Asia   Low Income Asia   NA/ME[a]   Non-OPEC NA/ME   Sub-Saharan Africa   Latin America   Latin America (excluding Argentina)   Total DMEs[b]   Low and Middle Income DMEs

■ Additional population projected to fall below calorie requirement in 1985, assuming market demand is met

■ Population below the calorie requirement in 1975

[a] North Africa/Middle East.
[b] Developing market economies.
* See Annex 4, Table 6.

SOURCE: International Food Policy Research Institute, *Recent and Prospective Developments in Food Consumption: Some Policy Issues* (Washington: International Food Policy Research Institute, 1977), p. 17.

above, to think of the law as being applied by the state against its citizens, in which case the overwhelming power of the state is easily brought to bear against the private individual. As we have noted, however, much law is applied to entities other than individuals. Sometimes the law is applied by one public authority against another. In this latter type of situation, which is found not only in international but also in national law, sanctions are difficult to apply.

When the U.S. Congress seeks to legally direct the executive branch, the executive sometimes disobeys. For example, in 1974 the Congress instructed the executive to compile human rights reports on countries receiving American security assistance. The executive refused to comply during 1975 and most of 1976. The State Department was not hauled off to jail, nor was Secretary of State Kissinger—who was responsible for the policy of non-compliance. The Congress proceeded to write a tougher law on human rights, one that was even more distasteful to Kissinger. Traditional sanctions were difficult if not impossible to apply, so Congress found an unofficial sanction.

It is precisely this type of national situation that is analogous to the international problem of applying sanctions in support of human rights norms. There is no question but that most of the norms are law, just as there was no question but that the congressional act noted above, duly signed by the president, was law. But problems remain concerning how to secure compliance from powerful public authorities.

Compliance is sometimes sought through the argument that continued violation of the norm will work against the violator's self-interest. The argument here is that violation produces an automatic and self-activating sanction, in that the interests of the violator are inherently damaged by breaking the law.[6] For example, State Department internal memos in the mid-1970s suggested to Kissinger that he should cooperate with congressional acts on human rights. Otherwise, Congress would take over that aspect of foreign policy from the executive branch.[7] State Department defiance of Congress would automatically hurt State Department interest in remaining the manager of American foreign policy. This argument resurfaced in 1981, when officials in the State Department again advised the White House that it would have to come up with a human rights policy or yield the issue to Congress.

Likewise, efforts are sometimes made to persuade states to follow human rights norms because of state interest in the rule of law, a good image, domestic support, foreign support, or some other value of interest to the violator. The argument, in sum, is that state violation of the norm(s) hurts the real interest of that state; and this is said to be a sanction that is automatically applied.

Of course, more traditional sanctions are available in principle and are sometimes applied in fact. The United Nations, as we have earlier noted, applied mandatory economic sanctions on Rhodesia and mandatory arms sanctions on South Africa, both because of human rights violations. The United States applied a trade embargo against Uganda in 1978. And so forth. One of the general problems here is that some other value must be sacrificed in order to pursue the value of human rights. The United States had to give up importing coffee from Uganda. Countries were supposed to give up military sales to South Africa. Countries were obligated to give up Rhodesian beef, sugar, minerals, etc.

Similar problems inhere in national legal systems when the decision is made whether to prosecute or not. When the U.S. Justice Department decided to move against the IBM Corporation in an antitrust action, it had to agree to pay a high price in terms of resources that it would commit to a long and costly trial. Likewise, when the Justice Department decided to move against ITT or the former director of the CIA (Richard Helms), it had to evaluate the cost it would pay in terms either of dollars or of classified information released to the defense attorneys and hence to the public.[8] Defendents, especially those with something to hide, always try to increase the cost of applying the law. Thus Oliver North, a member of Reagan's national security council staff involved in providing weapons to the Nicaraguan rebels after Congress banned such provisions, threatened to have the highest officials—perhaps including the Vice President and President—testify at his trial.

We can therefore see that sanctions are frequently applied only with great difficulty, even in national legal systems, but certainly in the international legal system. Sanctions against powerful actors carry a high price tag.

These two initial and fundamental points—the size of the task confronting human rights efforts as they seek to bring about change, and the difficulty of bringing law to bear on powerful actors—should serve to keep our expectations appropriately restrained. We return to our question: what is the condition and prognosis of human rights in the world?

TO RECAPITULATE

1. In chapter 1 we saw that the sum total of the human rights agreements constituted a visionary ideal and legal ideology. Most of these accords are indeed law; there is a legal obligation to comply on the part of those states which have adhered. Yet the obligations are so broad and apparently demanding that it is more reasonable to view them as goals to be achieved over considerable time than as governmental policy that can be implemented tomorrow. Of course, as the Chinese proverb states, the longest journey begins with the smallest step.

The international law of human rights should be viewed not only as a command or injunction for immediate action, but as a legal language communicating fundamental values to states and other actors in world politics.[9] This law can be used in courts, and on occasion it is. But at the same time the law of human rights is an agent of political socialization, communicating basic assumptions about the desired nature of world politics and society in the future. While revolutionary, since it challenges the notion of national sovereignty, the international law of human rights actually works to consolidate the nation-state system of world politics, for the states that implement the law enhance their legitimacy.[10] And the legitimate state is a stable and secure state, although with reduced autonomy.

As suggested in chapter 2, the human rights norms represent a fundamentally different way of thinking not just about human dignity but also about world politics. For some three hundred years the notion of national sovereignty has been widely accepted. It has been believed that states had the right to do as they pleased within their territorial jurisdiction. The human rights movement reflects the notion that states are obligated to meet certain standards in how they treat their nationals even within their own territory and that non-national bodies as specified in the treaties are entitled to comment or take action on human rights issues. This is a revolutionary change which has been accelerating in the period of 1945 to 1990, but which still confronts a tradition of three centuries. This modern period, as well as its historical background, shows that the promotion of human rights moves according to irregular dynamics. Rules are put forward in response to particular situations, and particular rules are emphasized according to concerns of the moment. This is common to all legal systems, and to the evolution of rights in all societies.

As of the 1980s the largest number of states in the world seemed more interested in socioeconomic rights than in civil-political rights. At least there was more rhetoric at the United Nations about socio-economic rights, although most of the concrete action taken by U.N. bodies was on civil and political rights.[11] Such a rhetorical orientation was understandable on the part of Marxists, because of their belief in economic determinism (not to mention their emphasis on dictator-ship). The poor could also be expected to be more interested in bread than votes. But parts of the West contributed to this trend by accepting socioeconomic rights.

These socioeconomic rights, like the civil-political ones to be re-viewed shortly, are emphasized by different parties for three basic rea-sons. First, the socioeconomic rights are said to be important in and of themselves as a major contributor to human dignity. Richard Fagen has written a concise statement of the lack of socioeconomic dignity in Latin America which nicely reinforces what has been said at the start of this chapter about socioeconomic deprivation in the world:

> The actual situation with respect to income distribution and social equity is, in general, appalling. Fifty percent of the re-gion's citizens have incomes of less than $200 per year; one-third receive less than $100. The top five percent of the popula-tion controls one-third of the total income. The emphasis on industrialization and export-led growth almost everywhere re-inforces and accelerates the neglect of agriculture—at least ag-riculture in basic food-stuffs for domestic consumption. Large sectors of the countryside and those who live there are ne-glected. In the countryside—as well as in the fringe and slum areas of the cities—high infant mortality, high levels of illit-eracy, and abominable housing are the norm. Although the sta-tistics are in dispute, the situation of the poorest one-quarter or one-third of the population may actually be worsening—a situ-ation exacerbated in certain countries by rapid population in-crease. Certainly the gaps between those who profit from growth and those who do not are widening. A short walk through the poor areas of almost any city in Latin America will reveal the human meaning of these statistics.[12]

Thus the advocates of socioeconomic rights ask, how can persons have human dignity in material conditions such as this? They can only have dignity if they are guaranteed minimum conditions of health, housing, food, and education.

Second, a revolution of rising entitlement in the socioeconomic area is fueled by the argument that socioeconomic rights are necessary for meaningful civil-political rights. This argument, or theory about what produces democratic rights, has never been proved or disproved conclusively. Research on the question continues, and the present author is sceptical,[13] but there is a school of thought which argues that democracy is closely tied to a certain degree of affluence as well as the emergence of a sizable middle class. Whatever the elusive truth on the question of whether certain socioeconomic foundations are necessary for stable democracies (entailing civil and political rights), there is a smaller argument. Some social rights seem to contribute to the kind of world that the law on human rights seeks to produce. The social right to education can be shown to be correlated with a number of values—such as tolerance and desire to limit violence—which seem essential to a stable system of civil-political rights.[14]

Third, the argument is made that socioeconomic rights contribute to peace. Again, social science research has not been spectacularly successful in documenting the exact causes of war, but the belief persists that denial of socioeconomic rights can lead to war. According to Pope John Paul II, speaking at the United Nations, one should link war, structural justice, and socioeconomic rights:

> The universal declaration of human rights has struck a real
> blow against the many deep roots of war since the spirit of war
> in its basic primordial meaning springs up and grows up, grows
> to maturity where the inalienable rights of men are violated.
> This is a new and deeply relevant vision of the cause of peace.
> One that goes deeper and is more radical. It is a vision that sees
> a genesis and in essence the substance of war. . . . The first of
> these systematic threats against human rights is linked in an
> overall sense with the distribution of material goods. This dis-
> tribution is frequently unjust, both within individual societies
> and on the planet as a whole. . . . People must become aware
> that economic tensions within countries and in the relation-
> ships between states and even between entire continents con-
> tain within themselves substantial elements that restrict or
> violate human rights.[15]

These three reasons for supporting socioeconomic rights—namely, that they contribute to human dignity, that they contribute to civil and political rights, and that they contribute to peace—may or may not be true from the scientific viewpoint. But as long as actors in world politics believe them to be true, they are important politically whatever their scientific validity.

Precisely the same arguments are made in behalf of civil-political rights. First it is said that they contribute to human dignity; just as persons require food, housing, health care, and education, so they require freedom and civil justice for a life of dignity.

Second, just as socioeconomic rights are said to be necessary for civil-political rights, so the reverse is argued. In chapter two we noted Professor Eide's general argument to this effect. Precisely the same argument appeared elsewhere, namely that the poor remained poor most fundamentally because they lacked the political rights which led to power which in turn could lead to material improvement:

> Similarly, the official aid agencies' diagnosis is that the poor are poor because they lack certain things—irrigation, credit, better seeds, good roads, etc. But, we ask: *Why* are they lacking these things? We have concluded that the poor are poor because they are prevented from achieving the power to secure these things. The first diagnosis focuses on the material lack; the second focuses on the lack of power. Therein lies the fundamental difference.[16]

Third, civil-political rights were also said to contribute to peace. In addition to Pope John Paul II, this argument has been made in contemporary times by the Russian dissident Andrei Sakharov:

> The most serious defect of a "closed" society is the total lack of democratic control over the upper echelons of the party and government in their conduct of domestic affairs, and foreign policy. The latter is especially dangerous, for here we are talking about the finger poised on the nuclear button. The "closed" nature of our society is intrinsically related to the question of civil and political rights. The human rights issue, therefore, is not simply a moral one, but also a paramount, practical ingredient of international trust and security. This thesis has been

the leitmotif of my public statements over the last several years.[17]

Again we note that the supporting arguments for civil-political rights—as contributing to human dignity, socioeconomic rights, and peace—are important for understanding current human rights developments, whatever their scientific standing.

The intertwined emphasis on socioeconomic and civil-political rights, best reflected in the two 1966 U.N. covenants, gives a tremendously broad scope to the human rights movement. The movement for human rights is really a movement for world reform. Nevertheless, there is the claimed third generation of internationally recognized human rights focusing on solidarity rights to peace, development, humanitarian assistance, and the like. Debate on the third generation of rights aside, it would seem that we have enough rules on human rights in the approximately two dozen treaties extant. What seems needed is more attention to implementing the rules already on the books.

2. It is not wrong to regard official protection efforts as weak, but it is not right to assume that the extensive diplomatic—and limited judicial—action to implement human rights has no impact on states. In evaluating international action for human rights we should recall that most of this action is promotional, or a matter of indirect protection. While some international steps seek direct and immediate impact, most of them seek to educate or socialize states into action in their own jurisdictions.

In chapters 3 and 4 we saw that when human rights action is left to intergovernmental organizations, the control of human rights runs a very high risk of becoming politicized. States vote and act with a high regard for defending their power and perceived national interests, and with a relatively low regard for human rights per se. This is especially true within the U.N. framework. For a time only the few pariahs of world politics became targets for intensive—and not entirely impartial—action. More recent modification of this pattern coexists with continued political bias.[18] We also saw that the independent or uninstructed U.N. bodies were restricted in their activities, with the UNHCR a notable example of independent action within an IGO system. It is true, however, that many specialized U.N. agencies could play a constructive role in implementing socioeconomic rights.[19] We found that the independent regional agencies in Western Europe and the Americas, but not yet in Africa, had been more dynamic in their protection efforts, with the European Human Rights Commission and Court compiling a record of implementation in the civil-political field worthy of imitation.

The difficulty of precise evaluation, and of striking the proper balance between optimism and pessimism, is seen in the example of the activity in the late 1970s of the Inter-American Commission on Human Rights in Argentina. That country probably constituted the worst human rights situation in the Western Hemisphere in the late 1970s.[20] Yet the junta there felt compelled—for whatever reasons—to admit the commission into its territory for "on-site inspection" and the unfettered taking of testimony. Widespread publicity was given to the commission's visit. Critical reports were issued by the commission. The OAS General Assembly eventually voted, 19–2, to condemn Argentina and three other states (Chile, Uruguay, and Paraguay) for violating human rights. According to some observers, some human rights violations were reduced in Argentina.[21] Yet structurally, gross violations of human rights, including torture and political murder, continued until the fall of the junta after the war with Britain in the south Atlantic.

A half-filled glass may be described as half-empty or half-full. The reality of human rights protection, especially by formal international means, is that more diplomacy is being expended than ever before, and with some impact, while at the same time all of that activity is incapable of preventing—or correcting in the short run—the gross violations that have obtained in places like Amin's Uganda, Pol Pot's Kampuchea, and Indonesian-occupied East Timor. Whatever the deficiencies of international formal action in the short term, there is also the cumulative and incremental effect over time—which is especially difficult to analyze precisely at any given point in time.

Unofficial protection efforts were usually cited with some enthusiasm by the optimists. In the Argentine situation of the late 1970s, not only Amnesty International but also the Permanent Assembly for Human Rights and a group called Relatives for Missing Political Prisoners were important sources of information for the Inter-American Commission. We saw in Chapter 4 that these types of unofficial groups were active in almost all regions on a wide variety of issues. One could hardly read the newspapers covering world politics without coming across examples of private pressure to protect human rights. For example, after the broad network of the Presbyterian Church of the United States had contacted congressional circles about human rights violations in Taiwan, a congressional delegation took up the question with Taiwanese authorities. There was no doubt that parts of the Catholic Church were playing important roles in defense of human rights in most of Latin America (a change of immense historical proportions, given the Church's support for the repressive status quo in the past). And a small core of secular human rights groups, such as Amnesty International, had some impact in both international and national political circles.

In the discussion of unofficial protection of human rights, it is important to observe that private banks and corporations were generally *not* as active as churches, unions, and other private groups. This was one reason why certain repressive regimes preferred private loans to those of the World Bank, with its sometime emphasis on meeting the basic needs of the rural poor, and with the U.S. delegation to the Bank mandated by U.S. law to take into account the human rights situation in applicant countries. Even with regard to the International Monetary Fund, whose drawing rights (loans) were sometimes scrutinized by the U.S. Congress for its impact on human dignity, there was some effort to link IMF activity to internationally recognized human rights. While it was true that economic IGOs like the World Bank and the IMF had never fully incorporated human rights concerns into their calculations, applicant countries frequently preferred private bank loans in order to bypass what little concern there was in behalf of human rights and/or human dignity.

That repressive regimes seeking foreign loans preferred private banks operating strictly according to profit motives was clear in Chile in the late 1970s. Private loans and investments flowed into Pinochet's Chile, with the result that the military regime was able to flout the weak and largely symbolic pressures attempted by the Carter administration when Pinochet refused to extradite ex-officials indicted in the United States for political murder.[22] State terrorism and violations of human rights were of no concern to American banks.

Yet there were many more private groups working for human rights around the globe than ever before. Religious and secular, rights-based and ethnicly oriented, global and regional, they made some difference—difficult to calculate precisely—in policy-making in Washington, New York, Geneva, and other political and diplomatic centers. They confronted not only powerful states but also powerful economic interests. A number of American business concerns, for example, opposed U.S. trade sanctions on communist Romania for violating human rights, because their business interests would be adversely affected. Even the factor of communism made no difference, such was the strength of the profit motive. Thus the rights groups faced formidable odds.

3. The United States has taken a number of unilateral steps to try to protect human rights, especially during the Carter administration. But as shown in chapter 5, even the second Reagan administration found that the issue would not go away—and could not be simply collapsed into traditional American concern with Soviet-led communism.

The most general level of debate in the U.S. concerns how human rights relates to other values in U.S. foreign policy. If, like Henry Kissinger, one views world politics as a struggle for domination between revolutionary forces and forces of order, with the revolutionary forces constantly seizing every opportunity to press for more power, then the forces of order will have little alternative but to emphasize their security to the exclusion of other values. If, like Kissinger, one sees Soviet expansionism inherent in tactical decisions by Palestinian guerillas, then there will be little room in U.S. policy for human rights per se. Almost no issue will receive attention other than as part of U.S. resistance to Soviet-led communism. It was not by accident, as we saw, that Kissinger refused to take up the question of human rights with Chile's military government in the 1970s, despite his public posturing otherwise.[23]

On the other hand, if, like Jimmy Carter in his first three years as president, one believes that Soviet-led communism is only one of the problems faced by the United States in world politics, then attention to human rights can have independent status. If one believes that government by extreme conservatives poses a danger to some values equal to that posed by government by extreme communalists, and if one believes that American core security is protected despite certain setbacks to other foreign policy objectives, then one can give almost as much attention to human rights as to any other issue. Hence it was not by accident that Carter initially spoke of moving away from the "inordinate fear" of communism and of not linking every issue in world politics to Soviet-American relations.[24]

The Soviet invasion of Afghanistan in December 1979 brought about a reorientation of U.S. foreign policy. Carter's policies became more in line with previous administrations, despite the fact that the Soviets were to eventually withdraw from Afghanistan in 1989. In retrospect it was clear that the Soviet Union was not interested in expansion via armed force, whether for warm water ports, Middle East oil, or any other reason. Yet the damage had been done by Soviet policies, and the last years of Carter's one term saw a downgrading of the human rights issue in general, although it received continuing attention in some cases.

Until the invasion of Afghanistan and the seizure of U.S. nationals in Tehran as part of revolution in that country, the rhetoric of the Carter team had been boldly supportive of international human rights— including socioeconomic rights. But we also saw that the reality of policy had not measured up to the rhetoric on a number of points. There was no questioning the large number of actual human rights policies authorized and implemented by both Congress and the executive between 1973 and 1980. But there is reason to question whether the U.S. focus on violations of the integrity of the person and other civil-political rights could have been effective in the long run if "business as usual" by the private sector continued as in the past.[25] As long as capitalism, including Latin American state-capitalism, continued to lead to massive socioeconomic deprivation, the deprived would lack socioeconomic rights and would demand greater political rights to change the situation.

This demand for rights had been historically resisted with repression by many elites, especially in the Third World, and with much U.S. support.[26] The Carter administration and Congress had never favored extensive and consistent restrictions on private banking and commercial transactions for reasons of human rights, as demonstrated by the Chilean case among others (and a panel of distinguished citizens recommended precisely that narrow course of action).[27] But analysis showed that relatively pure capitalism in the Third World probably could not duplicate the sharing of benefits obtained in North America; the historical factors were too different.[28] Thus as long as the reality of American policy largely ignored the type of fundamental change in the foreign transactions of the private economic sector required to protect directly socioeconomic rights and indirectly civil-political rights, U.S. rhetoric would be suspect in many quarters. (Somewhat ironically, the Reagan administrations, despite an ideological orientation toward pure capitalism when it came to Nestle and the infant formula controversy at the WHO, saw no difficulty in extensive governmental intervention into the economy when the issue was General Noriega in Panama, the natural gas pipeline between Western Europe and the Soviet Union, or the Sandinistas in Nicaragua.)

The Reagan administrations categorically rejected the entire notion of socioeconomic rights. It also sought to use the human rights issue primarily if not exclusively as a weapon against communist adversaries. Challenged by members of Congress and a number of private
human rights groups, as well as by United Nations bodies and simply
world events, the Reagan team progressively moved toward a more
balanced position about human rights—if only because it found that
human rights violations did not make for stable allies against the Soviet Union. Hence by 1988 the U.S. government under Reagan had intervened against human rights violations in such friendly authoritarian states as South Korea, the Philippines, Paraguay, and more
ambivalently in Haiti and Chile. Naturally it had taken an equally or
more vigorous stand against violations in leftist regimes such as Grenada, Nicaragua, Romania, Democratic Yemen, Angola, and Ethiopia.

By the end of the Reagan era human rights seemed a permanent part
of the U.S. foreign policy agenda, although this was probably less because of international developments and more because of traditional
American versions of morality as manifested through congressional
sentiment. (It was difficult to be precise about how much congressio-

nal action stemmed from international learning and how much from domestic traditions.)[29] Nevertheless, the Reagan team did finally support ratification of the Genocide Treaty, and did make some use of U.N. bodies on human rights, thus setting the stage for perhaps a more cosmopolitan foreign policy by its successor.

4. It was clear by 1988 that the issue of human rights was not a creation of Jimmy Carter and would remain on the political agenda after the demise of his administration. The private, nonprofit, unofficial human rights groups had played a secondary but significant role in Washington in setting the background for the explosion in attention to human rights in the 1970s, and in helping to keep the issue alive in the 1980s when the Reagan first team preferred to emphasize great power rivalries. They had remained active after Carter had left Washington, teaming with interested members of Congress to scrutinize Reagan policies, as demonstrated in chapter 6.

They had first shown the ability between 1973 and 1977 to seize upon a public mood wearied of war and Watergate to push their concerns. Utilizing above all this public mood and the sympathy it evoked among public officials, and overcoming a weak financial and membership base, the nonprofit lobbies found themselves with a new legitimacy to which they added excellent information, leadership, and tactical expertise in order to help place on the books a number of new laws concerning human rights. The groups had also monitored executive performance, although their ability to shape executive decisions seemed not so great as their influence on the congressional side.

During the Carter period they had allies within the Executive branch, but they still seemed to have more clout, relatively speaking, in Congress. They did battle with that administration on a number of issues, as they prodded it toward more attention to rights in competition with strategic and economic interests.

Most of the rights-based groups were highly critical of the Reagan treatment of human rights during his first administration, preferring a more balanced approach to the subject—viz., one less affected by cold war rivalry. The groups figured in a running series of battles over U.S. human rights policy between the administration and Congress. Most importantly, the groups provided interested, and frequently critical, members of Congress with alternative sources of information and expert opinion on a variety of human rights issues. While nonprofit influence was difficult to pinpoint, it was almost surely the case that congressional oversight of Reagan actions functioned better because of group activity than would have been the case had the groups not existed. It is not completely clear that the change in Reagan policies on human rights during his second administration stemmed from Congress and/or the nonprofit lobbying. Yet by 1988 U.S. foreign policy on human rights was more in keeping with what most of the groups wanted than had been the case in 1981.

Most of the private human rights groups had long lobbied for U.S. adherence to most human rights treaties, especially the two U.N. Covenants on socioeconomic and civil-political rights. This objective remained unreached, as did that of having the U.S. adhere to the American Convention on Human Rights. Thus, despite extensive group lobbying on the subject, the U.S. remained in the position of lecturing other countries about their human rights performance while the U.S. itself refused to undertake the obligations to act on human rights as found in international law. This situation brought home the fundamental truth about human rights lobbying: the lobbies could not take U.S. officials where they did not want to go.

5. The global debate about human rights is not entirely new, of course. It is a newly emphasized part of the age-old debate about citizen, government, and international society. This we saw in chapter 7. The U.N. core of human rights instruments reflects some version of equality, and thus conservatism, as a philosophy of unequal rights, has been rejected as an official ideology in world politics. This does not mean that states like Uruguay under military rule, which practiced (a brutal form of) conservatism via preferred rights (and benefits) for the few, did not accept the treaties. Uruguay was (and is) a party to both 1966 covenants. But it was an early focal point of the Human Rights Committee under the Civil-Political Covenant precisely because its practice of rights did not square with the ideology of equal civil-political rights it had promised to uphold.[30]

The promotion of international human rights, through legal standard-setting, in the 1940s and 1950s was led by Western liberals—primarily the classical variety. Differences over the ultimate source of rights, whether in natural law or utilitarianism, did not prevent mention of human rights in the U.N. Charter or emergence of the Universal Declaration. Thus metaphysical debate did not preclude international action. As seen in the contents of the Universal Declaration, there was agreement to emphasize civil and political rights.

Since that time the expanded membership of the U.N. has meant that much rhetoric in that body is based not on liberalism but on some form of communalism in which the professed equality derives not from individual human characteristics per se but rather from the individual's membership in some group—either an economic class or a national people. And we have observed the tendency among Marxists and national community advocates to stress socioeconomic rights, to the extent that they stress rights at all (as compared to benefits awarded for political conformity).

Looking at the complex of major human rights treaties, one would not be entirely wrong in linking them to Nyerere's speeches on combining national and individual freedom with socioeconomic justice. Nor would one be entirely wrong in saying the international human rights documents call for Sweden writ large.[31] The legal instruments, on their face, call for some version of either democratic socialism or extensive state-capitalism. Equal participatory rights are to be combined with equal rights to adequate health, education, and welfare—at least with regards to a minimum threshhold.

One of the major reasons both liberals and communalists find difficulty in implementing these rights internationally is fear of foreign opponents. Traditional (now called by reformers vulgar) Marxists argue that dictatorship, or "democratic centralism," is necessary to fight the reactionary capitalists and imperialists who are trying to undo the gains of the progressive revolution. Liberals usually argue some limits on implementing rights in order to maintain defense against a revolution that would destroy freedom. It is ironic that liberalism and communism both profess ultimate interest in individual human dignity but—to varying degrees—sacrifice that ultimate value to protecting the nation-state and its ruling elite in the short and intermediate run.

Despite the very real philosophical differences which underlie the modern debate over human rights, it is provocative to consider whether Sweden, Yugoslavia, and Senegal might not be, as abstractly described by their ruling elites, an amalgam which represents the closest meaning of the human rights ideology found in the treaties.[32]

Particularly if planet earth continues to exist in an age of scarcity and environmental decay, both the rampant individualism of classical liberalism, particularly as it entails the notion of unregulated economic freedom, and the repressive centralism of totalitarian communism may become irrelevant to future human dignity. Neither the spirit of the American frontier, with its emphasis on private profit and public poverty (e.g., of public services, of the environment), nor the spirit of Leninist oppression will—or can—be generally attractive to the many persons demanding rights to freedom and rights to material minimum standards as called for by human rights instruments. (The freedom that will have to be restricted is not the freedom to participate in the crucial decisions which affect our lives but rather the freedom of economic choice in which the pursuit of private profit damages the collective welfare.)

It is possible that many past differences in the debate over the philosophy of human rights will yield to a new sharing of values in the actual practice of rights. In this regard it was particularly interesting that most of the communist systems as of 1988 were showing an emphasis on individual freedom in the arts, in economic activity, in religion, and even—in an erratic way—in politics, as reflected by elite encouragement of diversity and even dissent.[33] It is very clear historically that even decades of communist authoritarianism have not erased the demand for freedom in parts of Eastern Europe—and even Asia which is not western culturally speaking.

We may arrive at a time when Leninist centralization looks in retrospect like an historical accident imposed by traditional Russian culture rather than "scientific" Marxist necessity. In the meantime it should be recognized that the dictatorship of the proletariat is a communist rationale for those dictators—perhaps like Castro—more interested in maintaining personal privilege than in Marxism as "scientific truth." That is but one reason the struggle to protect civil-political rights will continue for a very long time, for certain communalist ideologies are very comfortable to elites who have no interest in implementing human rights. At the time of writing the situation in many communist and Third World regimes was quite unsettled, with considerable movement toward both personal and property rights.

On the other side of the same coin, it is even more clear historically that the experience of the capitalistic West has been to move toward more public regulation of socioeconomic matters and away from unfettered economic activity.[34] All liberal states are now committed to some version of public responsibility for, and management of, socioeconomic matters. And all liberal states save the United States officially accept the idea of socioeconomic rights. Only the true conservatives, in places like Paraguay, remain apart (and even there one sees growing demand for liberal change). Thus an international consensus on practicing socioeconomic rights exists already to some extent. What the debate is about frequently is not socioeconomic rights per se. After all, even the Reagan administration and the Thatcher government maintained a minimum welfare state (although the former regime refused to acknowledge economic rights). The debate, rather, was mostly about the size of the welfare state, and what rights the nation could afford (be those rights called economic or civil).[35]

FINAL THOUGHTS

One should not underestimate the importance of internationally recognized human rights. However visionary and apparently utopian they may seem, and however much international action may seek only indirect protection with national action remaining primary, the human rights treaties and resolutions give every indication of exerting influence *over time* in world politics. There will be, no doubt, waxing and waning of impact depending on personalities and crises. It does make a difference who exactly is U.S. President or First Secretary of the Communist Party of the Soviet Union, for example. Strategic nuclear war would obliterate, among other things, most of the concerns treated in this book. But short of this latter catastrophe, human rights is likely to remain a subject of fundamental political importance. This is so for three basic reasons.

First, we noted that true respect for human rights implies a new way of life. The political significance of this truth can be formulated in two ways. Either one can say that protection of human rights now constitutes a new source of legitimacy for a regime.[36] Or one can say that we are now required to manage the issue of human rights as a way of managing system change in the world political system.[37]

In the first formulation, human rights becomes a new standard for evaluating a government's right to rule. It is a standard overarching traditional ideologies. In the long run it tends to replace debates—and wars—over communism versus capitalism, nationalism versus colonialism, forces of order versus forces of revolution, Islam versus the Satanic infidels. The human rights instruments become guidelines for evaluating the impact of all regimes on their peoples regardless of ideological label. As such, human rights standards bypass much sterile argument which in the past has encouraged governments to rationalize all sorts of injustices to their nationals in the name of some "higher" ideological goal. It is increasingly a political fact that a regime which tortures its people will not be regarded as still having the right to rule, whether that standard be applied to the Shah of Iran, Idi Amin of Uganda, or Anastasio Somoza of Nicaragua.

In the second formulation, human rights standards become a way of managing system change from a traditional nation-state system of world politics based on the principle of national sovereignty to a system of world politics based on humanitarian values as supervised by international organizations. In the traditional nation-state system a government had the right to do as it pleased within its jurisdiction. In the emerging global political system a government must adhere to internationally adopted values even in its area of national jurisdiction. Hence human rights standards become a main bridge for moving from one type of political system to another.[38]

In sum, our first reason for the continuing importance of human rights is that it signifies a major effort at defining new standards of legitimacy and hence a new push for systematic change in world politics. The law is on the books now. It would be embarrassing for anyone to come out and overtly say that the law should be repealed—that one is against human rights. While some may wish to ignore the law or interpret it in a self-serving way, many others will oppose. The subject will remain.

Second, human rights will not quietly fade away as an issue in world politics because a number of political actors are convinced that a government's security is linked to protection of human rights. This will be an increasingly demonstrable truth to the extent that the first point above is also accepted. That is to say, if legitimacy depends increasingly on protecting human rights, then a government that denies human rights calls into question its own security by subjecting itself to international pressures. But beyond this, a government that in practice denies human rights undermines its own security from within. Similarly, a foreign policy that seeks security but ignores human rights is destined for difficulties.

One can demonstrate this second point by reference to recent policies of either of the two superpowers. While the U.S. government was remarkably secure at home, in some degree due to its commitment to political rights and a distribution of material benefits seen by most of its people as tolerably fair, its foreign policy periodically defined national security largely in terms of military might.[39] U.S. foreign policy encountered a number of difficulties precisely because it aligned the United States with regimes insensitive to, or ineffective in dealing with, matters of rights and justice.

The culmination of the American effort to contain communism in South Vietnam was a collapse from within that alleged nation caused by the failure of southern authorities to respond to the needs and wants of the people. The culmination of the American effort to lean on the Shah of Iran as the anticommunist policeman of the Persian Gulf area was a collapse from within brought on by the Shah's failure to respond to the religious, social, and political aspirations of important segments of that nation. The culmination of the American effort to

By permission of Johnny Hart and Field Enterprises, Inc.

lean on Greater Pakistan in the early 1970s was a collapse from within engendered by brutal repression, if not genocide, in East Pakistan, which in turn led to the creation of Bangladesh. And the U.S. had great difficulty in trying to stamp out rebellion in El Salvador, given the long history of rights violations in that country.

The same problem reappeared in the 1980s for the United States. Why was it so difficult to rely on Pakistan to stop any Soviet movement to the south of Afghanistan through the Pakistani province of Baluchistan? Consider this description of the situation in the *New York Times:*

> Tribal and political leaders here believe the Kremlin's move on Kabul has forced Pakistan's military rulers to pay serious attention to their now-strategic province, in the western part of the country. The moderates among them hope for enough political respect and developmental aid to assuage the hatred toward the central government that has been allowed to fester over decades of social neglect, economic exploitation and political repression.[40]

In other words, denial of human rights in Baluchistan made Pakistan internally insecure and thus a weak reed for the United States to lean upon.

Modern U.S. foreign policy had in effect taken a wartime necessity and transformed it into an everyday pattern. Faced with a clearly expansionist Nazi Germany which committed some of the worst atrocities known in history, the United States formed alliances with the likes of Stalin's Russia and Salazar's Portugal. The United States continued this practice after the war, ignoring in effect the advice of George Kennan and others that containment of communism was

bound to fail if that strategy were only a geo-military device devoid of positive appeal. Outside of democratic Europe and a few other democratic places, the United States sought military cooperation with conservative regimes but did not seek consistently and effectively the socioeconomic and civil-political changes that would have made those regimes, in places like Iran and Pakistan, internally secure as well as powerful toward foreigners.

Predictable problems arose in the Philippines, South Korea, and Haiti, along with El Salvador and Nicaragua, for the same reasons. Domestic elites ruled without attention to human rights, and the U.S. aligned itself with those elites in the mistaken notion that U.S. security would be so enhanced.

There is no denying that commitment to human rights can prove politically disabling in the short and intermediate run. Freedom, where education and consensus are lacking, can lead to disorder. Some social welfare can lead to unrealistic demands for much more too soon. But the alternative, tried in places like South Vietnam and Iran, is to deny significant human rights at the expense of long-range security, stability, and power. Architects of American policy like Henry Kissinger stress the short run problems of controlling change, but they ignore the long-run problems of trying to build a geopolitical order on state power while ignoring deprivation and repression within nations.[41] In effect, they ignore the effect of keeping a tight lid on a boiling pot, which is the same as ignoring the old adage that you can do a lot of things with bayonets, but you cannot sit on them.

Without denying the reality that the United States and other liberal states will make alliances with conservative regimes, one can ask the liberals to define national security interests broadly enough to include movement toward more human rights, for such a policy, although troublesome in the short run, can help to create the most solid building block of world order—a powerful *and progressive* state. Former Senator John Culver of Iowa, a member of the Senate Armed Services Committee, articulated this view concisely with regard to American power and security: "Security is more than just your military budget. It is the health of the economy, the well-being and welfare of the people, their morale. . . . An army of 7.5 million unemployed doesn't really scare the Russians. Clearly any nation state, to maintain a strong security position, does require both guns and butter. But the mix is what is crucial."[42]

As for the Soviet Union, it is clear that in many ways the Soviet denial of civil-political rights at home and in its satellite states constitutes a weakness rather than a strength. In attempts to project its power, the Kremlin has to be constantly concerned about restless minorities, religious groups, and dissidents at home. It has to be equally concerned about the reliability of its Warsaw Pact allies, who chafe under Soviet restrictions. Even the reliability of individual Soviet soldiers may be at issue, when they are Muslim and sent to conquer a Muslim people, or when they are Muscovite and have not been told the truth about what they are ordered to do and why.

In sum of our second point, a persuasive case can be made that in the long run a commitment to human rights is compatible with—even necessary for—governmental security. However much the United States may find it desirable to enter an arrangement in the short run with an authoritarian and exploitative Marcos government in the Philippines, it will meet difficulties in the long run; and the ultimate success of its foreign policy probably depends on its careful attention to human rights. A number of politically important actors know this. The subject of human rights will remain.

The third reason why human rights will remain an important subject in world politics is that certain people and private groups demand attention to their needs and aspirations. In their perspective human rights should be pursued not because they are necessary to the security of a governing elite and not because the U.N. Human Rights Committee should gain more authority at the expense of states, but because human rights are necessary for a life with human dignity.

Has the unregulated nation-state system led to horribly destructive wars? Has the principle of national sovereignty allowed Idi Amin and Pol Pot to engage in mass political murder and genocide? Do the "laws of the market" seem to operate internationally so that trade and investment by private corporations in much of the Third World do not benefit the masses in those countries? Does the advance of technology seem to give repressive governments even more control over their people for the benefit of the ruling elite? Does the introduction of more science and technology lead to more—but more unemployed—people gravitating to the cities of the world, where their frustrations are magnified by their being uprooted from their traditional life-styles?

Is there not a global demand for an improvement in the way people live and governments govern? Did not Robert Heilbroner identify a widespread "malaise" in the form of disenchantment with modern industrial and technocratic life, whether capitalistic or socialistic,[43] a psychological sickness only temporarily assuaged by appeals to historic nationalism whether in mother Russia or Reagan's United States?

For many people there are forces at work in the modern world which are profoundly disturbing. They are forces which exploit, dehumanize, and crush the opportunity and even the will to live, to develop, to make a better environment for one's children. For these people, whether dissidents in the Soviet Union, members of Solidarity in Poland, readers of "democracy" wall in China, guerrilla fighters in Namibia, opposition forces in El Salvador, or critics of unregulated capitalism in the West, human rights is an important subject. For these and others, human rights is a subject which reminds us of humanitarian values—principally, that forces and situations and developments should be evaluated on the basis of their impact on the person rather than on the basis of profit or privilege. These humanitarian standards can have a religious or secular underpinning; to endorse human rights it is not necessary to delve into the religion-versus-secular humanism debate. The overriding point is that for many people the demand for human rights is a counterpoint to the disaffections with modern life. The subject will remain.

While the subject of human rights will remain an important part of world politics for these three reasons—namely, it is an established standard of legitimacy and change, a source of governmental security, and an appealing standard for people sensitive to humanitarian values—the crucial questions about the future of human rights center on precise interpretation and effective implementation. But interpretation cannot be made precise and implementation cannot be made effective until there are improved guidelines about what is and is not acceptable. Only then will the gap between "what is" and "what ought to be" become narrowed. To borrow from the language of regime theory, the human rights norms must be translated into rules; then there can be interpretation and application.

The highest priority in protecting human rights should be the subject of assessing human rights violations.[44] This requires two related steps—the first instrumental for the second. The first step is to strengthen independent human rights agencies whether public or private. This entails increased funding and other support for such agencies. The private human rights NGOs, for example, should be supported in their struggle to gain unfettered access to international organizations where debates on human rights occur. Those states which prevent U.N. consultative status for such groups as the International League for Human Rights should be pressured to change their policies. Likewise, efforts to curtail independent public agencies, such as the U.N. Human Rights Subcommission, should be resisted.

Relatedly, the effort should be resumed to create a U.S. Human Rights Institute for the objective compilation of human rights information. William F. Buckley, Jr., among others, has supported the idea of what would be, in effect, a public corporation to disseminate human rights information.[45] The advance of human rights is largely dependent upon acceptance of an idea.[46] Efforts to promote acceptance of human rights as a ruling ideology should be encouraged. Such a U.S. Human Rights Institute could take over some of the summary reporting functions of the State Department's Human Rights Bureau (although the HA Bureau would still contribute to the annual summary reports and would be responsible for more specific reporting to Congress so as not to lose the socialization effect from reporting). In the late 1970s such an independent body, similar to the U.S. Civil Rights Commission, was almost funded by the Congress. If finally established, its role would be to add to the public knowledge about human rights in the hopes that this would generate in and of itself pressure on the U.S. government, among others, to protect human rights when possible. It should also lay before the policy-making branches arguments about desired priorities in U.S. human rights policy abroad.

A second needed step, following from the first, is to move toward a better understanding of appropriate standards of violations concerning human rights. The lead could be taken by the NGOs and independent public agencies, but eventually any consensus on standards would have to entail intergovernmental international organizations. There cannot be a neat and orderly process in this regard. Standards will emerge over time through the give-and-take of the formal political process as well as through the arguments of churches and other NGOs. This disorganized and pluralistic process can be seen at work in the development of the global consensus identifying apartheid as a gross violation of internationally recognized human rights. Reports by various NGOs as well as resolutions by the U.N. General Assembly and the Organization of African Unity contributed to that overwhelming consensus, as did books by private authors such as Donald Woods.[47]

Most probably what would expedite a better understanding of real human rights violations would be studies of the subject by the NGOs. This could be the start of a general debate about human rights violations that might affect governmental and IGO public policy. We have mentioned already the Overseas Development Council and its Physical Quality of Life Index, an index which was reprinted in one State Department report on human violations abroad and published by the Congress.[48] If more NGOs would give more time to the tough question of defining violations in relation to legal language, that could be the beginning of an important shift in the public's awareness and mood—especially in open societies.

For example, data exist concerning governmental spending per capita on the military compared to health and education. Taking this data, one could establish, say, a Latin American or Black African median for spending in each category. One could then establish a median ratio between median military spending and the other two categories. A state in the region which fell below this ratio would be under an obligation to show why its spending for health and education was so low. A government not recently facing civil war or foreign attack would be under a special obligation to justify its spending priorities in the light of the requirements of the socioeconomic covenant. The new expert committee under ECOSOC, which reviews state reports under that covenant, could eventually use NGO data to press the offending state. Such a process would center on the effort to compel a state to rationalize and justify its policies before an international body of control, with NGO data ultimately used to embarrass a target state. This process, not dissimilar to what is already extant in embryonic form, is more feasible than court judgments requiring supranational authority.

To further illustrate this point, one could take Latin American data on military and health expenditures per capita published by the United Nations. One could then compare these data with the U.N. Covenant on Economic, Social, and Cultural Rights, say, Article 12:

1. The States Parties to the present Covenant recognize the right of everyone to the enjoyment of the highest attainable standard of physical and mental health.
2. The steps to be taken by the States Parties to the present Covenant to achieve the full realization of this right shall include those necessary for: . . .
   (d) The creation of conditions which would assure to all medical service and medical attention in the event of sickness.

The Latin American data indicate the following, selected from information on twenty-four Latin countries (including Cuba):

TABLE 9
Median Spending per Capita

	Military	Health	Ratio
Region	$21	$24	1.1
Argentina	55	11	−5.0
Bolivia	18	8	−2.3
Chile	73	34	−2.2
Ecuador	22	9	−2.4
El Salvador	13	9	−1.4
Paraguay	13	3	−4.4
Peru	33	6	−5.5
United States	499	341	−1.2
Canada	174	469	1.8

Thus certain states stand out as making very little effort to manage resources in order to meet the broad objectives of Article 12. This broad-gauge first step directs attention especially to Argentina when under military rule, and Paraguay. These two states in particular, one a historical example and the other a contemporary one, have been internally stable by any reasonable standard, and especially by Latin standards. (Argentina did manifest some terrorism during the 1970s, but not to the extent claimed by military authorities.) Neither had fought an international armed conflict of any size for decades. (The Argentine junta engaged in armed conflict with Britian *after* its seizure of power, not before.) Moreover, only Bolivia among Latin states has a lower Physical Quality of Life as measured on the ODC index. Hence this approach is useful for helping to identify certain states which can then become the focal point of more specific questions about health policies—such as what emphasis is given to rural health clinics, or whether there are medical services to Indian and other minority groups. (Peru's low ranking should be discussed in the context of domestic rebellion by the brutal Shining Path group.)

It might be recalled at this point that much national law is being written so as to require a public authority to justify its policies. That is, the law is broadly permissive, but those covered by the law must explain their actions under the law. For example, the Congress may permit the executive to provide military assistance to El Salvador if the executive explains in writing to the Congress why it believes the government there is correcting violations of human rights. Or the Congress may permit the continuation of U.S. economic assistance if the executive declares in writing that such assistance benefits needy people or is otherwise in the U.S. national interest. If the executive gives an unpersuasive justification, the Congress can ask for further information, demand that executive officials appear before congressional committees, write a tougher law, or exercise the power of the purse. While this process has not worked in a way satisfactory to many advocates of human rights in the U.S., it seems to generate some pressure in behalf of human rights.[49]

Especially under the social and economic covenant one can pursue this line of questioning according to numerous indices. Another fruitful approach is to look at the distribution of wealth intranationally. Particularly in those countries where food and nutrition, or health services, are made available in the private sector under principles of capitalism, it is important to inquire into the buying power of various parts of the population. If private stores and private medicine respond basically to the "laws" of supply and demand, adequate service hinges on effective demand—that is, demand backed by money. Again using United Nations statistics, one can target certain countries for follow-up questions about whether the state is indeed meeting its obligations, under Articles 2 and 11 of the socioeconomic covenant, to "take steps . . . to the maximum of its available resources" to make its citizens "free from hunger."

TABLE 10
Percentage Distribution of Income (figures derived from the late 1960s)

State	Bottom 40%	Middle 40%	Top 40%
India	11	24	65
Mexico	10	30	60
Sweden	13	41	47
United States	17	41	42

There is no avoiding specific questions which deal with a particular context. It may be that certain states have specific policies to compensate for the inequities apparently shown by income distribution figures. No doubt the Swedish welfare-state provides a number of services to those unable to buy needed food or medical care. The question then becomes, Does India (or Mexico) have similar services, in proportion to its gross national product or number of trained physicians or some other indicator of state capability? It is important to use relative, realistic, and reasonable standards for judgments rather than absolute and abstract values. But ultimately a comparative judgment can be made.

Under the Civil and Political Covenant the questions perhaps do not permit the use of such statistical guidelines, yet certain steps toward general standards can be made. The International Commission of Jurists has done so on the basis of its African meetings and reports of human rights in one-party states. The point here is that the commission tried to clarify that there could be protection of many civil and political rights even if one accepted the argument that African culture tended to produce something other than the two-party or multi-party systems found in Western culture.[50]

One of the very desirable things that might result from the development of the indices talked about here is the avoidance of blanket judgments against a regime because of its ideology. Once one recognizes that there are socioeconomic rights, that Kadaffi's Libya has done a great deal for the material welfare of the average Libyan, or that Cuba has spent more on literacy campaigns than most Latin governments, one is forced to acknowledge certain improvements in human dignity. At the same time, to the extent that Kadaffi arranges the assassination of political opponents, or Castro engages in torture and/or mistreatment of political prisoners, those policies remain unacceptable by international standards whatever the other progressive policies. But the debate centers on specific policies rather than over political ideologies.[51]

Implicit in all these final pages is the idea that states—by which we mean political elites, those who make decisions in the name of the state—can engage in political learning, meaning that they can adapt their policies to human rights standards and are not frozen into policies by culture or economic condition.[52] This idea runs counter to the notion that states are the fixed and finalized product of their culture; it has been argued that advocacy of human rights stems from Western culture and will be limited largely to Western states. (This argument overlooks the fact that some Western states like Spain and Portugal were not receptive to most human rights until very recently.) Similarly, it has been argued that Third World states in particular are dependent on a global economic market; they are supposedly locked into repressive and oppressive policies by this condition of dependency.

Space does not permit a full exposition of the possibility of political change according to human rights standards. A historical cultural tradition exerts a powerful pull on contemporary elites; they are not completely free to institute policies at whim. It is certainly relevant to note that Russia, even prior to 1917, never successfully sustained democratic forms of government. Yet there are numerous countries which have managed to implement civil and political rights despite a cultural history with ample authoritarian periods: India, Botswana, Senegal, Venezuela, Costa Rica, Lebanon, Thailand, Malaysia, etc. And while economic factors are also relevant to the fate of human rights, there are numerous countries that have provided socioeconomic rights, or growth with equity, despite considerable poverty: Sri Lanka, South Korea, Taiwan, and others. Particular examples from the contemporary experiences of Yugoslavia, Hungary, Czechoslovakia, and Poland show that various rights can be implemented when national policies are allowed to evolve of their own dynamics. The three years, at the time of writing, of the Gorbachev era in the Soviet Union indicate that striking changes can occur if and when the political elite desires new policies.

It seems that a very strong case can be made that states of whatever culture and economic condition can implement many of the internationally recognized human rights if the political culture of the national people is supportive of the basic idea of human rights. This may mean, depending on particulars, that an elite can lead a people, or that a people may have to wrest recognition of rights from an elite. Some national political cultures are certainly more supportive of rights than others (compare Poland with the Soviet Union, or many Latin countries with Arab-Islamic ones). The basic argument remains that change can occur over time, under stimulus of international action, although national variations of a cultural or economic nature are important.

Thus the struggle for the advancement of human rights can be justified, although such a struggle is certainly not without its frustrations. Some persons, such as Jerome J. Shestack, who is active in several human rights groups and causes, has drawn an interesting parallel. There is much about working to protect human rights in an imperfect world that seems absurd, but Sisyphus—condemned by the gods to forever push a boulder uphill—may be more of an example here than the strong men of history. According to Shestack:

> Still, Sisyphus may turn out to be a more enduring hero than Hercules. For if, as Camus taught, life itself is absurd, Sisyphus represents the only triumph possible over that absurdity. In his constancy to reach that summit, even with failure preordained, Sisyphus demonstrated that the human spirit is indomitable and that dedication to a higher goal is in itself man's reason for living. So, like Sisyphus, the non-governmental organizations do what they must. The realities of the world may foredoom a great part of the struggle to failure and make most of the effort seem abysmal. Yet, the very struggle itself takes on symbolic meaning, enhancing human dignity. And when all is said and done, there is no other humane course to pursue.[53]

As long as people and organizations exist—and their number is growing—who think that life can be made less absurd by implementing the international law of human rights, they will continue to have some effect. The struggle may indeed be never ending, for the law would transform an imperfect world into a perfect place. Thus the law may remain for some time more an educational tool than an immediately effective directive. The law may serve basically as a background condition against which national debates take place. But little by little one can trace not only the growth of an idea but also the beginnings of its implementation in actuality. The growing number of states adhering to the International Bill of Human Rights; the creation of new committees, commissions, and agencies; the Peña case holding torture to be barred everywhere by customary international law; the defeat of Ernest Lefever and his distortion of human rights in the name of ideological preference; the continued demand for self-determination and human dignity in places like Namibia and South Africa; the continued attacks on communist and capitalist and Islamic repression—all indicate efforts to implement the basic idea inherent in the international law of human rights: public authority and private transactions should exist to enhance the dignity of persons, not exploit them. Human rights is a powerful means to this end.

Notes

1. Vladimir Bukovsky, *To Build a Castle: My Life as a Dissenter* (London: André Deutsch, 1978), p. 187.
2. Ibid., p. 230.

1. For an overview of the origins of the idea of national sovereignty tracing its roots to Roman and papal times, see Alan James, *Sovereign Statehood: The Basis of International Society* (Boston: Allen and Unwin, 1986).
2. Statements and actions by the Carter administration are examined in detail in chapter 5. On the subject of animal rights in international diplomacy, see the *International Herald Tribune*, 14–15 October 1978, p. 2. The U.S. funding of studies on livestock rights was reported by the Associated Press in August 1981. For a serious argument that human rights should be defined broadly to include what surrounds humans, see W. Paul Gormley, *Human Rights and Environment: The Need for International Cooperation* (Leyden: A. W. Sijthoff, 1976).
3. The statement by Henry Kissinger is quoted in David P. Forsythe, *Humanitarian Politics: The International Committee of the Red Cross* (Baltimore: The Johns Hopkins University Press, 1977), pp. 279–80. For the views of Ernest Lefever, see not only the 1981 Senate hearings on his nomination but also his earlier book, *Ethics and United States Foreign Policy*, 8th ed. (Cleveland: World Publishing Company, 1967). That Richard Nixon can discuss world politics and not stress human rights is made clear in his *The Real War* (New York: Warner Books, 1980). Professor Hans Morgenthau has presented his views in many works, but perhaps the most important on ethics is *Scientific Man and Power Politics* (Chicago: University of Chicago Press, 1946), where he argues that it is morally courageous for the statesman to undertake an evil act.

4. Richard P. Claude, "The Case of Joelito Filartiga," *Human Rights Quarterly* 5, no. 3 (August 1983): 275–301.

5. Concerning an intermediate case between Filartiga and Suarez-Mason which appeared to put a brake on human rights protection, see "Agora: What Does Tel-Oren Tell Lawyers?," *American Journal of International Law* 79, no. 1 (January 1985): 92–114. For an early and brief synopsis of *Suarez-Mason* see *Human Rights Internet Reporter* 12, no. 3 (Spring, 1988).

6. Ronald Dworkin, *Taking Rights Seriously* (Cambridge, Ma: Harvard University Press, 1977).

7. Jack Donnelly, "Human Rights and Human Dignity," *American Political Science Review* 76, no. 2 (June 1982): 433–49.

8. Burns Weston, *Encyclopedia Britannica* (London: Encyclopedia Britannica, 1985), 15th ed., p. 713. Reprinted in the *Human Rights Quarterly* 6, no. 3 (August 1984): 257–83.

9. Jack Donnelly, "International Human Rights: A Regime Approach," *International Organization* 40, no. 3 (Summer 1986): 599–642.

10. R. J. Vincent, *Human Rights and International Relations* (Cambridge: Cambridge University Press, 1986), p. 151.

11. See, among others, Inis L. Claude, *National Minorities: An International Problem* (New York: Greenwood, 1969).

12. See Louis Sohn and Thomas Buergenthal, *International Protection of Human Rights* (New York: Bobbs-Merrill, 1973).

13. There are two primary sources of international law: treaties and customary law. It is theoretically possible for a U.N. recommendation to become part of customary law over time and when repeatedly endorsed without significant opposition. We know for sure when something that is simply diplomatic becomes legally binding only when a court tells us so. Slightly short of this process is the process in which a U.N. recommendation does not become law directly itself, but becomes an accepted guide to the meaning or requirements of law.

On the important subject of the legal status of the 1948 Universal Declaration see further John P. Humphrey (former director of the U.N. Division of Human Rights), "The International Bill of Human Rights: Scope and Implementation," *William and Mary Law Review* 17, no. 3 (Spring 1976): 527–42. Note p. 529 and especially p. 540: "Because the Universal Declaration of Human Rights is now part of the customary law of nations. . . ."

But for the important *Peña* case (referred to in note 4) based on customary international law, which says that the 1948 declaration is one guide to law, see the *American Journal of International Law* 75, no. 1 (January 1981): 49–53. Note especially the other scholarly literature on the status of the declaration cited by the U.S. court.

14. See further Vernon Van Dyke, *Human Rights, the United States, and World Community* (New York: Oxford University Press, 1970), pp. 58–59. On the "positive" actions to implement "negative" rights see especially Henry Shue, *Basic Rights* (Princeton: Princeton University Press, 1980), chap. 2, and particularly note 8.

15. Jack Donnelly, *Universal Human Rights: Interdisciplinary Essays on Theory and Practice*, forthcoming.

16. Quoted in Margaret E. Galey, "The Implications of Science and Technology," Paper presented at the 18th annual meeting of the International Studies Association, March 1977, mimeographed.

17. A. Glenn Mower, Jr., *International Cooperation for Social Justice: Global and Regional Protection of Economic/Social Rights* (Westport, Conn.: Greenwood Press, 1985), pp. 17–18.

18. "Human Rights in the World Community," *Report*, Subcommittee on Foreign Affairs, House, 93d Cong., 2d sess., 27 March 1974 (Washington: Government Printing Office, 1974).

19. U.N. Centre for Human Rights, *Human Rights: Status of International Instruments* (New York and Geneva: the U.N., 1987).

20. A multilateral treaty can also be called a charter, a convention, or a covenant. A protocol is an additional treaty. States may sign and ratify, accede to, or declare acceptance of a treaty. A state may adhere to a treaty in one of these ways, but reserve against one or more treaty provisions, unless prohibited by the treaty.

21. Theo van Boven, "Human Rights and Development: The U.N. Experience," in David P. Forsythe, ed., *Human Rights and Development: International Views* (London: Macmillan Press Ltd., 1989). Van Boven was a Director of the U.N. Centre on Human Rights.

22. The subject of legal regulation of internal war is important both because of the prevalence of this form of conflict in the last quarter of the twentieth century and because such current regulation lays a basis for improved human rights in the future. See David P. Forsythe, "Legal Regulation of Internal War," *American Journal of International Law* 72, no. 2 (April 1978): 272–95.

23. "Agora: The U.S. Decision Not to Ratify Protocol 1 to the Geneva Conventions on the Protection of War Victims," *American Journal of International Law* 81, no. 4 (October 1987): 910–25.

24. On the subject of European political culture as it relates to human rights, see especially Stephen F. Szabo, "Contemporary French Orientations toward Economic and Political Dimensions of Human Rights," *Universal Human Rights* 1, no. 3 (July–September 1979): 61–76; and his "Social Perspectives and Support for Human Rights in West Germany," in ibid., no. 2 (March 1979).

25. See Richard Gittleman, "The Banjul Charter on Human and People's Rights," in Claude E. Welch, Jr. and Ronald I. Meltzer, eds., *Human Rights and Development in Africa* (Albany, NY: SUNY Press, 1984).

CHAPTER TWO

1. Ivo Duchacek, *Rights and Liberties in the World Today* (Santa Barbara, Calif.: ABC-Clio, 1973), p. 9.

2. Wolfgang Friedmann, *Law in a Changing Society* (Baltimore: Penguin Books, 1964).

3. Lyndon Johnson, quoted in Vernon Van Dyke, *Human Rights, The United States, and World Community* (New York: Oxford University Press, 1970), p. 62.

4. Bertram Gross, "Economic Rights in the United States," paper presented to the International Political Science Association, Washington World Congress, August 28–September 1, 1988, mimeographed.

5. George Kennan, *Cloud of Danger* (London: Hutchinson, 1978), p. 44. It should be noted that Kennan is speaking of promoting democracy rather than human rights per se, and he would approve of some representation to the Soviet government concerning human rights (see pp. 216–18).

6. Joshua Muravchik, *The Uncertain Crusade: Jimmy Carter and the Dilemmas of Human Rights Policy* (Lantham, MD: Hamilton Press, 1986).

7. "The question whether a certain matter is or is not solely with the jurisdiction of a State is an essentially relative question; it depends upon the development of international relations. . . . [J]urisdiction which, in principle, belongs solely to the State, is limited by rules of international law. . . ." Permanent Court of International Justice, *Nationality Decrees in Tunis and Morocco*, PCIJ, Ser. B, No. 4; 1 Hudson, World Court Reports, 143, 1923.

8. On the goal of enforcement of international human rights by impartial tribunal see Louis Henkin, *The Rights of Man Today* (Boulder: Westview Press, 1978).

9. Ernst B. Haas, "Dilemmas of Protecting Human Rights Abroad: Global Constraints and the Carter Administration," mimeographed (1978), p. 24. A revised version of this unpublished paper was published as "Human Rights: To Act or Not to Act?," in Kenneth A. Oye, et al., *Eagle Entangled: U.S. Foreign Policy in a Complex World* (New York and London: Longman, 1979). Still another version of the paper was published as *Global Evangelism Rides Again: How to Protect Human Rights without Really Trying*, Policy Papers in International Affairs no. 5 (Berkeley, Calif.: Institute of International Studies, University of California, 1978).

10. One of the best legal compendia is Louis Sohn and Thomas

Buergenthal, *International Protection of Human Rights* (New York: Bobbs-Merrill, 1973). One of the best discussions of the abstract logic of the norms is Van Dyke's in *Human Rights*.

11. This view is analyzed in Kenneth Waltz, *Man, the State, and War* (New York: Columbia University Press, 1959).

12. Franklin Delano Roosevelt, quoted in Van Dyke, *Human Rights*, p. 41.

13. George Marshall, quoted in Van Dyke, *Human Rights*, p. 155. Marshall also refers to natural rights.

14. Jimmy Carter, Inaugural Address, 1977.

15. Stanley Hoffmann, "The Hell of Good Intentions," *Foreign Policy* 29 (Winter 1977–78): 5.

16. Michael W. Doyle, "Liberalism and World Politics," *American Political Science Review* 80, no. 4 (December 1986): 1151–70.

17. See Stanley Hoffmann, *Duties beyond Borders* (Syracuse: Syracuse University Press, 1981), especially pp. 111, 114.

18. See further Richard B. Lillich, ed., *Humanitarian Intervention and the United Nations* (Charlottesville: University of Virginia Press, 1973).

19. "The United States Action in Grenada," *American Journal of International Law* 78, no. 1 (January 1984): 131–200; and Lloyd N. Cutler, "The Right to Intervene," *Foreign Affairs* 64, no. 1 (Fall 1985): 96–112.

20. Given the strength of nationalism and the cost of military action, purely humanitarian intervention, like the U.S. raid to free the hostages in Iran, is likely to remain rare, as the example of starvation in Kampuchea shows. There, virtually all states were maneuvering politically rather than acting simply on the basis of humanitarian need.

21. See Michla Pomerance, "The United States and Self-Determination," *American Journal of International Law* 70, no. 1 (January 1976): 1–27.

22. 1970 Declaration on Principles of International Law concerning Friendly Relations and Cooperation among States in Accordance with the Charter of the United Nations.

23. The Security Council has made only two other binding decisions: one ordering a cease-fire in the Middle East war of 1948, and one ordering an arms embargo against South Africa in 1977. Two of the three decisions concern human rights—Rhodesia and South Africa.

24. David P. Forsythe, "The 1974 Geneva Diplomatic Conference on Humanitarian Law: Some Observations," *American Journal of International Law* 69, no. 1 (January 1975): 77–91.

25. Namibia is a territory declared independent by the U.N. General Assembly but ruled by South Africa. See further Elna Schoeman, *Namibia—An International Issue, 1920–1977* (Braamfontein: South African Institute of International Affairs, 1978).

26. Akram Chowdhury, "The Chittagong Hill Tract Peoples and Self-Determination," in Forsythe, ed., *Human Rights and Development.*

27. Hoffmann, "The Hell of Good Intentions," p. 8.

28. See chapter one at about note 8.

29. See Louis Henkin, "The United Nations and Human Rights," *International Organization* 19, no. 3 (Summer 1965): 504–17.

30. Asborn Eide, *Human Rights in the World Society* (NOU, 1977), no. 23, p. 24. There is a misprint in the original, corrected here.

31. Ibid., p. 62.

32. Van Dyke uses the distinction between assuring a right and taking steps to fulfill a right to good advantage, *Human Rights,* p. 107.

33. Newsletter, Human Rights Internet, March 1978, p. 11.

34. Donnelly, *Universal Human Rights.*

35. Henry Shue, *Basic Rights: Subsistence, Affluence, and U.S. Foreign Policy* (Princeton: Princeton University Press, 1980).

36. Richard P. Claude, *Comparative Human Rights* (Baltimore: The Johns Hopkins University Press, 1976), p. 40. And Theodor Meron, "On a Hierarchy of International Human Rights," *American Journal of International Law* 80, no. 1 (January 1986): 1–24.

37. Eide, *Human Rights in the World Society,* pp. 23–29, p. 29.

38. Ibid., p. 28.

39. See further David P. Forsythe and Laurie Wiseberg, "A Research Agenda on Human Rights Protection," *Universal Human Rights* 1, no. 4 (Fall 1979): 1–25.

40. See further Claude, *Comparative Human Rights.*

41. See Duchacek, *Rights and Liberties,* p. 118.

42. Hoffmann, *Duties beyond Borders,* p. 133.

43. See Duchacek, *Rights and Liberties.* For the same point in international context, see Myers S. McDougal and Florentino P. Feliciano, *Law and Minimum World Public Order: The Legal Regulation of International Coercion* (New Haven: Yale University Press, 1961).

44. Vernon Van Dyke, "Human Rights without Distinction," *American Political Science Review* 67, no. 4 (December 1973): 1274; Eide, *Human Rights in the World Society,* p. 7; Richard Falk, "Comparative Protection of Human Rights in Capitalist and Socialist Third World Countries," (Paper presented to the 1978 annual meeting of the American Political Science Association, August–September 1978), mimeographed.

45. Duchacek, *Rights and Liberties,* p. 105.

46. Management of contradictions is discussed by Hoffmann, "The Hell of Good Intentions."

CHAPTER THREE

1. I use the term "law" because most of the agreements discussed in this chapter are law. Where agreements are not treaty law, such as the Universal Declaration and the Helsinki Accord, it is clear they perform the functions of law. They set standards for permissible and impermissible behavior, or in other words they specify the rules for orderly behavior. For those who prefer a sharper distinction between law and nonlegal standards, other reading is available—e.g., Thomas Buergenthal, ed., *Human Rights, International Law and the Helsinki Accord* (Montclair, N. J.: Allanheld, 1978).

2. Stuart A. Scheingold, *The Politics of Rights: Lawyers, Public Policy, and Political Change* (New Haven: Yale University Press, 1974), p. 8.

3. For an excellent discussion of the several functions of international law see William P. Coplin, "International Law and Assumptions about the State System," *World Politics* 17, no. 4 (December 1964): 615–35.

4. Thomas Buergenthal and Judith Torney, *International Human Rights and International Education* (Washington: U.S. Committee for UNESCO, 1976).

5. Ibid., chap. 4.

6. Jerome B. Elkind, "Application of the International Covenant on Civil and Political Rights in New Zealand," *American Journal of International Law* 75, no. 1 (January 1981): 169–71. More generally on the process of state reporting see Oscar Schachter, "The Obligation of the Parties to Give Effect to the Covenant on Civil and Political Rights," *American Journal of International Law* 73, no. 3 (July 1979): 462–64.

7. David P. Forsythe, *Human Rights and U.S. Foreign Policy: Congress Reconsidered* (Gainesville, Fla.: University of Florida Press, 1988), chap. 6, drawing in part on Judith Innes de Neufville, "Human Rights Reporting as a Policy Tool: An Examination of the State Department Country Reports," *Human Rights Quarterly* 8, no. 4 (November 1986), pp. 681–99.

8. Johan Nordenfelt, "Conventions in Crisis," *Human Rights Internet Reporter* 11, nos. 5/6 (winter/spring 1987): 61.

9. See further Helge Ole Bergesen, "Human Rights—the Property of the Nation State or a Concern for the International Community? A Study of the Soviet Positions concerning U.N. Protection of Civil and Political Rights since 1975," *Cooperation and Conflict* 4 (1979): 239–54 and Farrokh Jhabvala, "The Soviet-Bloc's View of the Implementation of Human Rights Accords," *Human Rights Quarterly* 7, no. 4 (November 1985): 461–91.

10. Ibid., and Leonid Brezhnev, *Socialism, Democracy, and Human Rights* (New York: Pergamon Press, 1980); V. Czhikvadze, "Human Rights and Non-Interference in the Internal Affairs of States," *International Af-*

fairs (Moscow), no. 4 (1978): 22–31; and V. Kartashkiv, *The International Defense of Human Rights* (Moscow: The International Relations Publishing House, 1977). A concise summary of the traditional Soviet view is found in V. Katzskin, "Human Rights and the Modern World," *International Affairs* (Moscow), no. 1 (1979): 48–56: the USSR is the champion of human rights; no defense is made of its record on civil-political rights; Western policies are vigorously attacked; implementation must be left to the state.

11. Philip Alston, "Out of the Abyss: The Challenges Confronting the New U.N. Committee on Economic, Social and Cultural Rights," *Human Rights Quarterly* 9, no. 3 (August 1987): 332–81. And David P. Forsythe, book review in *Human Rights Quarterly* 8, no. 3: 541, drawing on the unpublished paper by Yvetta Pass, "The Problems of Implementing the International Covenant on Economic, Social and Cultural Rights," typed, 1985.

12. Howard Tolley, Jr., *The U.N. Commission on Human Rights* (Boulder and London: Westview Press, 1987).

13. For a brief overview of the U.N. process, see Theo C. van Boven, "The United Nations and Human Rights: A Critical Appraisal," *Bulletin of Peace Proposals*, no. 3 (1977): 198–208. The subject of U.N. supervision of international human rights accords is incredibly complex; see the useful chart concerning the U.N. and human rights in Tom J. Farer, "The United Nations and Human Rights: More than a Whimper Less than a Roar," *Human Rights Quarterly* 9, no. 4 (November 1987): 550–86.

14. See further Thomas M. Franck and H. Scott Fairley. "Procedural Due Process in Human Rights Fact-finding by International Agencies," *American Journal of International Law* 74, no. 2 (April 1980): 308–45. And Jack Donnelly, "Human Rights at the U.N. 1955–1985: The Question of Bias," *International Studies Quarterly* 32, no. 3 (September 1988): 275–304.

15. In addition to Donnelly, "Human Rights at the U.N. 1955–1985," see David P. Forsythe, "The United Nations and Human Rights, 1945–1985," *Political Science Quarterly* 100, no. 2 (Summer 1985): 249–70; and Tolley, *The U.N. Human Rights Commission.*

16. Ernst B. Haas, *Human Rights and International Action* (Stanford: Stanford University Press, 1970), p. 24.

17. Ibid., pp. 91, 115.

18. Ibid., pp. 82, 92, 115.

19. See further Richard Melansin, "Human Rights and the American Withdrawal from the I.L.O.," *Universal Human Rights* 1, no. 1 (February 1979).

20. B. G. Ramcharan, "The Good Offices of the United Nations Secretary-General in the Field of Human Rights," *American Journal of International Law* 76, no. 1 (January 1982): 130–41.

21. See further David P. Forsythe, "The Political Economy of U.N. Refu-

gee Programs," in Forsythe, ed., *The United Nations in the World Political Economy* (London: Macmillan Ltd., 1989).

22. The ICRC is one agency in the Red Cross transnational movement. For clarification of this complex picture as well as a discussion of the ICRC's strengths and weaknesses, support and criticism, see David Forsythe, *Humanitarian Politics: The International Committee of the Red Cross* (Baltimore: The Johns Hopkins University Press, 1977); and Forsythe, "The Red Cross as Transnational Movement: Conserving and Changing the Nation-State System," *International Organization* 30, no. 4 (Autumn 1976): 607–30.

23. Lawrence J. Le Blanc, *The OAS and the Promotion and Protection of Human Rights* (The Hague: Martinus Nijhoff, 1977). For striking details of the Inter-American Commission in Nicaragua see the *International Herald Tribune*, 10 October 1978, p. 4, and 20 November 1978, p. 6. See further Thomas Buergenthal, "The Inter-American System for the Protection of Human Rights," in Theodore Meron, ed., *Human Rights in International Law: Legal and Policy Issues* (Oxford: Clarendon Press, 1984).

24. For details see Glenda da Fonseca, *How to File Complaints of Human Rights Violations: A Practical Guide to Intergovernmental Procedures* (Geneva: World Council of Churches, 1975). And Tolley, *The U.N. Human Rights Commission.*

25. Forsythe, "The United Nations and Human Rights, 1945–1985."

26. See Margaret P. Doxey, *Economic Sanctions and International Enforcement* (New York: Oxford University Press, 1980). Cf. Robin Renwick, *Economic Sanctions* (Cambridge, Mass.: Harvard University Press, 1981).

27. The United States voted for a binding trade embargo in the Security Council. Subsequently the Congress permitted extensive trade with Rhodesia. American courts refused to move away from the U.S. doctrine that Congress has the right, in American law, to negate certain treaty obligations. (The same domestic legal issue was to arise ten years later when the Congress mandated closing of the U.N. office of the Palestine Liberation Organization.) Such action remains illegal under international law. The politics of U.S. violation of Rhodesian sanctions is explained in Anthony Lake, *The "Tar Baby" Option* (New York: Columbia University Press, 1976). The Carter administration successfully lobbied for repeal of the trade amendment, citing among other arguments the fact of U.S. violation of international law.

28. A. H. Robertson, *Human Rights in National and International Law* (Manchester: Manchester University Press, 1968), pp. 292–93. In 1980 the World Court, at the request of the United States, issued an interim judgment demanding the release of the American hostages seized by Iranian militant students at the American embassy. In terms of the letter of the law, this was not a human rights case but rather one of consular and diplo-

matic immunity covered by the Vienna Conventions of 1961, under which the court assumed jurisdiction of the dispute. Many American citizens viewed the matter as one involving the human rights of the hostages.

29. The Statute of the International Court of Justice, which is the court's controlling document, indicates that states may give their consent in several ways: a blanket grant, a grant for particular types of disputes, an ad hoc grant for one dispute, etc. A number of states play legal games with this issue. The United States, for example, has agreed to accept the jurisdiction of the court in general. But to this blanket grant the United States attaches the so-called Connally Amendment, which states that the United States will not accept the jurisdiction of the court over legal disputes involving the internal affairs of the United States, as determined by the United States. This, of course, negates the original American consent to let the court handle legal disputes. In the mid-1980s case of *Nicaragua* v. *the U.S.*, the U.S. walked out of the World Court when it accepted jurisdiction over Nicaragua's petition to the Court, claiming among other things that Nicaragua had never given its legal consent to be bound by the Court, thus the U.S. did not have to respond.

30. "Military and Paramilitary Activities in and against Nicaragua," *Nicaragua* v. *the United States, International Court of Justice Reports* 14, 1986 (Judgment of 27 June).

31. For a summary of the case involving journalists see the *New York Times*, November 29, 1985, p. 8. With regard to the case concerning death squads, see the *New York Times*, 30 July 1988, p. 1. See also Buergenthal, "The Inter-American System for the Protection of Human Rights."

32. Richard B. Lillich and Hurst Hannum, "Linkages Between International Human Rights and U.S. Constitutional Law," *American Journal of International Law* 79, no. 1 (January 1985): 158–63. For the historical trend see Richard B. Lillich, "The Role of Domestic Courts in Promoting International Human Rights Norms," in James C. Tutle, ed., *International Human Rights Law and Practice*, rev. ed. (Philadelphia: International Printing Co., for the ABA, 1978), pp. 105–31.

33. Howard Tolley, Jr., "International Human Rights Law in U.S. Courts: Public Interest Groups and Private Attorneys," paper prepared for the American Political Science Association, Chicago, 1987, 30 pp.

34. European Commission on Human Rights, *Stock-Taking on the European Convention on Human Rights* (Strasbourg, France: The Council of Europe, 1984). See also Ralph Beddard, *Human Rights and Europe: A Study of the Machinery of Human Rights Protection of the Council of Europe* (London: Sweet and Maxwell, 1980), 2nd ed.

35. This is the central theme in Louis Henkin, *The Rights of Man Today* (Boulder: Westview Press, 1978).

36. The impact of the regional machinery on the British government is

well explained in the *New York Times,* 9 February 1977, p. A-3. Unofficial groups were also active on the question within the United Kingdom.

37. *Washington Post: National Weekly Edition,* 27 March 1988, p. 3.

38. *The Nation,* 27 December 1980, p. 691.

39. Henry Kissinger, *The White House Years* (Boston: Little, Brown & Co., 1979): 151. A more accurate view is presented in Stanley Hoffmann, *Duties beyond Borders* (Syracuse: Syracuse University Press, 1981), especially pp. 114–15.

40. There are two official U.S. sources which chart violations of human rights in the USSR and Eastern Europe. One is written by the State Department and published by Congress: the *Annual Country Reports on Human Rights Practices,* noted above. The other one is written by the bi-branch U.S. Commission on Security and Cooperation in Europe, which publishes periodic reports. See also Vladimir Bukovsky, *To Build a Castle: My Life as a Dissenter* (London: Audré Deutsch, 1978). This leading critic of Soviet society not only details from the inside the repression of human rights activists but also expresses concern that he and other well-known figures are treated differently from the more obscure inmates of prisons, labor camps, and misused psychiatric hospitals. The fate of Bukovsky was clearly affected by foreign events.

41. For an unofficial view of violations of human rights in Eastern Europe, especially pertaining to the Helsinki Accord, see the publications by Helsinki Watch and affiliated private groups. See, eg., Helsinki Watch, *Violations of the Helsinki Accords* (New York: Helsinki Watch, November 26, 1986).

42. Changes at the time of writing were charted in the *Christian Science Monitor* 7 January 1988, p. 32; and the *New York Times,* October 21, 1987, p. 1.

43. Final documents from the Havana Conference did not mention civil-political rights in the Third World but rather spoke of human rights in relation to opposition to great-power intervention; some mention was made of socioeconomic rights *(New York Times,* 10 September 1979, p. A-8).

44. Jack Donnelly, "Repression and Development: The Political Contingency of Human Rights Tradeoffs," in David P. Forsythe, ed., *Human Rights and Development* (London: Macmillan, Ltd., forthcoming).

CHAPTER FOUR

1. Information presented here draws heavily from the following: Laurie S. Wiseberg and Harry M. Scoble, "The Human Rights Lobby in Washing-

ton," (Paper prepared for the American Political Science Association, September 1978); Scoble and Wiseberg, "Human Rights NGOs: Notes Towards Comparative Analysis," *Human Rights* 9, no. 4 (Winter 1976), pp. 611–44; Scoble and Wiseberg, "Amnesty International," *Intellect Magazine* (September–October 1976), pp. 79–82; Peter Archer, "Action by Unofficial Organizations on Human Rights," in *The International Protection of Human Rights*, Evan Luard, ed. (London: Thames Hudson, 1967); Arthur Blaser and Stephen Saunders, "Human Rights NGOs" (Paper prepared for the Mid-West Political Science Association, 1978); Antonio Cassese, "Progressive Transnational Promotion of Human Rights by NGOs," in *Human Rights*, B. G. Ramcharan, ed. (The Hague: Martinus Nijhoff, 1978); J. F Green, "NGOs," in *Human Rights and World Order*, Abdul Aziz Said, ed. (New Brunswick: Transaction Books, 1978).

2. See further Nigel Rodley, "Monitoring Human Rights Violations in the 1980's," in Jorge I. Dominguez et al., *Enhancing Global Human Rights* (New York: McGraw-Hill, 1979), p. 138. On American labor activity for a broad range of rights at home and abroad see the *Christian Science Monitor*, 18 February 1988, p. 3.

3. Various schema are discussed in David P. Forsythe and Laurie S. Wiseberg, "Human Rights Protection: A Research Agenda," *Universal Human Rights* 4, no. 1 (October–December 1979): 7–12.

4. Ibid.

5. *Human Rights in Developing Countries: A year-book on countries receiving Norwegian aid* (Oslo: Norwegian University Press, annual from 1985).

6. Eg., *Country Reports on Human Rights Practices for 1987*, Report to the House Committee on Foreign Affairs and Senate Committee on Foreign Relations, Department of State (Washington: GPO, 1988). For the process in which Congress and private human rights groups scrutinize this report see David P. Forsythe, *Human Rights and U.S. Foreign Policy: Congress Reconsidered* (Gainesville: University Press of Florida, 1988), chap. 6.

7. See especially Egon Larsen, *A Flame in Barbed Wire* (London: Frederick Muller Ltd., 1978).

8. See Antonio Cassese, "How Could Nongovernmental Organizations Use U.N. Bodies More Effectively," *Universal Human Rights* 1, no. 4 (October–December 1979), pp. 73–80.

9. David P. Forsythe, "The United Nations and Human Rights 1945–1985," *Political Science Quarterly* 100, no. 2 (Summer, 1985), pp. 249–69.

10. *New York Times*, 10 January 1980, p. A-10.

11. David P. Forsythe, *Humanitarian Politics: The International Committee of the Red Cross* (Baltimore: Johns Hopkins University Press, 1977), pp. 69, 70.

12. John G. Sommer, *Beyond Charity: U. S. Voluntary Aid for a Changing Third World* (New York: Prager, 1977).

13. On the issue of implementing human rights in situations of natural disasters it should be noted that there is some public policy emanating from the United Nations in the form of UNDRO (the U.N. Disaster Relief Organization) and various resolutions. But UNDRO has no grass-roots operating capacity and is basically an information and planning agency. Actual relief is in the hands of governments and private agencies. Thus there is no centralized, comprehensive global public policy. Such a policy would frequently have to accommodate the intertwining of natural and political disasters, as when agricultural disaster combined with armed conflict produced major denials of human rights in Kampuchea, East Timor, and Ethiopia in the 1970s. See David P. Forsythe, "Diplomatic Approaches to the Political Problems of Disaster Relief," in *Disaster Assistance,* Lynn Stephens and Stephen Greene, eds. (New York: New York University Press, 1979). See also David P. Forsythe, "U.S. Humanitarian Assistance," in Gil Loescher and Bruce Nichols, eds., *The Moral Nation* (South Bend, Ind.: Notre Dame Press, 1989).

15. Thomas E. Heneghan, "Human Rights Protests in Eastern Europe," *The World Today* 33 (March 1977), pp. 90–100.

16. Mariclaire Acosta, "Women's Human Rights Groups in Latin America," in Forsythe, ed., *Human Rights and Development.*

17. Kate Millet, an American activist in behalf of women's rights, was summarily taken to an airport and flown out of Iran by the authorities in the spring of 1979. For a review of the ups and downs of tolerance for rights in China, see the *New York Times,* 22 November 1987, p. 4. For an interesting argument as to why China has never become the focus of U.S. and other attention to human rights violations, see Roberta Cohen, "People's Republic of China: The Human Rights Exception," *Human Rights Quarterly 9,* no. 4 (1987), pp. 447–549.

18. See the chapters by Kothari, Rubin, and Medhi in Forsythe, ed., *Human Rights and Development.*

19. An excellent analysis of private health groups in the Philippines, linked to transnational actors, is found in Richard P. Claude, "The Right to Health: The Philippines, the AAAS, and Beyond," in Forsythe, ed., *Human Rights and Development.*

20. Regarding AI and Kenya see the *New York Times,* September 16, 1987, p. 5. More generally on the importance of private actors for the functioning of public actors, see A. H. Robertson, "A Global Assessment of Human Rights," *Notre Dame Lawyer* 53, no. 1 (October 1977): p. 32.

CHAPTER FIVE

1. Arthur Schlesinger, Jr., "Human Rights and the American Tradition," *Foreign Affairs* 57, no. 3 (America and the World, 1978): 503–26.

2. See Vernon Van Dyke, *Human Rights, the United States, and World Community* (New York: Oxford University Press, 1970).

3. See Kissinger's *American Foreign Policy: Three Essays* (New York: Norton, 1969). For clarification see John G. Stoessinger, *Henry Kissinger: The Anguish of Power* (New York: Norton, 1976), p. 77. And Kissinger, *The White House Years* (Boston: Little, Brown, 1979), p. 229.

4. For a classic statement from a "realist" about U.S. foreign policy read George Kennan, *American Diplomacy 1900–1950* (Chicago: University of Chicago Press), p. 1951.

5. For an overview see David P. Forsythe, *Human Rights and U.S. Foreign Policy: Congress Reconsidered* (Gainesville: University of Florida Press, 1988).

6. Henry Kissinger, speech in Santiago, Chile, 8 June 1976 (text from Bureau of Public Affairs, Department of State).

7. Kissinger, United Nations Speech.

8. Hugh Arnold, "Henry Kissinger and Human Rights," *Human Rights Quarterly* 2, no. 4 (Autumn 1980): 57–71.

9. Kissinger, United Nations Speech.

10. *Washington Post*, 27 February 1977, C-1.

11. Ibid.

12. Elizabeth Drew, "Reporter at Large: Human Rights," *The New Yorker*, 18 July 1977, starting at 36.

13. Jimmy Carter, *Keeping Faith* (New York: Bantam, 1982), p. 144 and passim.

14. Caleb Rossiter, "Human Rights: The Carter Record, The Reagan Reaction," *Report*, Center for International Policy, Washington: September 1984. Lincoln P. Bloomfield, "From Ideology to Program to Policy: Tracking the Carter Human Rights Policy," *Journal of Policy Analysis and Management* 2, no. 1 (Fall, 1982): 1–12.

15. Vance, "Human Rights and Foreign Policy," *Georgia Journal of International & Comparative Law* 7 (Supplement 1977): 223–30.

16. Lake, speech in Houston, Texas, 5 November 1977 (text provided by the Bureau of Public Affairs, Department of State). Goldberg, speech at Belgrade, 6 October 1977 (text provided by the Bureau of Public Affairs, Department of State). Vance, *Department of State Bulletin*, June 1978, p. 15.

17. The point is well made in Sandra Volgelgesang, *American Dream, Global Nightmare: The Dilemma of U.S. Human Rights Policy* (New York: Norton, 1980).

18. Richard Fagan, "The Carter Administration and Latin America:

Business as Usual?," *Foreign Affairs* 57, no. 3 (America and the World, 1978): 652–69.

19. Vogelgesang, *American Dream.*

20. Forsythe, *Human Rights and U.S. Foreign Policy.*

21. Compare Joshua Muravchik, *The Uncertain Crusade: Jimmy Carter and the Dilemmas of Human Rights Policy* (Lanham, Md.: Hamilton Press, 1986), with David Owen, *Human Rights* (London: Jonathan Cape, 1978).

22. Tammi R. Davis and Sean M. Lynn-Jones, "City Upon A Hill," *Foreign Policy* 66 (Spring 1987): 20–38.

23. "Introduction," *Country Reports On Human Rights Practices for 1981*, Report submitted to Committees on Foreign Affairs and Foreign Relations, Joint Committee Print, February 1982, Washington: GPO, 1982, pp. I–II.

24. Jean Kirkpatrick, *The Reagan Phenomenon and Other Speeches on Foreign Policy* (Washington: American Enterprise Institute, 1983).

25. "Nomination of Ernest W. Lefever," *Hearings*, Senate Committee on Foreign Relations, 97th Cong., 1st sess., May 18, 19, June 4, 5, 1981 (Washington: GPO, 1981).

26. Jean Kirkpatrick, "Dictatorships and Double Standards," *Commentary* 68, no. 5 (November 1979): 34–45.

27. The details are presented in Forsythe, *Human Rights and U.S. Foreign Policy.*

28. David Heaps, *Human Rights and U.S. Foreign Policy: The First Decade 1973–1984* (for the American Association for the International Commission of Jurists, no publisher indicated, 1984).

29. Tamar Jacoby, "Reagan's Turnaround on Human Rights," *Foreign Affairs* 64, no. 5 (Summer 1986): 1066–86.

30. After a military coup in Liberia, and despite continuing human rights violations, U.S. military aid increased 600%, economic aid 800%. Given Shultz's unwillingness to deal seriously with human rights violations there, the Congress began to focus on Liberia in its legislation.

31. Lars Schoultz, *Human Rights and United States Policy Toward Latin America* (Princeton: Princeton University Press, 1981).

32. On the American belief that non-democratic governments are inherently aggressive, see Kenneth Waltz, *Man, The State, and War* (New York: Columbia University Press, 1954).

33. See further Ved Nanda, "Development and Human Rights: The Role of International Law and Organizations," in George Shepherd and Ved Nanda, eds., *Human Rights and Third World Development* (Westport, Conn.: Greenwood Press, 1985).

34. Jahangir Amuzegar, "The IMF Under Fire," *Foreign Policy* 64 (fall 1986): 98–120.

35. *Duties Beyond Borders: On the Limits and Possibilities of Ethical International Politics* (Syracuse: Syracuse University Press, 1981), chap. 3. For the contrary argument that in most situations the U.S. government should not interfere with private markets read Richard Feinberg, *The Intemperate Zone: The Third World Challenge to U.S. Foreign Policy* (New York: Norton, 1983).

36. See further Fagan, "The Carter Administration and Latin America."

37. Cecil V. Crabb, Jr., and Pat M. Holt, *Invitation to Struggle: Congress, the President, and Foreign Policy,* 2nd ed. (Washington: Congressional Quarterly Press, 1984), p. 187.

38. Speech, Georgetown University, 12 October 1983 (text provided by Mr. Abrams office).

CHAPTER SIX

1. Much of the literature on the making of foreign policy has been reviewed in William P. Avery and David P. Forsythe, "Human Rights, National Security, and the U.S. Senate," *International Studies Quarterly* 23, no. 2 (June 1979): 303–20. See also note 13 below.

2. Human Rights Internet, *North American Human Rights Directory,* 3rd ed. (Boston: Internet, 1984). See also Technical Assistance Information Clearinghouse, *U.S. Non-Profit Organizations in Development Assistance Abroad* (New York: American Council of Voluntary Agencies for Foreign Services, 1978) for a 525-page directory covering 456 U.S. nonprofit organizations. See also Norman J. Ornstein and Shirley Elder, *Interest Groups, Lobbying and Policy Making* (Washington, D.C.: Congressional Quarterly Press, 1978): "Lobbying by domestic groups on foreign policy has clearly increased" (p. 51).

3. Peter Schuck, "Public Interest Groups and Policy Process," *Public Administration Review* (March/April 1977), p. 133. On the influence of public interest groups see also Ornstein and Elder, *Interest Groups;* Jeffrey M. Berry, *Lobbying for the People* (Princeton: Princeton University Press, 1977); Carol S. Greenwald, *Group Power: Lobbying and Public Policy* (New York: Praeger, 1978); Andrew McFarland, *Public Interest Lobbies* (Washington, D.C.: American Enterprise Institute, 1976); Andrew McFarland, "Recent Social Movements and Theories of Power in America," (Paper prepared for the Center for Health Studies Workshop, 1979), mimeographed, 23 pages.

4. Bernard C. Cohen, *The Public's Impact on Foreign Policy* (Boston: Little, Brown & Co., 1973).

5. Mobil Oil has run ads in leading newspapers charging that public interest lobbies are only another type of special interest; see, e.g., the *Wash-*

ington Post, 4 November 1979, p. C-2. The same argument had been made by a spokesman for the American Petroleum Institute, "Energy Lobby: New Voices at Ways and Means," *Congressional Quarterly* 33 (May 1975): 941. The general issue is treated in Berry, *Lobbying for the People*, p. 14; Greenwald, *Group Power*, p. 4 and thereafter; McFarland, *Public Interest Lobbies*, pp. 40–41; and John E. Sinclair, *Interest Groups in America* (Morristown, N.J.: General Learning Press, 1976). On foreign policy the dividing line between nonprofit and nonprofit public interest groups must necessarily remain hazy. For example, the category into which one puts the Zionist Organization of America depends upon personal perception. For an effort to make fine distinctions regarding domestic policy, see Schuck, "Public Interest Groups," p. 135.

6. At its August 1979 Executive Council meeting, the AFL-CIO took positions on human rights in Northern Ireland, Indochinese refugees, Nicaragua, Chile, and South African labor law, inter alia. Almost ten years later the agenda of this "labor" group was still full of international human rights issues.

7. Berry, *Lobbying for the People*, p. 45. My behavioral concept of lobbying is thus the one found in most of the social science literature referred to in notes 3 and 13. It is therefore nothing new to note lobbying by the tax exempt groups known to the IRS as 501(C)(3) groups—and nothing pernicious. See Schuck, "Public Interest Groups," p. 135.

8. A description of Freedom House activities on Rhodesia is found in "Rhodesia: What Role for the U.S.?" *Freedom at Issue* 52 (September–October 1979): 3–9.

9. President Carter, United Nations speech, 17 March 1977 (text from Bureau of Public Affairs, State Department).

10. It is increasingly difficult to separate foreign from domestic affairs. One can, however, focus on differing parts of a transnational process, as demonstrated by the domestic focus of Lennox S. Hinds, "Illusions of Justice: Human Rights Violation in the United States," (University of Iowa School of Social Work, 1979), mimeographed.

11. This essay does not address directly the question of whether this orientation is wise. The author's preferences are probably evident. It can be noted that there is an opposing argument, namely, that the nature of world politics imposes security requirements on nations which to a great extent preclude concern with human rights. For a blistering, and mostly irrational, attack on most American human rights groups, read Irving Kristol,"Human Rights: The Hidden Agenda," *The National Interest* (Winter 1986/87), pp. 3–11.

12. It is well to remember the dictum by two careful students of interest groups: "The classification of interest groups is always a difficult task and is of necessity somewhat arbitrary," L. Harmon Ziegler and G. Wayne

Peak, *Interest Groups in American Society,* 2nd ed. (Englewood Cliffs, N.J.: Prentice-Hall, 1972), p. 281. For attempts to categorize groups see McFarland, *Public Interest Lobbies,* pp. 40–41; Sinclair, *Interest Groups in America,* pp. 1–3; Berry, *Lobbying for the People,* pp. 7–10; Greenwald, *Group Power,* p. 17; and for the point that any type of group can be a human rights group see Nigel Rodley, "Monitoring Human Rights Violations in the 1980s," in Jorge I. Dominguez et al., *Enhancing Global Human Rights* (New York: McGraw-Hill, 1979), p. 138.

13. Lobbying is the same process whether on domestic, foreign, or mixed issues. See especially Ziegler and Peak, *Interest Groups in American Society;* L. Harmon Ziegler, "The Effects of Lobbying: A Comparative Assessment," in *Public Opinion and Public Policy,* Norman R. Luttberg, ed. (Homewood, Ill.: Dorsey Press, 1968); Graham Wooton, *Interest Groups* (Englewood Cliffs, N.J.: Prentice-Hall, 1970); Lester W. Milbrath, "The Impact of Lobbying on Governmental Decisions," in *Interest Group Politics in America,* Robert Salisbury, ed. (New York: Harper & Row, 1970); Lester W. Milbrath, *The Washington Lobbyists* (Chicago: Rand McNally, 1963); Robert Presthus, *Elites in the Policy Process* (New York: Cambridge University Press, 1974); see also the extensive bibliography in Greenwald, *Group Power.*

On lobbying and foreign policy see especially Cohen, *The Public's Impact on Foreign Policy;* Bernard C. Cohen, *The Influence of Non-Governmental Groups on Foreign Policy Making* (Boston: World Peace Foundation, 1959); Lester W. Milbrath, "Interest Groups and Policy," in James N. Rosenau, ed., *Domestic Sources of Foreign Policy* (New York: The Free Press, 1967); Theodore Lowi, "Making Democracy Safe for the World," in Rosenau, *Domestic Sources;* Raymond A. Bauer et al., *American Business and Public Policy: The Politics of Foreign Trade,* 2nd ed. (New York: Aldine Publications, 1972).

14. That lobbies focus on Congress is a clear finding in much of the literature which deals with national as compared to state lobbying. Congress is more open to group influence, being the representative branch and being decentralized in power, whereas the State Department sees itself as responsible to the national interest more than to public opinion. On the latter point, see William Chittick, *State Department, Press, and Pressure Groups* (New York: Wiley, 1970); on the former, see James C. Wilson, *Political Organizations* (New York: Basic Books, 1973), p. 337.

15. At times in U.S. history foreign policy lobbies have focused on the executive branch when congress was relatively passive and when the executive seemed sympathetic to group interests. See F. P. Lovell, *Foreign Policy in Perspective* (New York: Holt, Rinehart, and Winston, 1970), p. 259.

16. For one insider's view of interest group activity—including judicial

lobbying—concerning Rhodesia, see Anthony Lake, *The "Tar Baby" Option: American Policy toward Southern Rhodesia* (New York: Columbia University Press, 1976). For an example of a specific intervention, see IHRLG, "Amicus Curiae Brief in the case of Filartiga vs. Peña-Irala," 1976. On judicial lobbying and human rights in general, see Richard B. Lillich, "The Enforcement of International Human Rights Norms in Domestic Courts," in *International Human Rights Law and Practice*, James C. Tutle, ed., (Philadelphia: ARA, 1978), pp. 106–27.

17. *Washington Post*, 24 August 1984, p. A-3; *The New York Times*, 14 December 1985, p. 15.

18. In my questions I tried, following Ziegler, "The Effects of Lobbying," to distinguish factual information from ideas about policy. My respondents were generally unable to separate the two types of "information." Ziegler himself seemed to find the same situation (pp. 194, 195). Thus "information" has a broad and amorphous scope in this present study.

19. Cohen, *The Influence of Non-Governmental Groups*, p. 16.

20. *Public Opinion* 2, no. 2 (March–May 1979): 20–29. Gallup found in 1979 that promoting and defending human rights was very important to 42 percent and somewhat important to 43 percent of Americans sampled. Sixty-seven percent of those asked agreed or strongly agreed that the U.S. should pressure violators of human rights. But other research suggests American public opinion is opposed to paying the costs of pressuring South Africa. See Daniel Yankelovich, "Farewell to President Knows Best," *Foreign Affairs* 57, no. 3 (1979): 670–93.

21. The activities of U.S. for-profit and for-foreign government lobbies which focus on Latin American issues have been analyzed by Lars Schoultz, *Human Rights and United States Policy toward Latin America* (Princeton: Princeton University Press, 1981).

22. One of the potential strengths of aggregated nonprofit indirect lobbying on public opinion was that certain activist churches were strong in the Midwest, where unions and primary human rights groups were weak. On the general difficulty of mobilizing citizens on foreign policy see Milbrath, "Interest Groups," p. 243. On the weakness of unregistered lobbies who cannot mobilize voters see Greenwald, *Group Power*, p. 112.

23. For a view of the Coalition and its Working Group, see Harry M. Scoble and Laurie S. Wiseberg, "The Human Rights Lobby in Washington" (Paper prepared for the American Political Science Association, September 1978), mimeographed, 26 pages.

24. Some of the groups did have a tactical disagreement of some importance. In the late 1970s certain conservatives in Congress picked up the human rights issue to deny U.S. economic assistance to leftist regimes like Vietnam, Laos, Cambodia, Mozambique, and Angola. At that point

ADA and others quit pressing for country-specific restrictions by Congress and concentrated on general legislation. Other nonprofits continued to work on restrictions to Chile and other specific states.

25. Presthus, *Elites in the Policy Process*, p. 162.

26. See especially the studies by Ziegler; Milbrath, "Interest Groups,"; and Cohen, *Public Opinion*.

27. Berry, *Lobbying for the People*, p. 217, sums up much of the literature.

28. Bruce P. Cameron, "A Rough Outline of the Contours of the Decision-Making Process with Regard to the Emergence of a Progressive Human Rights Policy for the United States," (Paper presented to the Northeastern Political Science Association, 1978), mimeographed, 13 pages.

29. David Weissbrodt, "Human Rights Legislation and United States Foreign Policy," *Georgia Journal of Comparative and International Law* 7, Supplement (1977): 231–87. My essay does not try to deal with why groups form or why individuals join groups. On group origins see David B. Truman, *The Governmental Process* (New York: Knopf, 1971); Berry, *Lobbying for the People*, pp. 22–25; Greenwald, *Group Power*, p. 29; and McFarland, *Public Interest Lobbies*, pp. 1–24.

30. Elizabeth Drew, "A Reporter at Large: Human Rights," *New Yorker*, 18 July 1977, pp. 36–62.

31. This view is also found in subsequent quotations by Humanitarian Affairs officials. The general pattern of political opponents' attributing power to adversaries is found in much of the literature on interest groups.

32. Interview findings. See also Friends Committee on National Legislation, "Annual Report and Legislative Summary 1977," p. 3, for a brief reference.

33. Interview findings. See also Washington Office on Africa, "House Settles on Half a Loaf," 9 June 1978, mimeographed, for a brief reference.

34. Americans for Democratic Action, "Action for Human Rights," n.d. This publication quotes congressional sources as saying ADA's lobbying on an assistance cutoff to Uruguay by Congress in 1976 was "instrumental" and "decisive."

35. Interview findings. See also ADA, "Human rights—Part 2: The Battle Continues in Congress," *Legislative Newsletter* 7, no. 1 (1 June 1978).

36. David P. Forsythe, *Human Rights and U.S. Foreign Policy: Congress Reconsidered* (Gainesville, Fla.: University Press of Florida, 1988).

37. Harkin's office also worked with human rights nonprofits, such as the FCNL and the Coalition's Working Group, concerning legislation on the IFIS. See FCNL, "Annual Report, 1977," p. 4.

38. ADA and others, including the International League, had been concerned about human rights in East Timor for some time. Hearings were

held in the spring of 1978 and again in the fall of 1979. This is a good example of agenda setting by interest groups working against the background of press coverage. The position of State's Far Eastern bureau was that things were not so bad there: (New York Times, 5 December 1979, p. A-3).

39. ARA was reputed to be less interested in human rights than HA. The *Washington Post* reported ARA was "balky" over human rights in 1977 (25 October 1977, p. A-3). ARA had testified in 1979 contrary to HA testimony on the issue of military training for regimes violating human rights; ADA, "Human Rights and Foreign Aid," *Legislative Newsletter* 8, nos. 3 and 4 (15 June 1979), p. 2. ARA reportedly had opposed HA on the issue of U.S. economic pressures when Chile refused to extradite for trial the accused killers of a Chilean and an American in the U.S. (New York Times, 30 November 1979, pp. A-1, A-6). Several nonprofit interviewees indicated a belief that ARA was unreceptive to human rights concerns. The same view was found in some quarters of HA.

40. Caleb Rossiter, "Human Rights: The Carter Record, the Reagan Reaction," *International Report* (Washington: Center for International Policy, 1984).

41. However, in 1979 President Carter laid the failure of his energy policy at the door of "well-financed and powerful special interests." In the same year Harvard's President Bok expressed general concern about American pluralism: "America no longer seems diverse so much as it seems split into innumerable special interests" (*Harvard Gazette*, 7 June 1979, p. 15).

42. On the social science finding that interest groups lack decisive power, see especially Ziegler, "Effects of Lobbying," p. 186, and the literature cited there. On the general weakness of for-profit lobbying, see Wilson, *Political Organizations*, p. 342; Milbrath, "The Impact of Lobbying; and Bauer, *American Business and Public Policy;* but cf. Presthus, *Elites in the Policy Process*, p. 164.

43. This would seem to be especially true in crisis policy making or on policy of high political salience. Beyond this conventional wisdom, however, I have found attempts to link group influence to types of issues to be unhelpful. See Morton Berkowitz et al., *The Politics of American Foreign Policy* (Englewood Cliffs, N.J.: Prentice-Hall, 1977), pp. 275–76. But cf. Michael T. Hayes, "The Semi-Sovereign Pressure Groups," *Journal of Politics* 40, no. 1 (February 1978): 134–61.

44. Not only public interest groups but also for-profit lobbies frequently lack these raw materials, as especially the works of Ziegler demonstrate. On extensive and expensive lobbying by Chrysler, however, see *New York Times*, 11 December 1979, pp. D-1, D-7. But even the wealthiest for-profit groups cannot necessarily buy votes. According to a spokesman for the American Petroleum Institute, the biggest obstacle to his lobbying was

the lack of popular support for the oil companies, quoted in American Petroleum Institute, "Energy Lobby," p. 940.

45. On the supposed relative infrequency and unimportance of foreign policy lobbying, see John Spanier and Eric Uslaner, *How American Foreign Policy is Made* (New York: Praeger, 1976), pp. 83–91; Cohen, *The Influence of Non-Governmental Groups*, p. 20; Chittick, *State Department*, p. 238; and Milbrath, "Interest Groups," pp. 245–49. On the alleged superiority of information by State, see Chittick, *State Department*, p. 291.

46. On the importance of incremental change in politics, see Charles E. Lindblom, "The Science of Muddling Through," *Public Administration Review* 19 (Spring 1959): 79–98, and Lindblom, *The Policy Making Process* (Englewood Cliffs, N.J.: Prentice-Hall, 1980). Note the incremental changes in auto safety under pressure from Nader, 1965 on. On incremental influence by public interest groups in general, see Greenwald, *Group Power*, p. 314.

47. On the point that a certain degree of fragmentation does not vitiate lobbying efforts see Berry, *Lobbying for the People*, p. 78. According to Ziegler, "The Effect of Lobbying," p. 187, a central question is, would the policy process be the same if groups disappeared? This is a "what if" question and therefore unsatisfactory for social science analysis, but for reasons explained in the text it seems to me that the American process would not have been the same between during the 1970s and 1980s if the human rights nonprofits had not existed.

48. It is an important and tantalizing question to ask exactly how a dominant mood does get translated into policy decisions. The standard work on this subject concludes after careful analysis that political science cannot answer this question (Cohen , *The Public's Impact*, p. 199). It is essentially a chicken-and-egg dilemma to try to determine whether nonprofits created a mood or whether a mood allowed nonprofits to be effective. My argument is that since groups have weak electoral impact and must act in conjunction with sympathetic officials, it is the nature of officialdom and the mood it reflects which is the most important independent variable explaining resulting policy. The role of groups is an intervening or secondary variable.

49. Sandra Vogelgesang, "What Price Principle?" *Foreign Affairs* 56, no. 4 (July 1978): 820. Other interest groups in other issue areas have also had their ups and downs; see Greenwald, *Group Power*, p. 183.

50. Schuck, "Public Interest Groups and Policy Process," p. 132.

51. Common Cause and Nader's Raiders, among others, were said to have greatly increased their influence in early 1975 because of personnel changes among officials on the House Ways and Means Committee; see American Petroleum Institute, "Energy Lobby," pp. 939–45

52. Greenwald, *Group Power*, p. 80.

53. Schuck, "Public Interest Groups and Policy Process," p. 138, writes with reference to regulatory agencies that monitoring "vastly magnifies" a group's influence.

54. See especially McFarland, *Public Interest Lobbies*, pp. 4–24. It has been said that the new middle-class politics, and especially its single-issue approach, had made Congress even more cautious; Steven Roberts, "Slow Pace of Congress," *New York Times*, 5 October 1979, p. A-20. This thesis is not validated in the issue area of human rights 1973–80.

55. Sandra Vogelgesang, *American Dream, Global Nightmare: The Dilemma of U.S. Human Rights Policy* (New York: Norton, 1980), pp. 144, 147.

56. Forsythe, *Human Rights and U.S. Foreign Policy*.

57. Ziegler, "Effects of Lobbying," p. 204.

58. Research has shown that Americans—and especially young Americans—are relatively ignorant about human rights when compared with nationals in other democracies; Thomas Buergenthal and Judith Torney, *International Human Rights and International Education* (Washington, D.C.: Department of State for UNESCO, 1976), pp. 102–25. It is noteworthy that in 1979 the U.S. National Commission for UNESCO, a quasi-nonprofit group (private but appointed by the secretary of state), began to push for improved adult education on human rights. And some increased attention to human rights could be noted in the curricula of American colleges and universities, as documented by the American Political Science Association *(Political Science Teaching News, November 1980)*.

CHAPTER SEVEN

1. Stanley Hoffmann, *Duties beyond Borders* (Syracuse: Syracuse University Press, 1981), especially pp. 96–105. See further Thomas M. Scanlon, "Human Rights as a Neutral Concern," in *Human Rights and U. S. Foreign Policy: Principles and Applications*, Peter G. Brown and Douglas MacLean, eds. (Lexington, Mass.: D. C. Heath, 1979), pp. 83–92.

2. For a discussion of Paraguay as a blend of fascism and conservatism, see Penny Lernoux, "Behind Closed Borders," *Harper's*, February 1979, pp. 20–29.

3. See George Sabine, *A History of Political Theory*, 3rd ed. rev. (London: Harrap & Co., 1963).

4. But Plato thought communism the best society, too good for man. See Sabine, *History of Political Theory*, p. 80.

5. Jorge Videla, quoted in the *International Herald Tribune*, 29 November 1978, p. 1.

6. Fritz Stern, "Between Repression and Reform: A Stranger's Impres-

sions of Argentina and Brazil," *Foreign Affairs* 56, no. 4 (July 1978): 812.

7. Harry Browne, quoted in *Newsweek*, International Edition, 13 November 1978, p. 64.

8. The columnist George F. Will, for example, is known in the West as a conservative. He is actually a classical liberal, as this passage makes clear: "The United States is explicitly founded on the theory of atomistic individualism, and is aggressively dedicated to maintaining a society that is an arena of competition and ambition. Yet even in the U.S., the most thoroughly, self-consciously and proudly liberal nation. . . ." *(Newsweek,* International Edition, 5 February 1979, p. 16). The Will type of classical liberal parts company with other liberals over the issue of tempering individualism with some equal benefits (the latter desire some equality of results as well as of opportunity to compete). Wrote Will in his pop-chic style: "Equality of opportunity *and* equality of results. That is not a philosophy, that is a failure of nerve" *(Newsweek,* International Edition, 19 February 1979, p. 57).

9. Stern, "Between Repression and Reform," p. 802.

10. T. H. Green, quoted in Sabine, *History of Political Theory,* p. 728.

11. Hersch Lauterpacht, *International Law and Human Rights* (New York: Garland, 1973, 1950), p. 74. Compare Jack Donnelly, *The Concept of Human Rights* (London: Croom Helm, 1985).

12. Compare Sabine, *History of Political Theory,* p. 742, with Norman E. Bowie and Robert L. Simon, *The Individual and the Political Order* (Englewood Cliffs, N.J.: Prentice-Hall, 1977), pp. 46–48.

13. Much unites them as well. It is argued that F. A. Hayek, the classical liberal, shares a number of values with the nonconservative liberal John Rawls; see Sanford Levinson, *American Political Science Review* 72, no. 3 (September 1978): 1026–27. See further William Ryan, *Equality* (New York: Pantheon, 1981).

14. Bowie and Simon, *The Individual and the Political Order,* p. 85.

15. Maurice Cranston, *What Are Human Rights?* (London: Bodley Head, 1973), p. 85.

16. John Fowles, *Daniel Martin* (New York: Signet, 1977), p. 74.

17. Bowie and Simon, *The Individual and the Political Order,* p. 68.

18. William Ebenstein, *Today's Isms,* 7th ed. (Englewood Cliffs, N.J.: Prentice-Hall, 1973), p. 153. See further Walter Laqueur and Barry Rubin, eds., *The Human Rights Reader* (New York: New American Library, 1979).

19. Barrington Moore, Jr., *Reflections on the Causes of Human Misery and upon Certain Proposals to Eliminate Them* (London: Allen Lane, 1972), especially pp. 112–13.

20. Jack Donnelly and Rhoda Howard, "Human Dignity, Human Rights and Political Regimes," *American Political Science Review* 80, no. 3 (September, 1986): 801–17.

21. Karl Marx, quoted in Graeme Duncan, *Marx and Mill: Two Views of Social Conflict and Social Harmony* (Cambridge: At the University Press, 1973), pp. 88–89.

22. Duncan, *Marx and Mill*, p. 194.

23. Georgi Arbatov, quoted in the *International Herald Tribune*, 11–12 November 1978, p. 6.

24. Vladimir Kartashkin, "Research in the Field of Human Rights," (Paper prepared for the UNESCO Congress on Teaching Human Rights, September 1978, partially reproduced in Human Rights Internet *Newsletter*, September–October 1978, pp. 41–45). Kartaskin does not fail to give attention to individual rights.

25. Martin Nicholson, "The New Soviet Constitution," *The World Today* 34, no. 1 (January 1978): 14–20.

26. John Hazard, "Development and the 'New Law,'" *University of Chicago Law Review* 45, no. 3 (Spring 1978): 642.

27. On changes made by Gorbachev, and their implications for Eastern Europe, see Karen Dawisha, *Eastern Europe, Gorbachev, and Reform: The Great Challenge* (Cambridge: At the Press, 1988). For Gorbachev's ambiguous use of the term "democracy," see Mikhail Gorbachev, *Perestroika: New Thinking for Our Country and the World* (New York: Harper and Row, 1987).

28. Sabine, *History of Political Theory*, pp. 648–66, especially at p. 655, where the good German Hegel is quoted: "Freedom consists . . . in the adjustment of inclination and individual capacity to the performance of socially significant work."

29. Jahangir Amuzegar, quoted in the *New York Times*, 24 January 1977, p. 16.

30. *Alternatives* 3, no. 2 (December 1977): 280–82. I have given the first ten of thirty articles.

31. Daniel Patrick Moynihan, *A Dangerous Place* (New York: Atlantic Little Brown, 1978).

32. Zbigniew Brzezinski, *International Herald Tribune*, 11–12 November 1978, p. 6. This is the central criticism by Western philosophers such as Ebenstein.

33. Julius Nyerere, *Freedom and Development: A Selection From Writings and Speeches* (London: Oxford University Press, 1973), p. 58.

34. Julius Nyerere, *Freedom and Socialism* (London: Oxford University Press, 1968), p. 324. See also Nyerere, *Freedom and Unity* (London: Oxford University Press, 1966), especially pp. 128–29.

35. Henry Kissinger, Department of State news release 293, 8 June 1976, p. 1.

36. Jimmy Carter, Department of State news release, 4 January 1978, p. 1.

37. William Stevenson, *A Man Called Intrepid* (New York: Ballantine Books, 1978).

38. Henry Kissinger, Department of State news release 519, 19 October 1976, p. 7.

39. Reinhold Niebuhr, *Moral Man and Immoral Society: A Study in Ethics and Politics* (New York: Scribners, 1932, 1960), pp. 83, 4, 167.

40. N. K. Sullivan, *Conservatism* (New York: St. Martin's Press, 1976).

41. For another argument that rights arise out of practice, see Richard E. Flathman, *The Practice of Rights* (New York: Cambridge University Press, 1976).

42. Vernon Van Dyke, "Equality and Discrimination in Education," *International Studies Quarterly* 17, no. 4 (December 1973): 375–404; "Justice as Fairness: For groups?," *American Political Science Review* 69, no. 2 (June 1975): 607–14; "Human Rights without Distinction as to Language," *International Studies Quarterly* 20, no. 1 (March 1976): 3–38.

43. Van Dyke, "Human Rights without Distinction," p. 34.

44. Najdan Pasic, "The Yugoslav Experience," in *Self-Management: New Dimensions to Democracy,* Ichak Adizes and Elisabeth Mann Borgese, eds. (Santa Barbara, Calif.: ABC-Clio, 1975), pp. 118–20.

45. United States Congress, *Report on Human Rights Practices* (Washington, D.C.: Government Printing Office). Milovan Djilas, quoted in the *New York Times,* 9 February 1977, p. A-3. See further Edgar Owens, *The Future of Freedom in the Developing World* (Elmsford, NY: Pergamon Press, 1987), chapter 4.

46. On the general subject of individual rights in East Germany, see Inga Markowits, "Socialist and Bourgeois Rights—An East-West German Comparison," *University of Chicago Law Review* 45, no. 3 (Spring 1978): 612–36.

47. *International Herald Tribune,* 31 January 1979, p. 4.

48. See especially François Ponchaund, *Cambodia: Year Zero* (New York: Penguin, 1977).

49. Jacob Ben-Amittay, *The History of Political Thought* (New York: Philosophical Library, 1972), especially pp. 5–22.

50. Moore, *Reflections on the Causes of Human Misery,* p. xi.

CHAPTER EIGHT

1. *New York Times,* 12 December 1979, p. A-15, and 21 December 1979, p. A-7.

2. Karl Deutsch, "The Probability of International Law," in *The Relevance of International Law,* Karl Deutsch and Stanley Hoffmann, eds. (New York: Schenckman, 1968).

3. Ernst Haas, "Dilemmas of Protecting Human Rights Abroad: Global Constraints and the Carter Administration," mimeographed (1977); parenthetical classifications are mine.

4. Details drawn from *New York Times* accounts during February 1974.

5. J. L. Brierly, *The Law of Nations*, 6th ed. (London: Oxford University Press, 1973), p. 48.

6. On informal sanctions see Werner Levi, *Law and Politics in the International Society* (Beverly Hills, Calif.: Sage, 1976).

7. *Washington Post*, 27 February 1977, p. C-4. See further David P. Forsythe, *Human Rights and U.S. Foreign Policy: Congress Reconsidered* (Gainesville, Fla.: University Press of Florida, 1988).

8. The U.S. government in late 1979 refused to attempt to apply law to members of an international uranium cartel. Members like Gulf Oil were apparently too powerful. See further the *New York Times*, 4 December 1979, p. 1.

9. William Coplin, "International Law and Assumptions about the State System," *World Politics* 17, no. 4 (Summer 1965): 615–35.

10. R. J. Vincent, *Human Rights and International Relations* (Cambridge: At the University Press, 1986), p. 151 and passim.

11. Philip Alston, "The alleged demise of political human rights at the U.N.," *International Organization* 37, no. 3 (Summer 1983): 537–46.

12. Richard F. Fagen, "The Carter Administration and Latin America: Business as Usual," *Foreign Affairs* 53, no. 7 (special issue, 1978): 652–69.

13. See further David P. Forsythe, ed., *Human Rights and Development: International Views* (London: Macmillan, Ltd., 1989).

14. The literature on the socioeconomic determinants of democracy is vast. See especially Clyde Z. Nunn et al., *Tolerance for Non-Conformity* (London: Jossey-Bass, Ltd., 1978); and Rita J. Simon and Kenneth Mann, "Public Support for Civil Liberties in Israel," *Social Science Quarterly* 58 (September 1977): 283–92.

15. Pope John Paul II, *New York Times*, 3 October 1979, p. B-4.

16. Frances Moore Lappé and Joseph Collins, "Aid as Obstacle," *New York Times*, 15 February 1980, p. A-29; see also their book, *Aid as Obstacle* (San Francisco: Institute for Food and Development Policy, 1980). And see further Edgar Owens, *The Future of Freedom in the Developing World: Economic Development as Political Reform* (Elmsford, NY: Pergamon Press, 1987).

17. Andrei Sakharov, "A Sick Society," *New York Times*, 23 January 1980, p. A-23.

18. For the possibility of both bias and balance at the U.N. on human rights, compare Jack Donnelly, "Human Rights at the U.N., 1955–85: The Question of Bias," *International Studies Quarterly* (December 1988), forthcoming at time of writing, and David P. Forsythe, "The United Na-

tions and Human Rights, 1945–1985," *Political Science Quarterly* 100, no. 2 (Summer 1985): 249–70.

19. Philip Alston, "The United Nations Specialized Agencies and Implementation of the International Covenant on Economic, Social, and Cultural Rights," *Columbia Journal of Transnational Law* 18, no. 1 (January 1979): 79–119.

20. United States Congress, *Report on Human Rights Practices* (Washington, D.C.: Government Printing Office, annual).

21. *New York Times*, 31 October 1979, p. A-5; 7 September 1979, p. A-3; 15 September 1979, p. A-3; 16 September 1979, p. A-11. It is important to observe the deterioration of protection of human rights in Argentina—and Chile—in the early 1980s after the Reagan administration made clear to these two regimes that it would not pressure them on the issue.

22. *New York Times*, 31 January 1980, pp. D-1, D-3; 5 February 1980, pp. D-1, D-10; 2 October 1979, p. A-4; and 4 October 1979, p. A-16. See also the *Washington Post*, 2 January 1980, pp. A-1, A-13.

23. In *The White House Years* (Boston: Little, Brown & Co., 1979), volume 1 of his memoirs, Henry Kissinger places the election of Allende in the context of perceived Soviet expansionism in the Middle East and Cuba. Thus, even though Allende won a plurality of the Chilean vote (like the Italian Christian Democrats), Kissinger and Nixon challenged Allende's legitimacy and sought to have Chilean generals lead a coup against the civilian president. Hence the U.S. government, in the name of freedom, tried to suppress political rights that even the Chilean military—not to mention democratic politicians—were not interested initially in suppressing, on the basis of an extremely tenuous argument about Soviet behavior. See further Kissinger's "Continuity and Change in American Foreign Policy," in *Human Rights and World Order*, Abdul A. Said, ed. (New York: Praeger, 1978).

24. On the attitudes of Carter during his first three years as president, see Leslie H. Gelb, "Beyond the Carter Doctrine," *New York Times Magazine*, 10 February 1980, pp. 18ff.

25. This is argued convincingly by Fagen, "The Carter Administration and Latin America," especially pp. 663 and 669.

26. See the provocative interpretation in Noam Chomsky and Edward S. Herman, *The Washington Connection and Third World Fascism* (Boston: South End Press, 1979). The problem with this interpretation is that it assumes, rather than proves, a U.S. primary interest in economic affairs, and it downgrades, without explanation, political or security motivations. Thus the authors arrive at conclusions which are clear about U.S. support for extremely conservative regimes, but the motivations for such a policy are not so clear.

27. UNA-USA, *United States Foreign Policy and Human Rights: Princi-*

ples, Priorities, Practice (New York: UNA-USA, 1979).

28. Sylvia Ann Hewlett, "Human Rights and Economic Realities: Trade-offs in Historical Perspective," *Political Science Quarterly* 94, no. 3 (Fall 1979): 453–73.

29. Forsythe, *Human Rights and U.S. Foreign Policy.*

30. One can find periodic reports about events in the U.N. Human Rights Committee in, inter alia, *The American Journal of International Law.*

31. Haas, "Dilemmas of Protecting Human Rights Abroad."

32. I am aware of certain restrictions on especially civil and political rights in Yugoslavia, as well as uncertainty about the future of political stability and economic growth in Yugoslavia. I wish, however, to challenge students to think about new subjects, and also about the concept of economic democracy.

33. A Chinese official was quoted as saying in early 1980: "In the past we had too much egalitarianism," (*New York Times,* 31 January 1980, p. A-4); see also *New York Times,* 14 September 1979, p. A-3; 16 September 1979, p. A-1; but also 17 October 1979, p. A-3 on governmental crackdown on dissent. For an overview see Seymour Topping, "China's Long March Into the Future," *New York Times Magazine,* 3 February 1980, pp. 29ff. Compare Mikhail Gorbachev, *Perestroika: New Thinking for Our Country and the World* (New York: Harper & Row, 1987).

34. The electoral triumph in the 1970s of classical liberals (called conservatives) in Sweden, the United Kingdom, Canada, and later in the U.S. and West Germany did not fundamentally alter the historical movement "to the left" in social policy.

35. This is the real crux of the North-South conflict. For one example of discord over who's to pay, see the *New York Times* coverage of the New Delhi conference of the United Nations Industrial Development Organization, 10 February 1980, p. A-3. By the late 1980s the prospects for a NIEO had greatly faded, many Third World countries had moved toward privatization or more market mechanisms, and there was increased prospect of North-South cooperation along market or mixed economic lines.

36. See especially Sandy Vogelgesang, *American Dream, Global Nightmare: The Dilemma of U.S. Human Rights Policy* (New York: Norton, 1980).

37. See further Stanley Hoffmann, *Duties beyond Borders* (Syracuse: Syracuse University Press, 1981).

38. The point is made in ibid. On the general importance of human rights and system change, see Richard A. Falk, *A Study of Future Worlds* (New York: The Free Press, 1975). And Samuel S. Kim, *The Quest for a Just World Order* (Boulder, Colo.: Westview Press, 1984).

39. It can be argued with some plausibility that the U.S. government de-

rived internal security—i.e., support from the people—from nationalistic and hawkish policies. One of the apparent reasons for President Carter's unpopularity was his image as one unwilling to use power in the traditional military sense as well as his image as one willing to negotiate and seek compromise rather than demand superiority and dominance. The contrast is striking between the images of Carter and Reagan and the corresponding public mood. Nevertheless, it is doubtful that nationalistic and bellicose postures alone, without attention to economic equity aad political rights, can make a U.S. administration electorally secure.

40. *New York Times*, 15 February 1980, p. A-1.

41. See above, n. 30, for reference to Kissinger's views as an addition to his views analyzed in chap. 3.

42. Sen. John Culver, *New York Times*, 10 February 1980, p. E-4.

43. Robert L. Heilbroner, *An Inquiry into the Human Prospect* (New York: Norton, 1974).

44. See further Hoffmann, *Duties beyond Borders*.

45. William F. Buckley, Jr., "Human Rights and Foreign Policy: A Proposal," *Foreign Affairs* 54, no. 4 (Spring 1980): 775–96.

46. Rhoda Howard, "Human Rights and Foreign Policy," in Forsythe, ed., *Human Rights and Development*.

47. Donald Woods, *Asking for Trouble: The Autobiography of a Banned Journalist* (New York: Atheneum, 1981). See also another important book of this type with regard to Argentina, Jacobo Timerman, *Prisoner without a Name, Cell without a Number* (New York: Knopf, 1981).

48. Department of State, *Report Submitted to the Committee on Foreign Relations*, U.S. Senate, 96th Cong., 1st sess., 8 February 1979 (Washington, D.C.: Government Printing Office, 1979), appendix 2.

49. Forsythe, *Human Rights and U.S. Foreign Policy*. For a good study about how international law generates influence by compelling states to justify their policies, see Louis Henkin, *How Nations Behave: Law and Foreign Policy* (New York: Praeger, 1968).

50. International Commission of Jurists, *Human Rights in One-Party States* (London: Search, 1978).

51. Jorge I. Dominguez, "Assessing Human Rights Conditions," in Dominguez, et. al., *Enhancing Global Human Rights* (New York: McGraw-Hill, 1979).

52. Forsythe, *Human Rights and Development*. And Lawrence E. Harrison, *Under-Development Is A State Of Mind: The Latin American Case* (Lanham, MD: University Press of America, 1985).

53. Jerome J. Shestack, "Sisyphus Endures: The International Human Rights NGOs," *New York Law School Law Review* 24, no. 1 (January 1978): 89–124, especially p. 90.

Bibliography

The notes of this book constitute a detailed bibliography. Listed here are the most basic reference sources on human rights, along with some of the more recent books of general interest.

I .COLLECTIONS OF HUMAN RIGHTS DOCUMENTS.

Brownlie, Ian, ed. *Basic Documents on Human Rights.* New York: Oxford University Press, 1981.
Joyce, James Avery, ed. *Human Rights International Documents.* 2 vols. Dobbs Ferry, NY: Oceana Publications, 1978.
Sohn, Louis B., and Buergenthal, Thomas. *Basic Documents on International Protection of Human Rights.* New York: Bobbs-Merrill, 1973, with periodic supplements.
United Nations Publication. Sales No. E 78: Compilation of Human Rights Instruments (same as U. N. Document: ST/HR/1/Rev. 1).
United States Congress, Committee on Foreign Affairs. *Human Rights Documents.* Committee Print, September 1983, Washington: Government Printing Office, 1983.

II. REFERENCES TO HUMAN RIGHTS PUBLICATIONS.

American Journal of International Law. 2223 Massachusetts Ave., NW, Washington, DC 20008-2864. Articles, book reviews.
Bibliography on Human Rights. Center for Civil Rights, Notre Dame University, South Bend, IN.
Checklist of Human Rights Documents. Law Library, University of Texas, Austin, TX.
Foreign Affairs. 58 E 68th St., New York, N. Y. 10021. Section on book reviews and section on source materials. Documents and other publications.

Human Rights: A Topical Bibliography. Center on Human Rights, Columbia University, New York, NY.

Human Rights: An International and Comparative Law Bibliography. Julian R. Friedman and Marc I. Sherman, eds., Westport, CT: Greenwood Press, 1985.

Human Rights Internet Reporter. Pound Hall, Harvard Law School, Cambridge, MA, 02138. Survey of literature, update on public and private action, feature articles.

Human Rights Quarterly, formerly *Universal Human Rights.* Law School, University of Cincinnati, Cincinnati, OH 45221. Articles and book reviews.

III. OFFICIAL PUBLICATIONS BY PUBLIC AUTHORITIES.

Inter-American Yearbook on Human Rights. Washington: The Organization of American States, annual.

International Labour Standards. Geneva: International Labour Organization, 1984.

Report on Human Rights Practices in Countries Receiving U.S. Aid. Washington: U.S. Government Printing Office, annual. Title may vary. This is a report by the State Department but published jointly by the Senate and House of Representatives. Comprehensive reports date from 1978. Most recent title at time of publication: *Country Reports on Human Rights Practices.* Joint Congressional Print for the Senate Foreign Relations Committee and the House Foreign Affairs Committee.

United Nations Yearbook on Human Rights. Geneva: U. N., biennial.

Yearbook of the European Convention on Human Rights. The Hague, Netherlands: Martinus Nijhoff, annual.

IV. SOME RECENT BOOKS ON HUMAN RIGHTS

Brown, Peter G., and MacLean, Douglas, eds. *Human Rights and U.S. Foreign Policy.* Lexington, MA: D. C. Heath and Co., 1979.

Buergenthal, Thomas. *Human Rights, International Law, and the Helsinki Accord.* Montclair, NJ: Allanheld, Osmun, 1977.

Chomsky, Noam, and Herman, Edward S. *The Political Economy of Human Rights.* Vols. 1 and 2. Boston: South End Press, 1979.

Claude, Richard P., and Weston, Burns, eds. *Human Rights in the International Community: Issues and Action.* Philadelphia, PA: The University of Pennsylvania Press, 1989.

Dominguez, Jorge I., et al. *Enhancing Global Human Rights.* New York: McGraw Hill, for the Council on Foreign Relations, 1979.

Donnelly, Jack. *The Concept of Rights.* London: Croom, Helm, 1985.

Dugard, C. *Human Rights and the South African Legal Order.* Princeton: Princeton University Press, 1978.

Dworkin, Ronald. *Taking Rights Seriously.* Cambridge: Harvard University Press, 1977.

Farer, Thomas J., ed. *Toward a Humanitarian Diplomacy.* New York: NYU Press, 1980.

Forsythe, David P. *Human Rights and U.S. Foreign Policy: Congress Reconsidered.* Gainesville, Fla.: University of Florida Press, 1988.

Forsythe, David P., ed. *Human Rights and Development: International Views.* London: Macmillan Ltd., 1989.

Forsythe, David P. *Humanitarian Politics: The International Committee of the Red Cross.* Baltimore: The John Hopkins University Press, 1977.

Glaser, Kurt, and Possony, Stefan, *Victims of Politics: The State of Human Rights.* New York: Columbia University Press, 1979.

Heaps, David. *Human Rights and U. S. Foreign Policy: The First Decade, 1973–1983.* For the American Association of the International Commission of Jurists. New York: ICJ, 1984.

Henkin, Louis. *The Rights of Man Today.* Boulder, CO: Westview, 1978.

Hevener, Natalie K., ed. *The Dynamics of Human Rights in U. S. Foreign Policy.* New Brunswick, NJ: Transaction Books, 1981.

Hoffmann, Stanley. *Duties beyond Borders.* Syracuse: Syracuse University Press, 1981.

Howard, Rhoda. *Human Rights in Commonwealth Africa.* Totowa, NJ: Rowman & Littlefield, 1986.

Joyce, James Avery. *The New Politics of Human Rights.* New York: St. Martin's Press, 1979.

Laquer, Walter, and Rubin, Barry, eds. *The Human Rights Reader.* Philadelphia: Temple University Press, 1979.

Larsen, Egon. *A Flame in Barbed Wire: The Story of Amnesty International.* London: Frederick Muller, 1978.

LeBlanc, Lawrence J. *The OAS and the Protection of Human Rights.* The Hague: Martinus Nijhoff, 1977.

Lernoux, Penny. *Cry of the People: The Struggle for Human Rights in Latin America.* New York: Penguin, 1982.

Lillich, Richard, and Newman, Frank, eds. *International Human Rights.* New York: McGraw-Hill, 1977.

Luard, Evan. *Human Rights and Foreign Policy.* Oxford: Pergamon Press, 1981.

McDougal, Myres S., Lasswell, Harold D., and Chen, Lung-chu. *Human Rights and World Public Order.* New Haven: Yale University Press, 1980.

Meron, Theodor, ed. *Human Rights in International Law: Legal and Policy Issues.* Oxford: Clarendon Press, 1984.

Mower, A. Glenn, Jr. *International Cooperation for Social Justice: Global and Regional Protection of Economic/Social Rights.* Westport, CT: Greenwood Press, 1985.

Morgenthau, Hans. *Human Rights and Foreign Policy.* New York: Council on Religion and International Affairs, 1979.

Muravchik, Joshua. *The Uncertain Crusade: Jimmy Carter and the Dilemmas of Human Rights Policy.* Lanham, MD: Hamilton Press, 1986.

Nanda, Ved P., ed. *Global Human Rights.* Boulder, CO: Westview Press, 1981.

Newberg, Paula R., ed. *The Politics of Human Rights.* New York: NYU Press, 1981.

Newsome, David D., ed. *The Diplomacy of Human Rights.* Lanham, MD: University Press of America, 1986.

Nickel, James W. *Making Sense of Human Rights.* Berkeley: University of California Press, 1987.

Owen, Edgar. *The Future of Freedom in the Developing World.* New York: Pergamon Press, 1988.

Pollis, Adamantia, and Schwab, Peter, eds. *Human Rights: Cultural and Ideological Perspectives.* New York: Praeger Publishers, 1980.

Ramcharan, B. G. *Human Rights.* Boston: M. Nijhoff, 1979.

Rubin, Barry M., and Spiro, Elizabeth P., eds. *Human Rights and U. S. Foreign Policy.* Boulder, CO: Westview, 1979.

Robertson, A. H. *Human Rights in the World.* New York: St. Martin's Press, 1982, 2nd ed.

Schoultz, Lars. *Human Rights and United States Policy toward Latin America.* Princeton: Princeton University Press, 1981.

Shue, Henry. *Basic Rights.* Princeton: Princeton University Press, 1980.

Tolley, Howard Jr. *The United Nations Commission on Human Rights.* Boulder, CO: Westview Press, 1987.

Tutle, James C., ed. *International Human Rights Law and Practice.* Philadelphia: ABA, 1978.

Vasak, Karel, and Alston, Philip, eds. *The International Dimensions of Human Rights.* Westport, CT: Greenwood Press, 1982.

Vincent, R. J. *Human Rights and International Relations.* Cambridge, UK: Cambridge University Press, 1986.

Vogelgesang, Sandra. *American Dream, Global Nightmare: The Dilemma of U. S. Human Rights Policy.* New York: Norton, 1980.

Welch, Claude E., and Meltzer, Ronald I., eds. *Human Rights and Development in Africa.* Albany, NY: SUNY Press, 1984.

Wiarda, Howard J., ed. *Human Rights and U. S. Human Rights Policy.* Washington, DC: American Enterprise Institute, 1982.

Appendix

The International Bill of Human Rights

A. UNIVERSAL DECLARATION OF HUMAN RIGHTS

Adopted and proclaimed by General Assembly resolution 217 A (III) of 10 December 1948

Preamble

Whereas recognition of the inherent dignity and of the equal and inalienable rights of all members of the human family is the foundation of freedom, justice and peace in the world,

Whereas disregard and contempt for human rights have resulted in barbarous acts which have outraged the conscience of mankind, and the advent of a world in which human beings shall enjoy freedom of speech and belief and freedom from fear and want has been proclaimed as the highest aspiration of the common people,

Whereas it is essential, if man is not to be compelled to have recourse, as a last resort, to rebellion against tyranny and oppression, that human rights should be protected by the rule of law,

Whereas it is essential to promote the development of friendly relations between nations,

Whereas the peoples of the United Nations have in the Charter reaffirmed their faith in fundamental human rights, in the dignity and worth of the human person and in the equal rights of men and women and have determined to promote social progress and better standards of life in larger freedom,

Whereas Member States have pledged themselves to achieve, in cooperation with the United Nations, the promotion of universal respect for and observance of human rights and fundamental freedoms,

Whereas a common understanding of these rights and freedoms is of the greatest importance for the full realization of this pledge,

Now, therefore,
The General Assembly

Proclaims this Universal Declaration of Human Rights as a common standard of achievement for all peoples and all nations, to the end that every individual and every organ of society, keeping this Declaration constantly in mind, shall strive by teaching and education to promote respect for these rights and freedoms and by progressive measures, national and international to secure their universal and effective recognition and observance, both among the peoples of Member States themselves and among the peoples of territories under their jurisdiction.

Article 1

All human beings are born free and equal in dignity and rights. They are endowed with reason and conscience and should act towards one another in a spirit of brotherhood.

Article 2

Everyone is entitled to all the rights and freedoms set forth in this Declaration, without distinction of any kind, such as race, colour, sex, language, religion, political or other opinion, national or social origin, property, birth or other status.

Furthermore, no distinction shall be made on the basis of the political, jurisdictional or international status of the country or territory to which a person belongs, whether it be independent, trust, non-self-governing or under any other limitation of sovereignty.

Article 3

Everyone has the right to life, liberty and the security of person.

Article 4

No one shall be held in slavery or servitude; slavery and the slave trade shall be prohibited in all their forms.

Article 5

No one shall be subjected to torture or to cruel, inhuman or degrading treatment or punishment.

Article 6

Everyone has the right to recognition everywhere as a person before the law.

Article 7

All are equal before the law and are entitled without any discrimination to equal protection of the law. All are entitled to equal protection against any discrimination in violation of this Declaration and against any incitement to such discrimination.

Article 8

Everyone has the right to an effective remedy by the competent national tribunals for acts violating the fundamental rights granted him by the constitution or by law.

Article 9

No one shall be subjected to arbitrary arrest, detention or exile.

Article 10

Everyone is entitled in full equality to a fair and public hearing by an independent and impartial tribunal, in the determination of his rights and obligations and of any criminal charge against him.

Article 11

1. Everyone charged with a penal offence has the right to be presumed innocent until proved guilty according to law in a public trial at which he has had all the guarantees necessary for his defence.

2. No one shall be held guilty of any penal offence on account of any act or omission which did not constitute a penal offence, under national or international law, at the time when it was committed. Nor shall a heavier penalty be imposed than the one that was applicable at the time the penal offence was committed.

Article 12

No one shall be subjected to arbitrary interference with his privacy, family, home or correspondence, nor to attacks upon his honour and reputation. Everyone has the right to the protection of the law against such interference or attacks.

Article 13

1. Everyone has the right to freedom of movement and residence within the borders of each State.

2. Everyone has the right to leave any country including his own, and to return to his country.

Article 14

1. Everyone has the right to seek and to enjoy in other countries asylum from persecution.
2. This right may not be invoked in the case of prosecutions genuinely arising from non-political crimes or from acts contrary to the purposes and principles of the United Nations.

Article 15

1. Everyone has the right to a nationality.
2. No one shall be arbitrarily deprived of his nationality nor denied the right to change his nationality.

Article 16

1. Men and women of full age, without any limitation due to race, nationality or religion, have the right to marry and to found a family. They are entitled to equal rights as to marriage, during marriage and at its dissolution.
2. Marriage shall be entered into only with the free and full consent of the intending spouses.
3. The family is the natural and fundamental group unit of society and is entitled to protection by society and the State.

Article 17

1. Everyone has the right to own property alone as well as in association with others.
2. No one shall be arbitrarily deprived of his property.

Article 18

Everyone has the right to freedom of thought, conscience and religion; this right includes freedom to change his religion or belief, and freedom, either alone or in community with others and in public or private, to manifest his religion or belief in teaching, practice, worship and observance.

Article 19

Everyone has the right to freedom of opinion and expression; this right includes freedom to hold opinions without interference and to seek, receive and impart information and ideas through any media and regardless of frontiers.

Article 20

1. Everyone has the right to freedom of peaceful assembly and association.
2. No one may be compelled to belong to an association.

Article 21

1. Everyone has the right to take part in the government of his country, directly or through freely chosen representatives.

2. Everyone has the right of equal access to public service in his country.

3. The will of the people shall be the basis of the authority of government; this will shall be expressed in periodic and genuine elections which shall be by universal and equal suffrage and shall be held by secret vote or by equivalent free voting procedures.

Article 22

Everyone, as a member of society, has the right to social security and is entitled to realization, through national effort and international co-operation and in accordance with the organization and resources of each State, of the economic, social and cultural rights indispensable for his dignity and the free development of his personality.

Article 23

1. Everyone has the right to work, to free choice of employment, to just and favourable conditions of work and to protection against unemployment.

2. Everyone, without any discrimination, has the right to equal pay for equal work.

3. Everyone who works has the right to just and favourable remuneration ensuring for himself and his family an existence worthy of human dignity, and supplemented, if necessary, by other means of social protection.

4. Everyone has the right to form and to join trade unions for the protection of his interests.

Article 24

Everyone has the right to rest and leisure, including reasonable limitation of working hours and periodic holidays with pay.

Article 25

1. Everyone has the right to a standard of living adequate for the health and well-being of himself and of his family, including food, clothing, housing, and medical care and necessary social services, and the right to security in the event of unemployment, sickness, disability, widowhood, old age or other lack of livelihood in circumstances beyond his control.

2. Motherhood and childhood are entitled to special care and assistance. All children, whether born in or out of wedlock, shall enjoy the same social protection.

Article 26

1. Everyone has the right to education. Education shall be free, at least in the elementary and fundamental stages. Elementary education shall be compulsory. Technical and professional education shall be made generally available and higher education shall be equally accessible to all on the basis of merit.

2. Education shall be directed to the full development of the human personality and to the strengthening of respect for human rights and fundamental freedoms. It shall promote understanding, tolerance and friendship among all nations, racial or religious groups, and shall further the activities of the United Nations for the maintenance of peace.

3. Parents have a prior right to choose the kind of education that shall be given to their children.

Article 27

1. Everyone has the right freely to participate in the cultural life of the community, to enjoy the arts and to share in scientific advancement and its benefits.

2. Everyone has the right to the protection of the moral and material interests resulting from any scientific, literary or artistic production of which he is the author.

Article 28

Everyone is entitled to a social and international order in which the rights and freedoms set forth in this Declaration can be fully realized.

Article 29

1. Everyone has duties to the community in which alone the free and full development of his personality is possible.

2. In the exercise of his rights and freedoms, everyone shall be subject only to such limitations as are determined by law solely for the purpose of securing due recognition and respect for the rights and freedoms of others and of meeting the just requirements of morality, public order and the general welfare in a democratic society.

3. These rights and freedoms may in no case be exercised contrary to the purposes and principles of the United Nations.

Article 30

Nothing in this Declaration may be interpreted as implying for any State, group or person any right to engage in any activity or to perform any act aimed at the destruction of any of the rights and freedoms set forth herein.

B. INTERNATIONAL COVENANT ON ECONOMIC, SOCIAL AND CULTURAL RIGHTS

Adopted and opened for signature, ratification and accession by General Assembly Resolution 2200 A (XXI) of 16 December 1966
Entry into force: 3 January 1976 (see article 27).

Preamble

The States Parties to the present Covenant,

Considering that, in accordance with the principles proclaimed in the Charter of the United Nations, recognition of the inherent dignity and of the equal and inalienable rights of all members of the human family is the foundation of freedom, justice and peace in the world,

Recognizing that these rights derive from the inherent dignity of the human person,

Recognizing that, in accordance with the Universal Declaration of Human Rights, the ideal of free human beings enjoying freedom from fear and want can only be achieved if conditions are created whereby everyone may enjoy his economic, social and cultural rights, as well as his civil and political rights,

Considering the obligation of States under the Charter of the United Nations to promote universal respect for, and observance of, human rights and freedoms,

Realizing that the individual, having duties to other individuals and to the community to which he belongs, is under a responsibility, to strive for the promotion and observance of the rights recognized in the present Covenant,

Agree upon the following articles:

Part I

Article 1

1. All peoples have the right of self-determination. By virtue of that right they freely determine their political status and freely pursue their economic, social and cultural development.

2. All peoples may, for their own ends, freely dispose of their natural wealth and resources without prejudice to any obligations arising out of international economic co-operation, based upon the principle of mutual benefit, and international law. In no case may a people be deprived of its own means of subsistence.

3. The States Parties to the present Covenant, including those having responsibility for the administration of Non-Self-Governing and Trust Territories, shall promote the realization of the right of self-determination, and shall respect that right, in conformity with the provisions of the Charter of the United Nations.

Part II

Article 2

1. Each State Party to the present Covenant undertakes to take steps, individually and through international assistance and co-operation, especially economic and technical, to the maximum of its available resources, with a view to achieving progressively the full realization of the rights recognized in the present Covenant by all appropriate means, including particularly the adoption of legislative measures.

2. The States Parties to the present Covenant undertake to guarantee that the rights enunciated in the present Covenant will be exercised without discrimination of any kind as to race, colour, sex, language, religion, political or other opinion, national or social origin, property, birth or other status.

3. Developing countries, with due regard to human rights and their national economy, may determine to what extent they would guarantee the economic rights recognized in the present Covenant to non-nationals.

Article 3

The States Parties to the present Covenant undertake to ensure the equal right of men and women to the enjoyment of all economic, social and cultural rights set forth in the present Covenant.

Article 4

The States Parties to the present Covenant recognize that, in the enjoyment of those rights provided by the State in conformity with the present Covenant, the State may subject such rights only to such limitations as are determined by law only in so far as this may be compatible with the nature of these rights and solely for the purpose of promoting the general welfare in a democratic society.

Article 5

1. Nothing in the present Covenant may be interpreted as implying for any State, group or person any right to engage in any activity or to perform any act aimed at the destruction of any of the rights or freedoms recognized herein, or at their limitation to a greater extent than is provided for in the present Covenant.

2. No restriction upon or derogation from any of the fundamental human rights recognized or existing in any country in virtue of law, conventions, regulations or custom shall be admitted on the pretext that the present Covenant does not recognize such rights or that it recognizes them to a lesser extent.

Part III

Article 6

1. The States Parties to the present Covenant recognize the right to work, which includes the right of everyone to the opportunity to gain his living by work which he freely chooses or accepts, and will take appropriate steps to safeguard this right.

2. The steps to be taken by a State Party to the present Covenant to achieve the full realization of this right shall include technical and vocational guidance and training programmes, policies and techniques to achieve steady economic, social and cultural development and full and productive employment under conditions safeguarding fundamental political and economic freedoms to the individual.

Article 7

The States Parties to the present Covenant recognize the right of everyone to the enjoyment of just and favourable conditions of work which ensure, in particular:
(a) Remuneration which provides all workers, as a minimum, with:
(i) Fair wages and equal remuneration for work of equal value without distinction of any kind, in particular women being guaranteed conditions of work not inferior to those enjoyed by men, with equal pay for equal work;
(ii) A decent living for themselves and their families in accordance with the provisions of the present Covenant;
(b) Safe and healthy working conditions;
(c) Equal opportunity for everyone to be promoted in his employment to an appropriate higher level, subject to no considerations other than those of seniority and competence;
(d) Rest, leisure and reasonable limitation of working hours and periodic holidays with pay, as well as remuneration for public holidays.

Article 8

1. The States Parties to the present Covenant undertake to ensure:
(a) The right of everyone to form trade unions and join the trade union of his choice, subject only to the rules of the organization concerned, for the promotion and protection of his economic and social interests. No restrictions may be placed on the exercise of this right other than those prescribed by law and which are necessary in a democratic society in the interests of national security or public order or for the protection of the rights and freedoms of others;
(b) The right of trade unions to establish national federations or confederations and the right of the latter to form or join international trade-union organizations;
(c) The right of trade unions to function freely subject to no limitation other than those prescribed by law and which are necessary in a democratic society in the interests of national security or public order or for the protection of the rights and freedoms of others;
(d) The right to strike, provided that it is exercised in conformity with the laws of the particular country.
2. This article shall not prevent the imposition of lawful restrictions on the exercise of these rights by members of the armed forces or of the police or of the administration of the State.
3. Nothing in this article shall authorize States Parties to the International Labour Organisation Convention of 1948 concerning Freedom of Association and Protection of the Right to Organize to take legislative measures which would prejudice, or apply the law in such a manner as

would prejudice, the guarantees provided for in that Convention.

Article 9

The States Parties to the present Covenant recognize the right of everyone to social security, including social insurance.

Article 10

The States Parties to the present Covenant recognize that:

1. The widest possible protection and assistance should be accorded to the family, which is the natural and fundamental group unit of society, particularly for its establishment and while it is responsible for the care and education of dependent children. Marriage must be entered into with the free consent of the intending spouses.

2. Special protection should be accorded to mothers during a reasonable period before and after childbirth. During such period working mothers should be accorded paid leave or leave with adequate social security benefits.

3. Special measures of protection and assistance should be taken on behalf of all children and young persons without any discrimination for reasons of parentage or other conditions. Children and young persons should be protected from economic and social exploitation. Their employment in work harmful to their morals or health or dangerous to life or likely to hamper their normal development should be punishable by law. States should also set age limits below which the paid employment of child labour should be prohibited and punishable by law.

Article 11

1. The States Parties to the present Covenant recognize the right of everyone to an adequate standard of living for himself and his family, including adequate food, clothing and housing, and to the continuous improvement of living conditions. The States Parties will take appropriate steps to ensure the realization of this right, recognizing to this effect the essential importance of international co-operation based on free consent.

2. The States Parties of the present Covenant, recognizing the fundamental right of everyone to be free from hunger, shall take, individually and through international co-operation, the measures, including specific programmes, which are needed:

(a) To improve methods of production, conservation and distribution of food by making full use of technical and scientific knowledge, by disseminating knowledge of the principles of nutrition and by developing or reforming agrarian systems in such a way as to achieve the most efficient development and utilization of natural resources;

(b) Taking into account the problems of both food-importing and food-exporting countries, to ensure an equitable distribution of world food supplies in relation to need.

Article 12

1. The States Parties to the present Covenant recognize the right of everyone to the enjoyment of the highest attainable standard of physical and mental health.

2. The steps to be taken by the States Parties to the present Covenant to achieve the full realization of this right shall include those necessary for:

(a) The provision for the reduction of the stillbirth-rate and of infant mortality and for the healthy development of the child;

(b) The improvement of all aspects of environmental and industrial hygiene;

(c) The prevention, treatment and control of epidemic, endemic, occupational and other diseases;

(d) The creation of conditions which would assure to all medical service and medical attention in the event of sickness.

Article 13

1. The States Parties to the present Covenant recognize the right of everyone to education. They agree that education shall be directed to the full development of the human personality and the sense of its dignity, and shall strengthen the respect for human rights and fundamental freedoms. They further agree that education shall enable all persons to participate effectively in a free society, promote understanding, tolerance and friendship among all nations and all racial, ethnic or religious groups, and further the activities of the United Nations for the maintenance of peace.

2. The States Parties to the present Covenant recognize that, with a view to achieving the full realization of this right:

(a) Primary education shall be compulsory and available free to all;

(b) Secondary education in its different forms, including technical and vocational secondary education, shall be made generally available and accessible to all by every appropriate means, and in particular by the progressive introduction of free education;

(c) Higher education shall be made equally accessible to all, on the basis of capacity, by every appropriate means, and in particular by the progressive introduction of free education;

(d) Fundamental education shall be encouraged or intensified as far as possible for those persons who have not received or completed the whole period of their primary education;

(e) The development of a system of schools at all levels shall be actively pursued, an adequate fellowship system shall be established, and the material conditions of teaching staff shall be continuously improved.

3. The States Parties to the present Covenant undertake to have respect for the liberty of parents and, when applicable, legal guardians to choose for their children schools, other than those established by the public authorities, which conform to such minimum educational standards as may be laid down or approved by the State and to ensure the religious and moral education of their children in conformity with their own convictions.

4. No part of this article shall be construed so as to interfere with the liberty of individuals and bodies to establish and direct educational institutions, subject always to the observance of the principles set forth in paragraph 1 of this article and to the requirement that the education given in such institutions shall conform to such minimum standards as may be laid down by the State.

Article 14

Each State Party to the present Covenant which, at the time of becoming a Party, has not been able to secure in its metropolitan territory or other territories under its jurisdiction compulsory primary education, free of charge, undertakes, within two years, to work out and adopt a detailed plan of action for the progressive implementation, within a reasonable number of years, to be fixed in the plan, of the principle of compulsory education free of charge for all.

Article 15

1. The States Parties to the present Covenant recognize the right of everyone:

(a) To take part in cultural life;

(b) To enjoy the benefits of scientific progress and its applications;

(c) To benefit from the protection of the moral and material interests resulting from any scientific, literary or artistic production of which he is the author.

2. The steps to be taken by the States Parties to the present Covenant to achieve the full realization of this right shall include those necessary for the conservation, the development and the diffusion of science and culture.

3. The States Parties to the present Covenant undertake to respect the freedom indispensable for scientific research and creative activity.

4. The States Parties to the present Covenant recognize the benefits to be derived from the encouragement and development of international contacts and co-operation in the scientific and cultural fields.

Part IV

Article 16

1. The States Parties to the present Covenant undertake to submit in conformity with this part of the Covenant reports on the measures which they have adopted and the progress made in achieving the observance of the rights recognized herein.

2. *(a)* All reports shall be submitted to the Secretary-General of the United Nations, who shall transmit copies to the Economic and Social Council for consideration in accordance with the provisions of the present Covenant;

(b) The Secretary-General of the United Nations shall also transmit to the specialized agencies copies of the reports, or any relevant parts therefrom, from States Parties to the present Covenant which are also members of these specialized agencies in so far as these reports, or parts therefrom, relate to any matters which fall within the responsibilities of the said agencies in accordance with their constitutional instruments.

Article 17

1. The States Parties to the present Covenant shall furnish their reports in stages, in accordance with a programme to be established by the Economic and Social Council within one year of the entry into force of the present Covenant after consultation with the States Parties and the specialized agencies concerned.

2. Reports may indicate factors and difficulties affecting the degree of fulfillment of obligations under the present Covenant.

3. Where relevant information has previously been furnished to the United Nations or to any specialized agency by any State Party to the present Covenant, it will not be necessary to reproduce that information, but a precise reference to the information so furnished will suffice.

Article 18

Pursuant to its responsibilities under the Charter of the United Nations in the field of human rights and fundamental freedoms, the Economic and

Social Council may make arrangements with the specialized agencies in respect of their reporting to it on the progress made in achieving the observance of the provisions of the present Covenant falling within the scope of their activities. These reports may include particulars of decisions and recommendations on such implementation adopted by their competent organs.

Article 19

The Economic and Social Council may transmit to the Commission on Human Rights for study and general recommendation or, as appropriate, for information the reports concerning human rights submitted by States in accordance with articles 16 and 17, and those concerning human rights submitted by the specialized agencies in accordance with article 18.

Article 20

The States Parties to the present Covenant and the specialized agencies concerned may submit comments to the Economic and Social Council on any general recommendation under article 19 or reference to such general recommendation in any report of the Commission on Human Rights or any documentation referred to therein.

Article 21

The Economic and Social Council may submit from time to time to the General Assembly reports with recommendations of a general nature and a summary of the information received from the States Parties to the present Covenant and the specialized agencies on the measures taken and the progress made in achieving general observance of the rights recognized in the present Covenant.

Article 22

The Economic and Social Council may bring to the attention of other organs of the United Nations, their subsidiary organs and specialized agencies concerned with furnishing technical assistance any matters arising out of the reports referred to in this part of the present Covenant which may assist such bodies in deciding each within its field of competence, on the advisability of international measures likely to contribute to the effective progressive implementation of the present Covenant.

Article 23

The States Parties to the present Covenant agree that international action for the achievement of the rights recognized in the present Covenant includes such methods as the conclusion of conventions, the adoption of recommendations, the furnishing of technical assistance and the holding of regional meetings and technical meetings for the purpose of consultation and study organized in conjunction with the Governments concerned.

Article 24

Nothing in the present Covenant shall be interpreted as impairing the provisions of the Charter of the United Nations and of the constitutions of the specialized agencies which define the respective responsibilities of the various organs of the United Nations and of the specialized agencies in regard to the matters dealt with in the present Covenant.

Article 25

Nothing in the present Covenant shall be interpreted as impairing the inherent right of all peoples to enjoy and utilize fully and freely their natural wealth and resources.

Part V

Article 26

1. The present Covenant is open for signature by any State Member of the United Nations or member of any of its specialized agencies, by any State Party to the Statute of the International Court of Justice, and by any other State which has been invited by the General Assembly of the United Nations to become a party to the present Covenant.

2. The present Covenant is subject to ratification. Instruments of ratification shall be deposited with the Secretary-General of the United Nations.

3. The present Covenant shall be open to accession by any State referred to in paragraph 1 of this article.

4. Accession shall be effected by the deposit of an instrument of accession with the Secretary-General of the United Nations.

5. The Secretary-General of the United Nations shall inform all States which have signed the present Covenant or acceded to it of the deposit of each instrument of ratification or accession.

Article 27

1. The present Covenant shall enter into force three months after the date of the deposit with the Secretary-General of the United Nations of the thirty-fifth instrument of ratification or instrument of accession.

2. For each State ratifying the present Covenant or acceding to it after the deposit of the thirty-fifth instrument of ratification or instrument of accession, the present Covenant shall enter into force three months after the date of the deposit of its own instrument of ratification or instrument of accession.

Article 28

The provisions of the present Covenant shall extend to all parts of federal States without any limitations or exceptions.

Article 29

1. Any State Party to the present Covenant may propose an amendment and file it with the Secretary-General of the United Nations. The Secretary-General shall thereupon communicate any proposed amendments to the States Parties to the present Covenant with a request that they notify him whether they favour a conference of States Parties for the purpose of considering and voting upon the proposals. In the event that at least one third of the State Parties favours such a conference, the Secretary-General shall convene the conference under the auspices of the United Nations. Any amendment adopted by a majority of the States Parties present and voting at the conference shall be submitted to the General Assembly of the United Nations for approval.

2. Amendments shall come into force when they have been approved by the General Assembly of the United Nations and accepted by a two-thirds majority of the States Parties to the present Covenant in accordance with their respective constitutional processes.

3. When amendments come into force they shall be binding on those States Parties which have accepted them, other States Parties still being bound by the provisions of the present Covenant and any earlier amendment which they have accepted.

Article 30

Irrespective of the notifications made under article 26, paragraph 5, the Secretary-General of the United Nations shall inform all States referred to in paragraph 1 of the same article of the following particulars:

(a) Signatures, ratifications and accessions under article 26;

(b) The date of the entry into force of the present Covenant under article 27 and the date of the entry into force of any amendments under article 29.

Article 31

1. The present Covenant, of which the Chinese, English, French, Russian and Spanish texts are equally authentic, shall be deposited in the archives of the United Nations.

2. The Secretary-General of the United Nations shall transmit certified copies of the present Covenant to all States referred to in article 26.

C. INTERNATIONAL COVENANT ON CIVIL AND POLITICAL RIGHTS

Adopted and opened for signature, ratification and accession by General Assembly Resolution 2200 A (XXI) of 16 December 1966
Entry into force: 26 March 1976 (see article 49).

Preamble

The States Parties to the present Covenant,

Considering that, in accordance with the principles proclaimed in the Charter of the United Nations recognition of the inherent dignity and of the equal and inalienable rights of all members of the human family is the foundation of freedom, justice and peace in the world,

Recognizing that these rights derive from the inherent dignity of the human person,

Recognizing that, in accordance with the Universal Declaration of Human Rights, the ideal of free human beings enjoying civil and political freedom and freedom from fear and want can only be achieved if conditions are created whereby everyone may enjoy his civil and political rights, as well as his economic, social and cultural rights,

Considering the obligation of States under the Charter of the United Nations to promote universal respect for, and observance of, human rights and freedoms,

Realizing that the individual, having duties to other individuals and to the community to which he belongs, is under a responsibility to strive for the promotion and observance of the rights recognized in the present Covenant,

Agree upon the following articles:

Part I

Article 1

1. All peoples have the right of self-determination. By virtue of that right they freely determine their political status and freely pursue their economic, social and cultural development.

2. All peoples may, for their own ends, freely dispose of their natural wealth and resources without prejudice to any obligations arising out of international economic co-operation, based upon the principle of mutual benefit, and international law. In no case may a people be deprived of its own means of subsistence.

3. The States Parties to the present Covenant, including those having responsibility for the administration of Non-Self-Governing and Trust Territories, shall promote the realization of the right of self-determination, and shall respect that right, in conformity with the provisions of the Charter of the United Nations.

Part II

Article 2

1. Each State Party to the present Covenant undertakes to respect and to ensure to all individuals within its territory and subject to its jurisdiction the rights recognized in the present Covenant, without distinction of any kind, such as race, colour, sex, language, religion, political or other opinion, national or social origin, property, birth or other status.

2. Where not already provided for by existing legislative or other measures, each State Party to the present Covenant undertakes to take the necessary steps, in accordance with its constitutional processes and with the provisions of the present Covenant, to adopt such legislative or other measures as may be necessary to give effect to the rights recognized in the present Covenant.

3. Each State Party to the present Covenant undertakes:

(a) To ensure that any person whose rights or freedoms as herein recognized are violated shall have an effective remedy, notwithstanding that the violation has been committed by persons acting in an official capacity;

(b) To ensure that any person claiming such a remedy shall have his right thereto determined by competent judicial, administrative or legisla-

tive authorities, or by any other competent authority provided for by the legal system of the State, and to develop the possibilities of judicial remedy;

(c) To ensure that the competent authorities shall enforce such remedies when granted.

Article 3

The States Parties to the present Covenent undertake to ensure the equal right of men and women to the enjoyment of all civil and political rights set forth in the present Covenant.

Article 4

1. In time of public emergency which threatens the life of the nation and the existence of which is officially proclaimed, the States Parties to the present Covenant may take measures derogating from their obligations under the present Covenant to the extent strictly required by the exigencies of the situation, provided that such measures are not inconsistent with their other obligations under international law and do not involve discrimination solely on the ground of race, colour, sex, language, religion or social origin.

2. No derogation from articles 6, 7, 8 (paragraphs 1 and 2), 11, 15, 16 and 18 may be made under this provision.

3. Any State Party to the present Covenant availing itself of the right of derogation shall immediately inform the other States Parties to the present Covenant, through the intermediary of the Secretary-General of the United Nations, of the provisions from which it has derogated and of the reasons by which it was actuated. A further communication shall be made, through the same intermediary, on the date on which it terminates such derogation.

Article 5

1. Nothing in the present Covenant may be interpreted as implying for any State, group or person any right to engage in any activity or perform any act aimed at the destruction of any of the rights and freedoms recognized herein or at their limitation to a greater extent than is provided for in the present Covenant.

2. There shall be no restriction upon or derogation from any of the fundamental human rights recognized or existing in any State Party to the present Covenant pursuant to law, conventions, regulations or custom on the pretext that the present Covenant does not recognize such rights or that it recognizes them to a lesser extent.

Part III

Article 6

1. Every human being has the inherent right to life. This right shall be protected by law. No one shall be arbitrarily deprived of his life.

2. In countries which have not abolished the death penalty, sentence of death may be imposed only for the most serious crimes in accordance with the law in force at the time of the commission of the crime and not contrary to the provisions of the present Covenant and to the Convention on the Prevention and Punishment of the Crime of Genocide. This penalty can only be carried out pursuant to a final judgement rendered by a competent court.

3. When deprivation of life constitutes the crime of genocide, it is understood that nothing in this article shall authorize any State Party to the present Covenant to derogate in any way from any obligation assumed under the provisions of the Convention on the Prevention and Punishment of the Crime of Genocide.

4. Anyone sentenced to death shall have the right to seek pardon or commutation of the sentence. Amnesty, pardon or commutation of the sentence of death may be granted in all cases.

5. Sentence of death shall not be imposed for crimes committed by persons below eighteen years of age and shall not be carried out on pregnant women.

6. Nothing in this article shall be invoked to delay or to prevent the abolition of capital punishment by any State Party to the present Covenant.

Article 7

No one shall be subjected to torture or to cruel, inhuman or degrading treatment or punishment. In particular, no one shall be subjected without his free consent to medical or scientific experimentation.

Article 8

1. No one shall be held in slavery; slavery and the slave-trade in all their forms shall be prohibited.

2. No one shall be held in servitude.

3. *(a)* No one shall be required to perform forced or compulsory labour;

(b) Paragraph 3 *(a)* shall not be held to preclude, in countries where imprisonment with hard labour may be imposed as a punishment for a crime, the performance of hard labour in pursuance of a sentence to such punishment by a competent court;

(c) For the purpose of this paragraph the term "forced or compulsory labour" shall not include:

(i) Any work or service, not referred to in subparagraph *(b)*, normally required of a person who is under detention in consequence of a lawful order of a court, or of a person during conditional release from such detention;

(ii) Any service of a military character and, in countries where conscientious objection is recognized, any national service required by law of conscientious objectors;

(iii) Any service exacted in cases of emergency or calamity threatening the life or well-being of the community;

(iv) Any work or service which forms part of normal civil obligations.

Article 9

1. Everyone has the right to liberty and security of person. No one shall be subjected to arbitrary arrest or detention. No one shall be deprived of his liberty except on such grounds and in accordance with such procedure as are established by law.

2. Anyone who is arrested shall be informed, at the time of arrest, of the reasons for his arrest and shall be promptly informed of any charges against him.

3. Anyone arrested or detained on a criminal charge shall be brought promptly before a judge or other officer authorized by law to exercise judicial power and shall be entitled to trial within a reasonable time or to release. It shall not be the general rule that persons awaiting trial shall be detained in custody, but release may be subject to guarantees to appear for trial, at any other stage of the judicial proceedings, and, should occasion arise, for execution of the judgement.

4. Anyone who is deprived of his liberty by arrest or detention shall be entitled to take proceedings before a court, in order that that court may decide without delay on the lawfulness of his detention and order his release if the detention is not lawful.

5. Anyone who has been the victim of unlawful arrest or detention shall have an enforceable right to compensation.

Article 10

1. All persons deprived of their liberty shall be treated with humanity and with respect for the inherent dignity of the human person.

2. *(a)* Accused persons shall, save in exceptional circumstances, be segregated from convicted persons and shall be subject to separate treatment appropriate to their status as unconvicted persons;

(b) Accused juvenile persons shall be separated from adults and brought as speedily as possible for adjudication.

3. The penitentiary system shall comprise treatment of prisoners the essential aim of which shall be their reformation and social rehabilitation. Juvenile offenders shall be segregated from adults and be accorded treatment appropriate to their age and legal status.

Article 11

No one shall be imprisoned merely on the ground of inability to fulfill a contractual obligation.

Article 12

1. Everyone lawfully within the territory of a State shall, within that territory, have the right to liberty of movement and freedom to choose his residence.

2. Everyone shall be free to leave any country, including his own.

3. The above-mentioned rights shall not be subject to any restrictions except those which are provided by law, are necessary to protect national security, public order *(ordre public)*, public health or morals or the rights and freedoms of others, and are consistent with the other rights recognized in the present Covenant.

4. No one shall be arbitrarily deprived of the right to enter his own country.

Article 13

An alien lawfully in the territory of a State Party to the present Covenant may be expelled therefrom only in pursuance of a decision reached in accordance with law and shall, except where compelling reasons of national security otherwise require, be allowed to submit the reasons against his expulsion and to have his case reviewed by, and be represented for the purpose before, the competent authority or a person or persons especially designated by the competent authority.

Article 14

1. All persons shall be equal before the courts and tribunals. In the determination of any criminal charge against him, or of his rights and obligations in a suit at law, everyone shall be entitled to a fair and public hearing by a competent, independent and impartial tribunal established by law. The Press and the public may be excluded from all or part of a trial for reasons of morals, public order *(ordre public)* or national security in a

democratic society, or when the interest of the private lives of the parties so requires, or to the extent strictly necessary in the opinion of the court in special circumstances where publicity would prejudice the interests of justice; but any judgement rendered in a criminal case or in a suit at law shall be made public except where the interest of juvenile persons otherwise requires or the proceedings concern matrimonial disputes or the guardianship of children.

2. Everyone charged with a criminal offense shall have the right to be presumed innocent until proved guilty according to law.

3. In the determination of any criminal charge against him, everyone shall be entitled to the following minimum guarantees, in full equality:

(a) To be informed promptly and in detail in a language which he understands of the nature and cause of the charge against him;

(b) To have adequate time and facilities for the preparation of his defence and to communicate with counsel of his own choosing;

(c) To be tried without undue delay;

(d) To be tried in his presence, and to defend himself in person or through legal assistance of his own choosing; to be informed, if he does not have legal assistance, of this right; and to have legal assistance assigned to him, in any case where the interests of justice so require, and without payment by him in any such case if he does not have sufficient means to pay for it;

(e) To examine, or have examined, the witnesses against him and to obtain the attendance and examination of witnesses on his behalf under the same conditions as witnesses against him;

(f) To have the free assistance of an interpreter if he cannot understand or speak the language used in court;

(g) Not to be compelled to testify against himself or to confess guilt.

4. In the case of juvenile persons, the procedure shall be such as will take account of their age and the desirability of promoting their rehabilitation.

5. Everyone convicted of a crime shall have the right to his conviction and sentence being reviewed by a higher tribunal according to law.

6. When a person has by a final decision been convicted of a criminal offence and when subsequently his conviction has been reversed or he has been pardoned on the ground that a new or newly discovered fact shows conclusively that there has been a miscarriage of justice, the person who has suffered punishment as a result of such conviction shall be compensated according to law, unless it is proved that the nondisclosure of the unknown fact in time is wholly or partly attributable to him.

7. No one shall be liable to be tried or punished again for an offence for which he has already been finally convicted or acquitted in accordance with the law and penal procedure of each country.

Article 15

1. No one shall be held guilty of any criminal offence on account of any act or omission which did not constitute a criminal offence, under national or international law, at the time when it was committed. Nor shall a heavier penalty be imposed than the one that was applicable at the time when the criminal offence was committed. If, subsequent to the commission of the offence, provision is made by law for the imposition of the lighter penalty, the offender shall benefit thereby.

2. Nothing in this article shall prejudice the trial and punishment of any person for any act or omission which, at the time when it was committed, was criminal according to the general principles of law recognized by the community of nations.

Article 16

Everyone shall have the right to recognition everywhere as a person before the law.

Article 17

1. No one shall be subjected to arbitrary or unlawful interference with his privacy, family, home or correspondence, nor to unlawful attacks on his honour and reputation.

2. Everyone has the right to the protection of the law against such interference or attacks.

Article 18

1. Everyone shall have the right to freedom of thought, conscience and religion. This right shall include freedom to have or to adopt a religion or belief of his choice, and freedom, either individually or in community with others and in public or private, to manifest his religion or belief in worship, observance, practice and teaching.

2. No one shall be subject to coercion which would impair his freedom to have or to adopt a religion or belief of his choice.

3. Freedom to manifest one's religion or beliefs may be subject only to such limitations as are prescribed by law and are necessary to protect public safety, order, health, or morals or the fundamental rights and freedoms of others.

4. The States Parties to the present Covenant undertake to have respect for the liberty of parents and, when applicable, legal guardians to ensure the religious and moral education of their children in conformity with their own convictions.

Article 19

1. Everyone shall have the right to hold opinions without interference.

2. Everyone shall have the right to freedom of expression; this right shall include freedom to seek, receive and impart information and ideas of all kinds, regardless of frontiers, either orally, in writing or in print, in the form of art, or through any other media of his choice.

3. The exercise of the rights provided for in paragraph 2 of this article carries with it special duties and responsibilities. It may therefore be subject to certain restrictions, but these shall only be such as are provided by law and are necessary:

    (a) For respect of the rights or reputations of others;

    (b) For the protection of national security or of public order (*ordre public*), or of public health or morals.

Article 20

1. Any propaganda for war shall be prohibited by law.

2. Any advocacy of national, racial or religious hatred that constitutes incitement to discrimination, hostility or violence shall be prohibited by law.

Article 21

The right of peaceful assembly shall be recognized. No restrictions may be placed on the exercise of this right other than those imposed in conformity with the law and which are necessary in a democratic society in the interests of national security or public safety, public order (*ordre public*), the protection of public health or morals or the protection of the rights and freedoms of others.

Article 22

1. Everyone shall have the right to freedom of association with others, including the right to form and join trade unions for the protection of his interests.

2. No restrictions may be placed on the exercise of this right other than those which are prescribed by law and which are necessary in a democratic society in the interests of national security or public safety, public order (*ordre public*), the protection of public health or morals or the protection of the rights and freedoms of others. This article shall not prevent the imposition of lawful restrictions on members of the armed forces and of the police in their exercise of this right.

3. Nothing in this article shall authorize States Parties to the International Labour Organisation Convention of 1948 concerning Freedom of

Association and Protection of the Right to Organize to take legislative measures which would prejudice, or to apply the law in such a manner as to prejudice the guarantees provided for in that Convention.

Article 23

1. The family is the natural and fundamental group unit of society and is entitled to protection by society and the State.

2. The right of men and women of marriageable age to marry and to found a family shall be recognized.

3. No marriage shall be entered into without the free and full consent of the intending spouses.

4. States Parties to the present Covenant shall take appropriate steps to ensure equality of rights and responsibilities of spouses as to marriage, during marriage and at its dissolution. In the case of dissolution, provision shall be made for the necessary protection of any children.

Article 24

1. Every child shall have, without any discrimination as to race, colour, sex, language, religion, national or social origin, property or birth, the right to such measures of protection as are required by his status as a minor, on the part of his family, society and the State.

2. Every child shall be registered immediately after birth and shall have a name.

3. Every child has the right to acquire a nationality.

Article 25

Every citizen shall have the right and the opportunity, without any of the distinctions mentioned in article 2 and without unreasonable restrictions:

(a) To take part in the conduct of public affairs, directly or through freely chosen representatives;

(b) To vote and to be elected at genuine periodic elections which shall be by universal and equal suffrage and shall be held by secret ballot, guaranteeing the free expression of the will of the electors;

(c) To have access, on general terms of equality, to public service in his country.

Article 26

All persons are equal before the law and are entitled without any discrimination to the equal protection of the law. In this respect, the law shall prohibit any discrimination and guarantee to all persons equal and effective protection against discrimination on any ground such as race, colour, sex, language, religion, political or other opinion, national or social origin, property, birth or other status.

Article 27

In those States in which ethnic, religious or linguistic minorities exist, persons belonging to such minorities shall not be denied the right, in community with the other members of their group, to enjoy their own culture, to profess and practice their own religion, or to use their own language.

Part IV

Article 28

1. There shall be established a Human Rights Committee (hereafter referred to in the present Covenant as the Committee). It shall consist of eighteen members and shall carry out the functions hereinafter provided.

2. The Committee shall be composed of nationals of the States Parties to the present Covenant who shall be persons of high moral character and recognized competence in the field of human rights, consideration being given to the usefulness of the participation of some persons having legal experience.

3. The members of the Committee shall be elected and shall serve in their personal capacity.

Article 29

1. The members of the Committee shall be elected by secret ballot from a list of persons possessing the qualifications prescribed in article 28 and nominated for the purpose by the States Parties to the present Covenant.

2. Each State Party to the present Covenant may nominate not more than two persons. These persons shall be nationals of the nominating State.

3. A person shall be eligible for renomination.

Article 30

1. The initial election shall be held no later than six months after the date of the entry into force of the present Covenant.

2. At least four months before the date of each election to the Committee, other than an election to fill a vacancy declared in accordance with article 34, the Secretary-General of the United Nations shall address a written invitation to the States Parties to the present Covenant to submit their nominations for membership of the Committee within three months.

3. The Secretary-General of the United Nations shall prepare a list in alphabetical order of all the persons thus nominated, with an indication of the States Parties which have nominated them, and shall submit it to the States Parties to the present Covenant no later than one month before the date of each election.

4. Elections of the members of the Committee shall be held at a meeting of the States Parties to the present Covenant convened by the Secretary-General of the United Nations at the Headquarters of the United Nations. At that meeting, for which two thirds of the States Parties to the present Covenant shall constitute a quorum, the persons elected to the Committee shall be those nominees who obtain the largest number of votes and an absolute majority of the votes of the representatives of States Parties present and voting.

Article 31

1. The Committee may not include more than one national of the same State.

2. In the election of the Committee, consideration shall be given to equitable geographical distribution of membership and to the representation of the different forms of civilization and of the principal legal systems.

Article 32

1. The members of the Committee shall be elected for a term of four years. They shall be eligible for re-election if renominated. However, the terms of nine of the members elected at the first election shall expire at the end of two years; immediately after the first election, the names of these nine members shall be chosen by lot by the Chairman of the meeting referred to in article 30, paragraph 4.

2. Elections at the expiry of office shall be held in accordance with the proceeding articles of this part of the present Covenant.

Article 33

1. If, in the unanimous opinion of the other members, a member of the Committee has ceased to carry out his functions for any cause other than

absence of a temporary character, the Chairman of the Committee shall notify the Secretary-General of the United Nations, who shall then declare the seat of that member to be vacant.

2. In the event of the death or the resignation of a member of the Committee, the Chairman shall immediately notify the Secretary-General of the United Nations, who shall declare the seat vacant from the date of death or the date on which the resignation takes effect.

Article 34

1. When a vacancy is declared in accordance with article 33 and if the term of office of the member to be replaced does not expire within six months of the declaration of the vacancy, the Secretary-General of the United Nations shall notify each of the States Parties to the present Covenant, which may within two months submit nominations in accordance with article 29 for the purpose of filling the vacancy.

2. The Secretary-General of the United Nations shall prepare a list in alphabetical order of the persons thus nominated and shall submit it to the States Parties to the present Covenant. The election to fill the vacancy shall then take place in accordance with the relevant provisions of this part of the present Covenant.

3. A member of the Committee elected to fill a vacancy declared in accordance with article 33 shall hold office for the remainder of the term of the member who vacated the seat on the Committee under the provisions of that article.

Article 35

The members of the Committee shall, with the approval of the General Assembly of the United Nations, receive emoluments from United Nations resources on such terms and conditions as the General Assembly may decide, having regard to the importance of the Committee's responsibilities.

Article 36

The Secretary-General of the United Nations shall provide the necessary staff and facilities for the effective performance of the functions of the Committee under the present Covenant.

Article 37

1. The Secretary-General of the United Nations shall convene the initial meeting of the Committee at the Headquarters of the United Nations.

2. After its initial meeting, the Committee shall meet at such times as shall be provided in its rules of procedure.

3. The Committee shall normally meet at the Headquarters of the United Nations or at the United Nations Office at Geneva.

Article 38

Every member of the Committee shall, before taking up his duties, make a solemn declaration in open committee that he will perform his functions impartially and conscientiously.

Article 39

1. The Committee shall elect its officers for a term of two years. They may be re-elected.

2. The Committee shall establish its own rules of procedure, but these rules shall provide, *inter alia*, that:

(a) Twelve members shall constitute a quorum;

(b) Decisions of the Committee shall be made by a majority vote of the members present.

Article 40

1. The States Parties to the present Covenant undertake to submit reports on the measures they have adopted which give effect to the rights recognized herein and on the progress made in the enjoyment of those rights:

(a) Within one year of the entry into force of the present Covenant for the States Parties concerned;

(b) Thereafter whenever the Committee so requests.

2. All reports shall be submitted to the Secretary-General of the United Nations, who shall transmit them to the Committee for consideration. Reports shall indicate the factors and difficulties, if any, affecting the implementation of the present Covenant.

3. The Secretary-General of the United Nations may, after consultation with the Committee, transmit to the specialized agencies concerned copies of such parts of the reports as may fall within their field of competence.

4. The Committee shall study the reports submitted by the States Parties to the present Covenant. It shall transmit its reports, and such general comments as it may consider appropriate, to the States Parties. The Committee may also transmit to the Economic and Social Council these comments along with the copies of the reports it has received from States Parties to the present Covenant.

5. The States Parties to the present Covenant may submit to the Committee observations on any comments that may be made in accordance with paragraph 4 of this article.

Article 41

1. A State Party to the present Covenant may at any time declare under this article that it recognizes the competence of the Committee to receive and consider communications to the effect that a State Party claims that another State Party is not fulfilling its obligations under the present Covenant. Communications under this article may be received and considered only if submitted by a State Party which has made a declaration recognizing in regard to itself the competence of the Committee. No communication shall be received by the Committee if it concerns a State Party which has not made such a declaration. Communications received under this article shall be dealt with in accordance with the following procedure:

(a) If a State Party to the present Covenant considers that another State Party is not giving effect to the provisions of the present Covenant, it may, by written communication, bring the matter to the attention of that State Party. Within three months after the receipt of the communication the receiving State shall afford the State which sent the communication an explanation or any other statement in writing clarifying the matter, which should include, to the extent possible and pertinent, reference to domestic procedures and remedies taken, pending, or available in the matter.

(b) If the matter is not adjusted to the satisfaction of both States Parties concerned within six months after the receipt by the receiving State of the initial communication, either State shall have the right to refer the matter to the Committee, by notice given to the Committee and to the other State.

(c) The Committee shall deal with a matter referred to it only after it has ascertained that all available domestic remedies have been invoked and exhausted in the matter, in conformity with the generally recognized principles of international law. This shall not be the rule where the application of the remedies is unreasonably prolonged.

(d) The Committee shall hold closed meetings when examining communications under this article.

(e) Subject to the provisions of sub-paragraph *(c)*, the Committee shall make available its good offices to the States Parties concerned with a view to a friendly solution of the matter on the basis of respect for human rights and fundamental freedoms as recognized in the present Covenant.

(f) In any matter referred to it, the Committee may call upon the States Parties concerned, referred to in sub-paragraph *(b)*, to supply any relevant information.

(g) The States Parties concerned, referred to in sub-paragraph *(b)*, shall have the right to be represented when the matter is being considered in the Committee and to make submissions orally and/or in writing.

(h) The Committee shall, within twelve months after the date of receipt of notice under sub-paragraph *(b)*, submit a report:

  (i) If a solution within the terms of sub-paragraph *(e)* is reached, the Committee shall confine its report to a brief statement of the facts and of the solution reached;

  (ii) If a solution within the terms of sub-paragraph *(e)* is not reached, the Committee shall confine its report to a brief statement of the facts; the written submissions and record of the oral submissions made by the States Parties concerned shall be attached to the report.

In every matter, the report shall be communicated to the States Parties concerned.

2. The provisions of this article shall come into force when ten States Parties to the present Covenant have made declarations under paragraph 1 of this article. Such declarations shall be deposited by the States Parties with the Secretary-General of the United Nations who shall transmit copies thereof to the other States Parties. A declaration may be withdrawn at any time by notification to the Secretary-General. Such a withdrawal shall not prejudice the consideration of any matter which is the subject of a communication already transmitted under this article; no further communication by any State Party shall be received after the notification of withdrawal of the declaration has been received by the Secretary-General, unless the State Party concerned has made a new declaration.

Article 42

1. *(a)* If a matter referred to the Committee in accordance with article 41 is not resolved to the satisfaction of the States Parties concerned, the Committee may, with the prior consent of the States Parties concerned, appoint an *ad hoc* Conciliation Commission (hereinafter referred to as the Commission). The good offices of the Commission shall be made available to the States Parties concerned with a view to an amicable solution of the matter on the basis of respect for the present Covenant;

(b) The Commission shall consist of five persons acceptable to the States Parties concerned. If the States Parties concerned fail to reach agreement within three months on all or part of the composition of the Commission, the members of the Commission concerning whom no agreement has been reached shall be elected by secret ballot by a two-thirds majority vote of the Committee from among its members.

2. The members of the Commission shall serve in their personal capacity. They shall not be nationals of the States Parties concerned, or of a

State not party to the present Covenant, or of a State Party which has not made a declaration under article 41.

3. The Commission shall elect its own Chairman and adopt its own rules of procedure.

4. The meetings of the Commission shall normally be held at the Headquarters of the United Nations or at the United Nations Office at Geneva. However, they may be held at such other convenient places as the Commission may determine in consultation with the Secretary-General of the United Nations and the States Parties concerned.

5. The secretariat provided in accordance with article 36 shall also service the commissions appointed under this article.

6. The information received and collated by the Committee shall be made available to the Commission and the Commission may call upon the States Parties concerned to supply any other relevant information.

7. When the Commission has fully considered the matter, but in any event not later than twelve months after having been seized of the matter, it shall submit to the Chairman of the Committee a report for communication to the States Parties concerned:

(a) If the Commission is unable to complete its consideration of the matter within twelve months, it shall confine its report to a brief statement of the status of its consideration of the matter;

(b) If an amicable solution to the matter on the basis of respect for human rights as recognized in the present Covenant is reached, the Commission shall confine its report to a brief statement of the facts and of the solution reached;

(c) If a solution within the terms of sub-paragraph *(b)* is not reached, the Commission's report shall embody its findings on all questions of fact relevant to the issues between the States Parties concerned, and its views on the possibilities of an amicable solution of the matter. This report shall also contain the written submissions and a record of the oral submissions made by the States Parties concerned;

(d) If the Commission's report is submitted under sub-paragraph *(c)*, the States Parties concerned shall, within three months of the receipt of the report, notify the Chairman of the Committee whether or not they accept the contents of the report of the Commission.

8. The provisions of this article are without prejudice to the responsibilities of the Committee under article 41.

9. The States Parties concerned shall share equally all the expenses of the members of the Commission in accordance with estimates to be provided by the Secretary-General of the United Nations.

10. The Secretary-General of the United Nations shall be empowered to pay the expenses of the members of the Commission, if necessary, before reimbursement by the States Parties concerned, in accordance with paragraph 9 of this article.

Article 43

The members of the Committee, and of the *ad hoc* conciliation commissions which may be appointed under article 42, shall be entitled to the facilities, privileges and immunities of experts on mission for the United Nations as laid down in the relevant sections of the Convention on the Privileges and Immunities of the United Nations.

Article 44

The provisions for the implementation of the present Covenant shall apply without prejudice to the procedures prescribed in the field of human rights by or under the constituent instruments and the conventions of the United Nations and of the specialized agencies and shall not prevent the States Parties to the present Covenant from having recourse to other procedures for settling a dispute in accordance with general or special international agreements in force between them.

Article 45

The Committee shall submit to the General Assembly of the United Nations, through the Economic and Social Council, an annual report on its activities.

Part V

Article 46

Nothing in the present Covenant shall be interpreted as impairing the provisions of the Charter of the United Nations and of the constitutions of the specialized agencies which define the respective responsibilities of the various organs of the United Nations and of the specialized agencies in regard to the matters dealt within the present Covenant.

Article 47

Nothing in the present Covenant shall be interpreted as impairing the inherent right of all peoples to enjoy and utilize fully and freely their natural wealth and resources.

Part VI

Article 48

1. The present Covenant is open for signature by any State Member of the United Nations or member of any of its specialized agencies, by any State Party to the Statute of the International Court of Justice, and by any other State which has been invited by the General Assembly of the United Nations to become a party to the present Covenant.

2. The present Covenant is subject to ratification. Instruments of ratification shall be deposited with the Secretary-General of the United Nations.

3. The present Covenant shall be open to accession by any State referred to in paragraph 1 of this article.

4. Accession shall be effected by the deposit of an instrument of accession with the Secretary-General of the United Nations.

5. The Secretary-General of the United Nations shall inform all States which have signed this Covenant or acceded to it of the deposit of each instrument of ratification or accession.

Article 49

1. The present Covenant shall enter into force three months after the date of the deposit with the Secretary-General of the United Nations of the thirty-fifth instrument of ratification or instrument of accession.

2. For each State ratifying the present Covenant or acceding to it after the deposit of the thirty-fifth instrument of ratification or instrument of accession, the present Covenant shall enter into force three months after the date of the deposit of its own instrument of ratification or instrument of accession.

Article 50

The provisions of the present Covenant shall extend to all parts of federal States without any limitations or exceptions.

Article 51

1. Any State Party to the present Covenant may propose an amendment and file it with the Secretary-General of the United Nations. The Secretary-General of the United Nations shall thereupon communicate any proposed amendments to the States Parties to the present Covenant with a request that they notify him whether they favour a conference of States Parties for the purpose of considering and voting upon the proposals. In

the event that at least one third of the States Parties favours such a conference, the Secretary-General shall convene the conference under the auspices of the United Nations. Any amendment adopted by a majority of the States Parties present and voting at the conference shall be submitted to the General Assembly of the United Nations for approval.

2. Amendments shall come into force when they have been approved by the General Assembly of the United Nations and accepted by a two-thirds majority of the States Parties to the present Covenant in accordance with their respective constitutional processes.

3. When amendments come into force, they shall be binding on those States Parties which have accepted them, other States Parties still being bound by the provisions of the present Covenant and any earlier amendment which they have accepted.

Article 52

Irrespective of the notifications made under article 48, paragraph 5, the Secretary-General of the United Nations shall inform all States referred to in paragraph 1 of the same article of the following particulars:

(a) Signatures, ratifications and accessions under article 48;

(b) The date of the entry into force of the present Covenant under article 49 and the date of the entry into force of any amendments under article 51.

Article 53

1. The present Covenant, of which the Chinese, English, French, Russian and Spanish texts are equally authentic, shall be deposited in the archives of the United Nations.

2. The Secretary-General of the United Nations shall transmit certified copies of the present Covenant to all States referred to in article 48.

D. OPTIONAL PROTOCOL TO THE INTERNATIONAL
COVENANT ON CIVIL AND POLITICAL RIGHTS

Adopted and opened for signature, ratification and accession by General Assembly Resolution 2200 A (XXI) of 16 December 1966
Entry into force: 26 March 1976

The States Parties to the present Protocol,
    Considering that in order further to achieve the purposes of the Covenant on Civil and Political Rights (hereinafter referred to as the Covenant)

and the implementation of its provisions it would be appropriate to enable the Human Rights Committee set up in part IV of the Covenant (hereinafter referred to as the Committee) to receive and consider, as provided in the present Protocol, communications from individuals claiming to be victims of violations of any of the rights set forth in the Covenant.

Have agreed as follows:

Article 1

A State Party to the Covenant that becomes a party to the present Protocol recognizes the competence of the Committee to receive and consider communications from individuals subject to its jurisdiction who claim to be victims of a violation by that State Party of any of the rights set forth in the Covenant. No communication shall be received by the Committee if it concerns a State Party to the Covenant which is not a party to the present Protocol.

Article 2

Subject to the provisions of article 1, individuals who claim that any of their rights enumerated in the Covenant have been violated and who have exhausted all available domestic remedies may submit a written communication to the Committee for consideration.

Article 3

The Committee shall consider inadmissible any communication under the present Protocol which is anonymous, or which it considers to be an abuse of the right of submission of such communications or to be incompatible with the provisions of the Covenant.

Article 4

1. Subject to the provisions of article 3, the Committee shall bring any communications submitted to it under the present Protocol to the attention of the State Party to the present Protocol alleged to be violating any provision of the Covenant.

2. Within six months, the receiving State shall submit to the Committee written explanations or statements clarifying the matter and the remedy, if any, that may have been taken by that State.

Article 5

1. The Committee shall consider communications received under the present Protocol in the light of all written information made available to it by the individual and by the State Party concerned.

2. The Committee shall not consider any communication from an individual unless it has ascertained that:

(a) The same matter is not being examined under another procedure of international investigation or settlement;

(b) The individual has exhausted all available domestic remedies. This shall not be the rule where the application of the remedies is unreasonably prolonged.

3. The Committee shall hold closed meetings when examining communications under the present Protocol.

4. The Committee shall forward its views to the State Party concerned and to the individual.

Article 6

The Committee shall include in its annual report under article 45 of the Covenant a summary of its activities under the present Protocol.

Article 7

Pending the achievement of the objectives of resolution 1514 (XV) adopted by the General Assembly of the United Nations on 14 December 1960 concerning the Declaration on the Granting of Independence to Colonial Countries and Peoples, the provisions of the present Protocol shall in no way limit the right of petition granted to these peoples by the Charter of the United Nations and other international conventions and instruments under the United Nations and its specialized agencies.

Article 8

1. The present Protocol is open for signature by any State which has signed the Covenant.

2. The present Protocol is subject to ratification by any State which has ratified or acceded to the Covenant. Instruments of ratification shall be deposited with the Secretary-General of the United Nations.

3. The present Protocol shall be open to accession by any State which has ratified or acceded to the Covenant.

4. Accession shall be effected by the deposit of an instrument of accession with the Secretary-General of the United Nations.

5. The Secretary-General of the United Nations shall inform all States which have signed the present Protocol or acceded to it of the deposit of

each instrument of ratification or accession.

Article 9

1. Subject to the entry into force of the Covenant, the present Protocol shall enter into force three months after the date of the deposit with the Secretary-General of the United Nations of the tenth instrument of ratification or instrument of accession.

2. For each State ratifying the present Protocol or acceding to it after the deposit of the tenth instrument of ratification or instrument of accession, the present Protocol shall enter into force three months after the date of the deposit of its own instrument of ratification or instrument of accession.

Article 10

The provisions of the present Protocol shall extend to all parts of federal States without any limitations or exceptions.

Article 11

1. Any State Party to the present Protocol may propose an amendment and file it with the Secretary-General of the United Nations. The Secretary-General shall thereupon communicate any proposed amendments to the States Parties to the present Protocol with a request that they notify him whether they favour a conference of States Parties for the purpose of considering and voting upon the proposal. In the event that at least one third of the States Parties favours such a conference, the Secretary-General shall convene the conference under the auspices of the United Nations. Any amendment adopted by a majority of the States Parties present and voting at the conference shall be submitted to the General Assembly of the United Nations for approval.

2. Amendments shall come into force when they have been approved by the General Assembly of the United Nations and accepted by a two-thirds majority of the States Parties to the present Protocol in accordance with their respective constitutional processes.

3. When amendments come into force, they shall be binding on those States Parties which have accepted them, other States Parties still being bound by the provisions of the present Protocol and any earlier amendment which they have accepted.

Article 12

1. Any State Party may denounce the present Protocol at any time by

written notification addressed to the Secretary-General of the United Nations. Denunciation shall take effect three months after the date of receipt of the notification by the Secretary-General.

2. Denunciation shall be without prejudice to the continued application of the provisions of the present Protocol to any communication submitted under article 2 before the effective date of denunciation.

Article 13

Irrespective of the notifications made under article 8, paragraph 5, of the present Protocol, the Secretary-General of the United Nations shall inform all States referred to in article 48, paragraph 1, of the Covenant of the following particulars:

(a) Signatures, ratifications and accessions under article 8;

(b) The date of the entry into force of the present Protocol under article 9 and the date of the entry into force of any amendments under article 11;

(c) Denunciations under article 12.

Article 14

1. The present Protocol, of which the Chinese, English, French, Russian and Spanish texts are equally authentic, shall be deposited in the archives of the United Nations.

2. The Secretary-General of the United Nations shall transmit certified copies of the present Protocol to all States referred to in article 48 of the Covenant.

Index

Abourezk, James, 142, 143
Abrams, Elliott, 116, 120, 134, 154
Ad Hoc Committee on the Human
    Rights and Genocide Treaties, 131
Advertising, freedom of, 42
Afghanistan, 53, 114, 157, 207, 208,
    218
AFL-CIO, 83, 86
African Charter on Individual and
    Peoples Rights (Banjul Charter),
    21, 51, 176
African Human Rights Commis-
    sion, 51
Agency for International Develop-
    ment (AID), 118, 136, 152, 153
Aggression and human rights, 30–
    31, 60
Albania, 63, 68, 186
Alfonsin, Raul, 81
Algeria, 16, 175
Allende, Salvadore, 52, 107, 187
Allis-Chalmers Corporation, 137,
    151
Amalgamated Meat Cutters and
    Butcher Workmens Union, 132
American Association for the Ad-
    vancement of Science (AAAS), 131
American Civil Liberties Union
    (ACLU), 87, 131
American Committee on Africa,
    135, 139
American Convention on Human
    Rights, 19, 63, 111, 211
American Enterprise Institute, 138
American Psychiatric Association,
    89, 131

Americans for Democratic Action
    (ADA), 84, 86, 135, 137, 139, 140,
    143, 144, 148, 150
America's Watch, 92
Amin, Idi, 33, 112, 186, 187, 205,
    215, 220
Amnesty International, 4, 50, 79, 85,
    87, 89, 90, 91, 93, 94, 96, 99, 101,
    129, 132, 134, 135, 137, 139, 142,
    145, 149, 150, 156, 157, 205, 206
Amuzegar, Jahangir, 175
Angola, 209
Anti-Slavery League (Society), 9, 85
Apartheid, 15, 98, 103, 122, 144, 165,
    222
Aquinas, Thomas, 167
Aquino, Corazon, 119
Arab League, 21
Arbatov, Georgi, 173
Argentina, 4, 81, 96, 107, 112, 116,
    121, 137, 148, 149, 151, 152, 165,
    166, 205, 223
Armed conflict and human rights,
    7–8, 10, 16, 30, 31, 32, 33, 34, 35,
    49, 56, 62, 63, 67, 80, 85, 91, 224
Armenians, 10, 34
Article 55, 11, 12, 13, 29
Association, freedom of. See Labor
    rights
Austria, 63

"Bakke case," 183
Baluchistan, 217
Bangladesh, 33, 35, 56, 81, 217
Banks, private, and human rights,
    125, 206

Basic human needs, 118, 124
Basques, 34
Belgian Congo, 32
Belgium, 183
Bentham, Jeremy, 168
Biko, Steven, 143
Bill of Rights, American, 13
Black Caucus, 143
Boeing Corporation, 147
Bolivia, 39, 81, 224
Bonker, Donald, 147
Botswana, 81, 186, 226
Brazil, 79, 142, 165, 166
Bread for the World, 148
Brezhnev, Leonid, 173
Brierly, J. L., 194, 196
Brzezinski, Zbigniew, 114, 153, 176
Buckley, William F., Jr., 221
Bukovsky, Vladimir, xiv
Bulgaria, 95, 196
Bureau of American Republics Af-
    fairs, U.S. Department of State
    (ARA), 148, 151, 152, 153
Bureau of Human Rights and Hu-
    manitarian Affairs, U.S. Depart-
    ment of State (HA), 2, 108, 116, 120,
    126, 133, 134, 135, 137, 142, 145,
    147, 148, 149, 151, 152, 153, 154,
    221; and attitudes toward non-
    governmental organizations, 145,
    147, 152
Burke, Edmund, 165, 166, 168

Cambodia. See Kampuchea
Canada, 21
CARITAS, 92
Carnegie Endowment, 142
Carter, Jimmy, xi, 1, 7, 74, 109, 118,
    120, 124, 125, 127, 128, 130, 133,
    135, 141, 142, 145, 146, 148, 149,
    152, 154, 156, 168, 176, 178, 179,
    206, 207, 208, 210; and foreign
    policy rhetoric, 2, 3, 30, 110–14,
    121; and foreign policy action, 59,
    65, 110–14; critique of views of,
    112–14
Case, Clifford, 146

Castro, Fidel, 213, 225
Catholic church, 26, 86, 95, 96, 183,
    206
Catholic Conference, 143
Center for International Policy, 135,
    137, 143
Central American Court on Human
    Rights, 10
Chamber of Commerce, 151
Chile, 15, 51, 53, 79, 82, 84, 96, 107,
    109, 112, 116, 118, 119, 120, 125,
    129, 144, 151, 152, 158, 187, 205,
    206, 207, 208, 209
Chiles, Lawton, 146, 147
China, Peoples Republic of, 27, 56,
    97, 105, 108, 112, 117, 123, 220
Christopher, Warren, 156
Church, Frank, 142
Church World Service, 92
Civil and political rights, xiv, 2, 6,
    13, 14, 19, 26, 31, 40, 41, 49, 50, 52,
    68, 74, 75, 76, 79, 81, 82, 88, 94,
    95, 98, 101, 108, 111, 112, 114, 115,
    119, 125, 131, 132, 166, 177, 179,
    190, 201, 202, 203, 204, 205, 208,
    211, 213, 214, 219, 225, 226. See
    also United Nations Covenant on
    Civil and Political Rights
Civil Rights Commission, U.S., 221
Coalition for a New Foreign and
    Military Policy, Working Group
    on Human Rights (the Coalition),
    132, 133, 135, 137, 139, 140
Collective rights. See communal
    rights
Colonialism, 34
Columbia, 81
Common Cause, 129
Common Market. See European
    Economic Community
Communal rights, xiv, 161, 163, 207,
    212; theory of, 14, 161, 172–77;
    theory of in international society,
    161, 177–81; practice of, 13, 21,
    181–87; western version of, 183
Communism, 2, 173, 176, 212, 213
Congress, U.S., xi, 4, 26, 60, 89, 107,

108, 109, 112, 116, 118, 124, 126,
129, 131, 132, 133, 135, 136, 137,
139, 141, 143, 145, 146, 149, 151,
152, 154, 155, 156, 158, 198, 199,
206, 208, 209, 210, 221, 222
Congress of Vienna, 105
Conscientious objection, 95
Conservatism, x, 161, 166, 211; theory of, 161, 163–67; theory of in international society, 161, 177–81; practice of, 165–67, 181–87
Constitution, U.S., 36
"Constructive engagement," 118, 122
"Contras," 120
Convention on Freedom of Association, 53
Convention on Racial Discrimination, 15, 36, 53
Costa Rica, 63, 80, 81, 226
Council of Europe, 18, 19
Council of Hemispheric Affairs, 137, 140
Country reports on human rights, U.S., 88, 114, 145, 149, 158, 221
Country-specific legislation, 107
Covenants. See United Nations covenants
Cranston, Maurice, 168
Crime-control equipment, 118
Cuba, 32, 92, 103, 117, 120, 225
Cultural rights, 2, 50, 114
Culver, John, 219
Customary law, 12
Czechoslovakia, 76, 77, 78, 90, 94, 95, 96, 122, 174, 184, 226; and Charter, 76, 77

Democratic Yemen, 209
Denmark, xiii, 170, 171, 178. See also Scandinavian states
Derian, Patricia, 110, 156, 157
Detention, political, 20, 76, 80, 91, 92, 97, 104, 179
Diggs v. Shultz, 134
Dijlas, Milovan, 185
Disappeared persons, 3, 20, 81, 96, 129, 187

Dissent, political, 4, 21, 28, 220
Doctrine of national sovereignty, 1, 4, 17, 60, 200, 228; contradiction of, 6
Domestic (state) jurisdiction, 22, 200, 215
Dominican Republic, 58, 81, 112, 141
Donnelly, Jack, 172
Drew, Elizabeth, 141
Dubcek, Alexander, 77, 122, 174, 183, 184
Duchacek, Ivo, 25, 43
Dunant, Henri, 7
Duvalier, "Baby Doc," 56, 79, 119

East Germany. See Germany, East
East Timor, 145, 148, 205. See also Indonesia
Ebenstein, William, 171
Economic rights. See Socio-economic rights
Education, right to, 38, 40
Egypt, 31
Eide, Asborn, 1, 37, 203
Eisenhower, Dwight, 104, 105
El Salvador, 33, 53, 81, 96, 107, 116, 122, 151, 158, 217, 218, 220, 224
Engels, Friedrich, 173
Enlightenment, 5
Entebbe airport, 32
Equal rights, 11, 161
Eritreans, 33, 35
Ethiopia, 34, 35, 79, 92, 93, 209
Ethnicity and human rights, 34, 35, 59
European Commission on Human Rights, 18, 56, 57, 58, 59, 66, 205
European Committee of Ministers, 57, 58
European Convention on Human Rights, 18, 19, 56, 58, 59, 63, 64, 65, 74
European Court of Human Rights, 18, 19, 57, 58, 59, 63, 66, 205
European Economic Community (EEC), 19

European Social Charter, 19
Evans, Thomas, 144
Execution, 85, 88, 110
Export-Import Bank, U.S., 107, 137, 143, 144, 151

Fagen, Richard, 201
Falklands (Malvinas) War, 121
Fascism, 10, 163, 165, 166. *See also* Nazism
Federal Bureau of Investigation (FBI), 74
Filartiga v. Pena, 3, 4, 64, 228
Food and Agricultural Organization (FAO), 15, 192
Forced labor, 31, 99
Ford, Gerald, 105
Ford Foundation, 157
Foreign Assistance Act, Section 116 (U.S.), 137, 143, 148
Fowles, John, 169
France, 31, 94, 119, 120
Fraser, Donald, 107, 141, 142, 147, 151, 156
Freedom fighters, 17. *See also* Guerilla fighters
Freedom House, 86, 130, 137, 139, 146, 148
Freedom of association and organization, 15, 40–41, 54, 95, 96, 129, 130, 174, 184
Freedom of expression, 63
Freedom of movement, 43
Freedom of religion, 42, 130
Freedom of speech, 5, 40, 43, 95, 174, 184
Freedom of the press, 43, 50, 95
Friedmen, Milton, 166
Friends Committee on National Legislation (Quakers), 129, 139, 142, 143
Friends of the Filipino People, 155
Function-specific legislation, 108

Gandhi, Indira, 97
Geneva Conventions, 7, 10, 16, 56, 80, 90, 106. *See also* Armed conflict and human rights
Geneva Protocols (1977), 17, 18, 56, 80, 90
Genocide, 10, 11, 15, 32, 186, 187, 217, 220
Genocide Treaty, 210
Germany, East, 22, 78, 95, 96, 184, 186
Germany, West, 22, 74, 94
Goldberg, Arthur J., 111
Gorbachev, Mikhail, 50, 77, 95, 123, 174, 226
Greece, 58, 66, 68, 104, 121
Green, T. H., 167, 168
Grenada, 2, 32, 209
Guatemala, 53, 81, 104, 107, 112, 116, 118, 120, 122, 129, 151, 158
Guerilla fighters, 17, 207

Haas, Ernest B., 29, 53, 54, 190
Haig, Alexander, 115, 116
Haiti, 56, 79, 107, 118, 119, 120, 154, 158, 209, 218
Hammarskjold, Dag, 55
Harkin, Tom, 143, 146, 147, 151, 156
Havana Conference of Non-Aligned States, 78
Hayek, F. A., 166
Hegel, George, 175
Heilbroner, Robert, 220
Helms, Jesse, 148
Helms, Richard, 199
Helsinki Accord, 21, 22, 47, 50, 76, 77, 78, 94, 106, 123; and Belgrade Conference, 22, 111, 149; and Madrid Conference, 22, 149; and Ottawa Conference, 22; and Stockholm Conference, 22
Helsinki Watch Committee, U.S., 85, 95
Heritage Foundation, 138, 154
Hoffmann, Stanley, 30, 42, 124, 162
Holtzman, Elizabeth, 145
Honduras, 3, 20, 81
Humanitarian intervention, 6, 32, 93

Human rights, definition of, 4–7
Human Rights Day, 189
Human Rights Institute, 221
Human Rights Working Group, 85
Hungary, 78, 95, 96, 123, 184, 186, 226
Hyde, Henry, 146, 148

IBM Corporation, 199
India, 33, 62, 81, 97, 98, 225, 226
Individual human rights, 3, 8, 14, 20, 22, 26, 33, 177, 184, 212, 213
Individual petition, 13, 19, 58–60, 65
Indonesia, 148, 149
Institute for Policy Studies, 135
Inter-American Bank, 111
Inter-American Commission on Human Rights, 19, 20, 57, 59, 79–80, 98, 151, 205
Inter-American Convention on Human Rights, 19, 63, 111, 211
Inter-American Court, 20, 63, 64
Internal Revenue Service, 129
Inter-Parliamentary Union, 90
International Bank for Reconstruction and Development. See World Bank
International Bill of Human Rights, 227
International Commission of Jurists, 84, 98, 129, 137, 150–51, 189, 225
International Committee of the Red Cross (ICRC), 7, 8, 9, 47, 56, 80, 85, 90, 91, 92, 93, 98, 99, 108
International Court of Justice. See World Court
International Defense and Aid Fund, 85
International Financial Institutions (IFI), 107, 124, 151, 152
International Human Rights Law Group (IHRLG), 133, 134
International Institute of Human Rights, 84
International Labor Organization

(ILO), 9, 14, 15, 50, 53, 54, 55, 98. See also Labor rights
International League of Human Rights, 85, 87, 127, 135, 137, 139, 142, 149, 221
International Monetary Fund (IMF), 148, 206
International Rescue Committee, 85
International Telephone and Telegraph, 199
Inter-Religious Task Force on U.S. Food Policy, 136
Iran, 31, 63, 67, 80, 91, 97, 104, 112, 121, 122, 157, 175, 179, 208, 215, 218
Iraq, 34, 80
Ireland, Republic of, 3, 26, 66, 74
Israel, 21, 31, 32, 51, 52, 55, 68, 78, 80, 92, 99
Italy, 94

Jackson, Henry: and Jackson-Vanik Amendment, 126
Jamaica, 81
Japan, 21, 88, 103, 191
Jefferson, Thomas, 167
John Paul II (pope), 202, 203
Johnson, Lyndon, 26, 105
Jung, Kim Dae, 118

Kadaffi, Muammar, 225
Kampuchea, Democratic, 32, 92, 107, 186, 205
Kennan, George, 27, 217
Kennedy, John F., 105
Kennedy, Ted, 145, 151, 156
Kenya, 27, 79, 90, 101
Khomeni, Ayatollah, 97
Kirkpatrick, Jeane, 115, 116, 120, 122; and Kirkpatrick Doctrine, 116, 118, 136, 138
Kissinger, Henry, 3, 105, 114, 121, 178, 179, 198, 207, 218; human rights views of, 105–10; critique of views of, 109–10
Koch, Ed, 151, 156

Korea. *See* South Korea
Kurds, 34

Labor rights, 8, 9, 15, 55, 83, 94, 99,
    129, 130, 144, 192. *See also* Inter-
    national Labor Organization
Lake, Anthony, 111
Laos, 107
Latvians, 35
Lauterpact, Hersch, 167
League Mandates Commission, 9
League of Nations, 8–9, 15
League of Red Cross Societies, 8
Lebanon, 81, 186, 226
Lefever, Ernest, 2, 115, 158, 228
Lenin, 173, 212, 213
Liberalism, x, xiv, 161, 165, 166,
    167–72, 173, 212; theory of in in-
    ternational society, 161, 177–81;
    practice of, 161, 181–87; Marxist
    version, 173, 177, 183–86
Liberia, 81, 107, 120, 158
Libya, 225
Lobbying: definition of, 129; for hu-
    man rights, 130–40
Locke, John, 167
Lugar, Richard, 120

McGovern, George, 143, 148
Malaysia, 81, 226
Malnutrition, 4, 37
Marcos, Ferdinand, 79, 97, 114, 119,
    120
Marshall, George, 30
Marxism, x, 22, 161, 162, 172, 173,
    176, 180, 212, 213
Mauritania, 4
Maurras, Charles, 167
Members of Congress for Peace
    through Law, 131
Mengistu Haile-Mariam, 79
Mexico, 26, 79, 103, 225
Michelsen Institute, 88
Mill, John Stuart, 168
Minorities, 8, 99
Minority Rights Group, 85
Mistreatment, 5, 40, 66, 92, 110, 225

Mitchell, Parren, 143
Mobil Oil Company, 129
Mobutu Sese Seko, 79
Moore, Barrington, 187
Morgenthau, Hans, 3
Morocco, 104, 112
Mothers of the Plaza del Mayo, 96
Moynihan, Daniel Patrick, 176
Mozambique, 91, 186
Mugabe, Robert, 177
Murder, 18, 20, 40, 96, 110, 205, 206,
    220

Namibia, 34, 35, 63, 78, 220, 228
National Council of Churches, 142
National Endowment for Democ-
    racy (U.S.), 98, 120
National Red Cross Societies, 8, 98
National security and human
    rights, 1–2, 103–10, 112–14, 142,
    145–46, 151, 152, 168–69, 178–79,
    207, 208, 215, 219, 220
National sovereignty. *See* Domes-
    tic (state) jurisdiction
Native Americans, 34, 35
Natural rights, 167–72, 211
Nazism, 9, 10, 11, 31, 74, 99, 218
Neal, Stephen, 143
Nestle Corportion, 41, 208
Network, the, 85, 132, 139
New Directions, 132, 134, 139
New International Economic Order
    (NIEO), 78
New Zealand, 49
Nicaragua, 32, 58, 67, 79, 80, 81,
    104, 107, 112, 117, 120, 122, 134,
    136, 148, 151, 152, 158, 208, 209,
    215, 218
Nicaragua v. the U.S., 63
Nickel, James W., 24
Niebuhr, Reinhold, 179, 180
Nigeria, 81
Nixon, Richard, 2, 105–10, 114, 121.
    See also Kissinger, Henry
Nobel Peace Prize, 56, 135
Non-governmental organizations
    (NGO's), 9, 90, 99, 100, 101, 127,

128, 134, 135, 136, 137, 140, 141,
142, 145, 146, 147, 148, 149, 150,
151, 152, 153, 155, 156, 157, 158,
159, 191, 210, 221, 222; and the
U.S., 85
Non-profit lobbies. *See* Non-
governmental organizations
Noriega, Gen. Manuel, 119, 208
North, Oliver, 199
North American Coalition on Ko-
rea, 149
North Atlantic Treaty Organization
(NATO), 104, 121
North Korea, 11
Norway, 40, 88, 101
Norwegian Peace Research Insti-
tute, 37
Nyerere, Julius, 177, 212

"Operation Stanleyville," 32
Organization of African Unity
(OAU), 20, 21, 51, 222
Organization of American States
(OAS), 20, 80, 108, 205. *See also*
American, and Inter-American
Orlov, Yuri, 86, 149
Overseas Development Council, 78,
88, 191, 222
Oxfam, 92

Pakistan, 33, 62, 107, 217, 218
Palestinians, 15, 207
Panama, 81, 118, 119, 120, 124
Paraguay, 4, 107, 119, 152, 163, 205,
209, 213, 223
Paraguay Watch, 132
Peace and human rights, 6, 30. *See
also* Aggression and human rights
Peace of Westphalia, 1
Peace through Law, 131
PEN (Poets, Essayists, Novelists), 85
People's Republic of China. *See*
China
Permanent Assembly for Human
Rights (Argentina), 205
Persian Gulf War, 80
Peru, 81, 224

Philippines, 79, 96, 97, 98, 103, 107,
114, 118, 119, 120, 140, 151, 154,
158, 209, 218
Physical Quality of Life Index. *See*
Quality of life index
Physicians for Human Rights, 92
Pinochet, Augusto, 79, 107, 109, 119,
125, 144, 206
Plato, 165
Poland, 22, 55, 91, 94, 95, 114, 123,
184, 226, 227. *See also* Solidarity
Political participation, 40; denial of,
191
Political prisoners, 50, 74, 90, 91, 94,
132, 134, 139, 149, 225; protection
of, 85
Politics and human rights, 24–25
Pol Pot, 32, 186, 205, 220
Portugal, 104, 217, 226
Positive and negative rights, 13, 14
Poverty and human rights, 37, 125
Presbyterian church, U.S., 205
Prisoners of conscience, 88. *See also*
Amnesty International
Prisoners of war, 8, 17. *See also*
Armed Conflict
Property rights, 13, 169, 191
Psychiatry, political, 76, 99, 131

Quality of life index, 78, 88, 191,
222, 224

Racial discrimination, 34, 40
Reagan, Ronald, xi, 42, 102, 112, 122,
124, 128, 157, 158, 183, 199, 207,
208, 209, 210, 211, 213; and human rights policies, 2, 3, 114–21;
views toward nongovernmental
organizations, 134, 135, 136, 138,
152, 153, 154
Red Cross, 17, 84. *See also names of
particular Red Cross agencies*
Refugees, 133, 145
Regional human rights law, 16, 18–
22; protection of, 85
Relatives for Missing Political Prisoners (Argentina), 205

Reporting system (state) and human rights, 47–50
Rhodesia, 16, 34, 60, 67, 124, 130, 134, 138, 142, 146, 148, 199. *See also* Zimbabwe
Ricardo, David, 168
Right to equality, 40
Right to life, 5, 37, 40, 94, 179, 191, 192
Rockefeller, Nelson, 109
Romania, 95, 107, 153, 206, 209
Roosevelt, Franklin, 26, 30
Rousseau, Jean Jacques, 167
Rudenko, Mykola, 86
Russia. *See* Soviet Union

Sakharov, Andrei, 77, 94, 203
Sandinistas, 120, 122, 208
Sarbanes, Paul, 147
Saudi Arabia, 112
Scandinavian states, xiii, 26, 31, 65, 74, 94
Scharansky, Anatoli, 86
Scheingold, Stuart A., 45
Schifter, Richard, 120, 134
Schlesinger, Arthur, Jr., 102
Schopenhauer, Arthur, 189
Schoultz, Lars, 83
Schultz, George, 120
Scots, 34
Security Assistance Act, Section 502, U.S., 144
Self-determination, 11, 15, 30, 33, 34, 35, 60, 78, 99, 103, 130, 174, 175
Senate, U.S., 83, 111; and Foreign Relations Committee, 116; and Appropriations Committee, 136–37
Senegal, 81, 182, 188, 212, 226
Shah of Iran, 31, 91, 121, 179, 215, 216
Shestack, Jerome J., 127, 227
Shining Path, 224
Slavery, 4, 7, 9–10, 99
Smith, Adam, 166, 168
Smith, Ian, 16, 34

Socioeconomic rights, xiv, 2, 6, 13, 14, 16, 19, 25, 26, 32, 35, 37, 39, 40, 41, 51, 52, 75, 78, 79, 82, 88, 92, 93, 101, 110, 111, 114, 115, 166, 190, 192, 201, 202, 203, 204, 208, 209, 212, 213, 214, 225, 226
Solarz, Steven, 120, 143
Solidarity (Poland), 55, 91, 95, 123, 184, 220
Solidarity rights, 26–27, 172, 174, 204
Somoza, Anastasio, 58, 79, 80, 112, 122, 134, 149, 151, 215
South Africa, Republic of, 15, 31, 52, 53, 60, 78, 98, 103, 107, 115, 116, 118, 119, 120, 122, 124, 142, 143, 144, 158, 165, 199, 228
South Korea, 11, 78, 96, 104, 107, 116, 118, 119, 120, 149, 151, 154, 158, 187, 209, 218, 226
Soviet Union, 2, 14, 22, 27, 29, 31, 35, 37, 49, 50, 51, 52, 66, 75, 76, 77, 78, 94, 95, 96, 104, 105, 106, 112, 114, 117, 120, 123, 129, 138, 149, 153, 157, 174, 182, 184, 185, 189, 207, 208, 209, 218, 219, 220, 226, 227
Spain, 31, 34, 88, 94, 103, 165, 226
Sri Lanka, 81, 82, 187, 226
Stalin, 27
Starvation, 4, 17
State Department Human Rights Bureau. *See* Bureau of Human Rights
State Department human rights reports. *See* Country reports on human rights, U.S.
State Department Policy Planning Staff, 111
Stewart, Donald, 147, 148
Stoessel, Walter J., 102
Stroessner, Alfredo, 119, 163
Structural violence, 41
Suarez-Mason, General, 4, 64
Sullivan principles re U.S. investment in South Africa, 144
Survival International, 85

Sweden, 41, 101, 182, 188, 212, 225
Switzerland, 11, 16, 27, 41, 82, 166
Syria, 80

Taiwan, 78, 88, 206, 226
Tanzania, 33, 177–78, 186
Task Force on Southern Africa, NAACP, 143
Terrorism, 116, 206
Thailand, 81, 226
Thatcher, Margaret, 146, 213
Third World, 12, 16, 28, 37, 40, 41, 43, 55, 63, 68, 78–82, 104, 125, 162, 175, 177, 182, 186–87, 208, 213, 220, 226
Timerman, Jocobo, 152
Tito, Josef, 185
Torture, 3, 5, 18, 20, 28, 40, 63, 66, 81, 85, 88, 92, 97, 104, 108, 110, 179, 187, 205, 225, 228
Transafrica, 133
Treaty of Versailles, 8
Trial observation and human rights, 90–91
Truman, Harry, 104
Tsongas, Paul, 143, 156
Turkey, 34, 66, 81
Turks, 10

Uganda, 27, 32, 33, 107, 112, 124, 186, 199, 205, 215
United Auto Workers, 138, 150
United Church of Christ (UCC), 132, 139, 140, 143
United Kingdom, 27, 31, 34, 40, 53, 63, 75, 85, 146, 192, 205, 224; and Northern Ireland, 3, 63, 66, 74
United Nations, 2, 10, 11, 13, 14, 15, 16, 25, 28, 33, 50, 52, 53, 60, 66, 78, 79, 88–89, 98, 99, 108, 126, 176, 199, 201, 202, 204, 210, 223, 224. See also names of particular U.N. agencies
United Nations Charter, 11–13, 29, 31, 32, 33, 35, 36, 46, 104, 211
United Nations Commissioner for Human Rights, 99

United Nations Covenant on Civil and Political Rights, 12, 13, 36, 37, 38, 39, 49, 50, 52, 59, 64, 66, 67, 68, 75, 76, 88, 98, 104, 111, 123, 187, 204, 211, 225
United Nations Covenant on Economic, Social, and Cultural Rights, 12, 13, 36, 38, 49, 51, 68, 75, 82, 88, 98, 104, 111, 123, 187, 204, 211, 222, 223, 224
United Nations Economic and Social Council (ECOSOC), 51, 52, 222
United Nations Educational, Scientific, and Cultural Organization (UNESCO), 2, 43, 55, 84; and Convention on Discrimination in Education, 15, 57
United Nations General Assembly, 11, 12, 15, 34, 51, 52, 54, 99, 117, 190, 222
United Nations High Commissioner for Refugees (UNHCR), 15, 56, 66, 145, 204
United Nations Human Rights Commission, 51, 52, 53, 54, 58, 59, 92, 98, 117, 119; and subcommission on Protection of Minorities, 58, 59, 66, 98
United Nations Human Rights Committee, 49, 50, 57, 59, 67, 211, 219
United Nations Prize for Human Rights, 56
United Nations Security Council, 15, 34, 35, 40, 60, 62, 67, 101
United Nations Treaty on Racial Discrimination, 49, 52, 67, 75, 111
United Nations Treaty Prohibiting Discrimination Against Women, 49
United Nations Treaty Prohibiting Torture, 49
United States, xiii, xiv, 3, 21, 28, 29, 31, 32, 34, 35, 38, 40, 41, 55, 56, 62, 63, 64, 65, 67, 74, 80, 90, 94, 98, 102–26, 131, 138, 142, 144, 151, 152, 153, 160, 169, 182, 183,

United States (cont.)
199, 207, 215, 217, 218, 219, 220;
and foreign assistance, 107, 108,
112, 116, 118, 120, 124, 125, 140,
143, 144, 145, 224; and foreign policy on human rights, 102–26
Universal Declaration of Human
Rights, 11, 12, 13, 47, 50, 104, 175,
189, 191, 211
Universal human rights, 6, 93, 95,
100, 162, 175
Uruguay, 59, 81, 82, 112, 149, 151,
205, 211
U.S.S.R. See Soviet Union
U Thant, 56
Utilitarianism, 168, 169, 211

Vance, Cyrus, 110, 111, 114, 149, 151,
156
Van Dyke, Vernon, 160, 183
Venezuela, 80, 81, 186, 226
Videla, Jorge, 165
Vietnam, 16, 32, 80, 91, 104, 105,
106, 107, 108, 114, 142, 156, 186,
187, 216, 218
Vogelgesang, Sandy, 157

War Powers Act, 110
Warsaw Pact, 219
Washington, George, 102
Washington Office on Africa (WOA),
133, 134, 137, 138, 139, 140, 143, 148
Washington Office on Latin Amer-
ica (WOLA), 132, 134, 137, 139, 140,
141, 143, 147, 148, 150, 152, 157

Webb, Sidney, 168
Weisbrodt, David, 141
West Germany. See Germany, West
Whalen, Charles, 146, 147
"Wilmington Ten," 74
Wilson, Charles, 135, 148
Wilson, Woodrow, 30, 33, 103
Women's rights, 15, 27, 42
Woods, Donald, 222
Worker's rights. See Labor rights
Working Group on Human Rights,
86
Working Group on the Internment
of Dissenters in Mental Hospi-
tals, 86
World Bank, 111, 124, 206
World Court, 15, 29, 35, 40, 62, 63,
67, 85, 89, 90, 101
World Health Organization (WHO),
15, 192, 208
World Psychiatric Association, 50
World War I, 10
World War II, 10, 16, 31

Yatron, Gus, 147
Young, Andrew, 74, 133
Yugoslavia, x, 78, 123, 182, 185, 186,
188, 212, 226

Zaire, 79, 107
Zimbabwe, 34, 81, 123, 177
Zionist-Jewish Lobbying Coalition,
138
Zorinsky, Edward, 146